Advanced Bookkeeping

Tutorial

David Cox

Published by Osborne Books Limited
Tel 01905 748071
Email books@osbornebooks.co.uk
Website www.osbornebooks.co.uk

Design by Laura Ingham

Printed by CPI Group (UK) Limited, Croydon, CR0 4YY, on environmentally friendly, acid-free paper from managed forests.

British Library Cataloguing in Publication Data
A catalogue record for this book is available from the British Library

ISBN 978 1909173 774

Contents

Also available from Osborne Books...

Workbooks

Practice questions and assessments
with answers

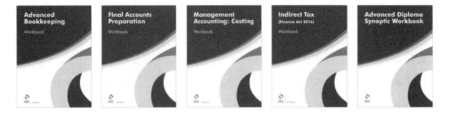

Wise Guides

Handy pocket-sized study and revision guides

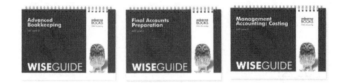

Student Zone

Login to access your free ebooks and
interactive revision crosswords

Download **Osborne Books App** free from the App Store or Google Play Store
to view your ebooks online or offline on your mobile or tablet.

www.osbornebooks.co.uk

Introduction

Qualifications covered

This book has been written specifically to cover the Unit 'Advanced Bookkeeping' which is mandatory for the following qualifications:

AAT Advanced Diploma in Accounting – Level 3

AAT Advanced Certificate in Bookkeeping – Level 3

AAT Advanced Diploma in Accounting at SCQF – Level 6

Further Education and Training Certificate: Accounting Technician (Level 4 AATSA)

The book contains a clear text with worked examples and case studies, chapter summaries and key terms to help with revision. Each chapter concludes with a wide range of activities, many in the style of AAT computer based assessments.

Osborne Study and Revision Materials

The materials featured on the previous page are tailored to the needs of students studying this unit and revising for the assessment. They include:

- **Workbooks:** paperback books with practice activities and exams
- **Wise Guides:** pocket-sized spiral bound revision cards
- **Student Zone:** access to Osborne Books online resources
- **Osborne Books App:** Osborne Books ebooks for mobiles and tablets

Visit www.osbornebooks.co.uk for details of study and revision resources and access to online material.

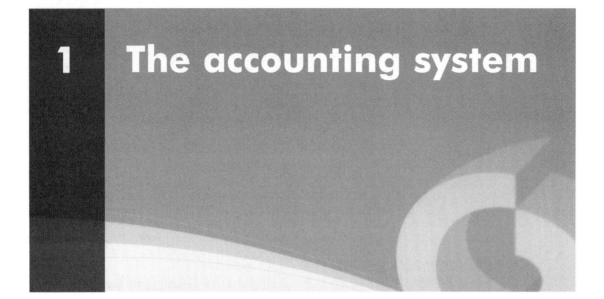

1 The accounting system

this chapter covers...

Before studying advanced bookkeeping in detail, it is important to take an overview of the accounting system. Every business is unique and therefore no one accounting system will be exactly the same as another. This chapter provides:

- *an introduction to financial transactions*

- *an explanation of how the transactions are recorded in an accounting system*

- *an introduction to some of the terms used in accounting*

This book deals with the accounting systems of sole trader businesses. Sole traders are people who run their own businesses — such as shops, factories, farms, garages, local franchises — which are often small businesses.

The other types of business in the private sector are partnerships and limited companies. These are not covered specifically in this book, but some financial transactions we will see may apply to partnerships and limited companies.

ACCOUNTING AND THE ACCOUNTING SYSTEM

what is accounting?

Accounting involves keeping financial records up-to-date and the preparation of financial statements (final accounts). It includes:

- recording business transactions in financial terms

- reporting financial information to the owner or managers of the business and other interested parties

- advising the owner how to use the financial reports to assess the past performance of the business, and to make decisions for the future

why keep accounts?

Accounting is essential to the recording and presentation of financial records and financial statements. It is important for:

- **internal control**, to ensure that all financial transactions are correctly recorded so as to show the true financial position of the business, and to help prevent fraud

- **measuring business performance**, by means of financial reports and the year-end financial statements

- **obtaining credit/financing**, by providing lenders with the current financial position of the business

- **statutory requirements**, to provide the information for VAT Returns and income tax returns to HM Revenue & Customs, and for other financial reports

the role of the accountant

The accountant's job is to check, summarise, present, analyse and interpret the accounts for the benefit of the owner and other interested parties. In particular, the function of the **financial accountant** is concerned with financial transactions, and with taking further the information produced by the person who 'keeps the books'. The financial accountant extracts information from the accounting records in order to provide a method of control, for instance over trade receivables, trade payables, cash and bank balances. The role also requires the preparation of year-end financial statements (final accounts).

It is especially important for those involved in accounting to ensure that they follow the policies and procedures of the business they work for.

manual and computer accounts

This book is concerned with the preparation of financial records and their use in the year-end financial statements. Financial records are kept either in handwritten form or on a computer. Computer accounting systems are sensibly backed up by handwritten records, in case of computer disasters such as total loss of data. The main record in a handwritten system is the **ledger** which, at one time, would be a weighty leather-bound volume, neatly ruled, into which the bookkeeper would handwrite each business transaction into individual accounts.

The major advantage of computer accounting is that it is a very accurate method of recording business transactions. The word 'ledger' has survived into the computer age but, instead of being a bound volume, it is used to describe data files held on a computer disk.

Whether business transactions are recorded by hand, or by using a computer, the basic principles remain the same. In the first few chapters of this book we will concentrate on these basic principles.

keeping accounts – practical points

When maintaining financial accounts you should bear in mind that they should be kept:

- accurately
- with integrity – in a straightforward and honest way
- up-to-date
- physically secure – eg computer passwords to prevent unauthorised persons accessing the accounts in order to enter false or fraudulent transactions
- with confidentiality:
  - not revealed to people outside the business (unless authorisation is given)
  - revealed only to those within the business who are entitled to the information

Maintaining financial accounts is a discipline, and you should develop disciplined accounting skills as you study with this book.

the stages of the accounting system

The diagram on the next page shows the stages of the accounting system – these will have been covered in your earlier studies. Topics such as financial documents, books of prime entry, and some aspects of double-entry bookkeeping will have been explained in Osborne Books' introductory texts. In this book we will focus on the double-entry accounts system and the trial balance in its extended form (showing figures transferred into the statement

the accounting system

FINANCIAL DOCUMENTS

invoices – issued and received

credit notes – issued and received

bank paying-in slips

cheques issued

BACS and Faster Payment documents

sources of accounting information

BOOKS OF PRIME ENTRY

day books

journal

cash book (also used in double-entry)

gathering and summarising accounting information

DOUBLE-ENTRY BOOKKEEPING

sales ledger – accounts of customers

purchases ledger – accounts of suppliers

general ledger

– income (revenue)

– expenses (costs)

– assets, eg non-current assets, inventory

– liabilities, eg loans

– capital (equity)

cash book

– cash book for bank and cash transactions

recording the dual aspect of business transactions in the accounting system

TRIAL BALANCE

a summary of the balances of all the accounts

– extended to produce data for financial statements

arithmetical checking of double-entry bookkeeping

FINANCIAL STATEMENTS (FINAL ACCOUNTS)

• statement of profit or loss

and

• statement of financial position

statement measuring profit or loss for an accounting period

statement of assets, liabilities and capital at the end of an accounting period of profit or loss and the statement of financial position). If you should at any time lose sight of where your studies are taking you, refer back to this chapter, and the diagram, and it should help to place your work in context.

We will now look at each of the stages of the accounting system in turn.

FINANCIAL DOCUMENTS

Financial transactions generate documents. In this section we link the main documents to the type of transaction involved.

sales and purchases – the invoice

When a business buys or sells goods or services the seller prepares an invoice stating:

- the amount owing
- when it should be paid
- details of the goods sold or service provided

cash and credit sales, cash and credit purchases

A sale by one business is a purchase by another business. The difference between cash and credit transactions is:

- **cash sales and cash purchases** – where payment is immediate, whether by cash or by bank payment
- **credit sales and credit purchases** – where payment is to be made at a later date (often 30 days later)

A **trade receivable** is a person who owes you money when you sell on credit.

A **trade payable** is a person to whom you owe money when you buy on credit.

Note that the total of sales, both cash and credit, for a particular time period is referred to as **revenue** or **sales revenue**.

return of goods – the credit note

If the buyer returns goods which are bought on credit (they may be faulty or incorrect) the seller will prepare a credit note which is sent to the buyer, reducing the amount of money owed. The credit note, like the invoice, states the money amount and the goods and services to which it relates.

bank transactions – cheques, BACS, Faster Payments

Businesses need to pay in money, draw out cash and make payments. Paying-in slips and cheques are used as financial documents for bank account transactions as are documents generated by BACS and the Faster Payments inter-bank computer payments systems.

BOOKS OF PRIME ENTRY

Many businesses issue and receive large quantities of invoices, credit notes and banking documents, and it is useful for them to list these in summary form, during the course of the working day. These summaries are known as **books of prime entry**. The books of prime entry include:

- **sales day book** – a list of credit sales made, compiled from invoices issued

- **purchases day book** – a list of credit purchases made, compiled from invoices received

- **sales returns day book** – a list of returns in, ie goods returned by credit customers, compiled from credit notes issued

- **purchases returns day book** – a list of returns out, ie goods returned by the business to credit suppliers, compiled from credit notes received

- **cash book** – the business's record of cash and bank transactions, compiled from receipts, paying-in slips, BACS and Faster Payment documents, and cheques

- **journal** – a record of non-regular transactions, which are not recorded in any other book of prime entry (the journal is covered in Chapter 11)

DOUBLE-ENTRY ACCOUNTS: THE LEDGER

The basis of many accounting systems is the **double-entry bookkeeping system** which is embodied in a series of records known as the **ledger**. This is divided into a number of separate **accounts**.

double-entry bookkeeping

Double-entry bookkeeping involves making two entries in the accounts for each transaction: for instance, if you are paying wages by BACS you will make an entry in bank account and an entry in wages account. If you are operating a manual accounting system you will make the two entries by hand, if you are operating a computer accounting system you will make *one* entry on the keyboard, but indicate to the machine where the other entry is to be made by means of a numerical code.

accounts

The books of prime entry are the sources for the entries you make in the accounts. The ledger into which you make the entries is divided into separate accounts, eg a separate account for sales, purchases, each type of expense, each trade receivable, each trade payable, and so on. Each account is given a specific name, and a number for reference purposes.

computer accounts

As noted earlier, many small businesses and all large businesses use computers to handle their financial transactions. Using an accounting program, transactions are input into the computer and stored on disk. The separate accounts are represented by data files held on disk. The principles of double-entry bookkeeping remain the same; an input code is used to identify the two accounts involved in each transaction.

division of the ledger

Because of the large number of accounts involved, the ledger has traditionally been divided into a number of sections. These same sections are used in computer accounting systems.

- **sales ledger** – personal accounts of trade receivables, ie customers to whom the business has sold on credit

- **purchases ledger** – personal accounts of trade payables, ie suppliers to whom the business owes money

- **cash book** – comprising cash account and bank account; note that cash book is also a book of prime entry for cash transactions

- **general ledger** – the remainder of the accounts: income (revenue), expenses (costs), assets (eg non-current assets, inventory), liabilities (eg loans), capital/equity

Note that, when control accounts (see Chapter 10) are in use, the sales ledger and purchases ledger are **subsidiary ledgers** (also known as **memorandum ledgers**) to the general ledger. When this happens, **sales ledger control account** and **purchases ledger control account** are used in general ledger as totals accounts to represent the accounts contained in sales ledger and purchases ledger. The diagrams in Chapter 10 – on pages 185 and 186 – show the relationship between general ledger and the subsidiary ledgers.

inventory records

Most businesses keep records of their inventories – either by using a computer inventory control system, or manually on individual inventory records. Under both methods a separate record is maintained for each type of inventory – whether materials held for resale by a retailer, or for use in production by a manufacturer.

When supplies of the inventory are received they are entered in the inventory record, and when items are sold, or issued to production, they are shown as issues on the inventory record.

At the financial year-end the value of inventory held is recorded in the inventory account in the general ledger of the double-entry system.

TRIAL BALANCE

Double-entry bookkeeping, because it involves making two entries for each transaction, is open to error. What if the person keeping the books writes £45 in one account and £54 in another? The trial balance – explained fully in Chapter 3 – effectively checks the entries made over a given period and will pick up most errors. It sets out the **balances** of all the double-entry accounts from the general ledger, ie the totals of the accounts to date. As well as being an arithmetical check, it is the source of valuable information which is used – in the **extended trial balance** – to help in the preparation of the **financial statements** of the business.

FINANCIAL STATEMENTS

The financial statements (final accounts) of a business comprise the statement of profit or loss and the statement of financial position.

statement of profit or loss

income	minus	**expenses**	equals	**profit/loss**
revenue from sales		*costs of running the business*		*which adds/subtracts to/from capital/equity*

The statement of profit or loss of a business calculates the profit or loss of the business after the cost of purchases and other expenses has been deducted from the sales revenue.

The figures for these calculations – sales, purchases, expenses of various kinds – are taken from the double-entry system. The statement of profit or loss is discussed in more detail in Chapter 4, and in the Advanced Diploma Unit 'Final Accounts Preparation'.

statement of financial position

The statement of financial position is so called because it shows the assets, liabilities and capital of a business in numerical (money) terms:

assets	minus	**liabilities**	equals	**capital/equity**
what a business owns		*what a business owes*		*how the business has been financed*

The double-entry system contains figures for:

assets items the business owns, which can be:

– non-current assets – items with a life span of more than one year which are bought for use in the business, eg premises, vehicles, computers

– current assets – items needed for the everyday running of the business, eg inventory, trade receivables ie money owed by customers, and money in the bank

Note that most assets are **tangible**, which means that you can see and touch them, ie they have material substance. A few assets are **intangible**, ie they do not have material substance, but belong to the business and have value. Goodwill is an example of an intangible non-current asset (goodwill is often paid for by the purchaser when buying an existing business).

liabilities items that the business owes, which can be :

– current liabilities – short-term liabilities repayable within twelve months, eg trade payables ie money owed to suppliers, bank overdrafts

– non-current liabilities – longer-term liabilities repayable in more than twelve months, eg bank loans, mortgages

capital/equity money or assets invested by the owner of the business, together with profits retained in the business, ie the owner's stake in the business

the financial statements of limited companies use the term 'equity' to describe the shareholders' stake in the company, being the share capital and retained profits

The statement of financial position is discussed in more detail in Chapter 4 and in the Advanced Diploma Unit 'Final Accounts Preparation'.

the accounting equation

The statement of financial position illustrates a principle important to accounting theory, known as the **accounting equation**. This equation has been explained above, namely:

assets   minus   **liabilities**   equals   **capital**

Every business transaction will change the statement of financial position and the equation, as each transaction has a **dual effect** on the accounts. However, the equation will always balance. Study the following financial transactions made through the business bank account and see how the accounting equation is affected by each of the transactions.

TRANSACTION	EFFECT ON EQUATION
Business pays a supplier	• decrease in asset (bank) • decrease in liability (money owed to supplier)
Comment: assets and liabilities both decrease by the amount of the payment; capital remains unchanged.	
Business buys a computer	• increase in asset (computer) • decrease in asset (bank)
Comment: assets remain the same because the two transactions cancel each other out in the assets section: value is transferred from the asset of bank to the asset of computer.	
The owner introduces new capital by paying a cheque into the bank	• increase in asset (bank) • increase in capital (the owner's investment in the business)
Comment: both sides of the equation increase by the amount of the capital introduced.	

In conclusion, every business transaction has a **dual aspect**, as two entries are involved: this is the basis of the theory of double-entry bookkeeping.

Note that the accounting equation is often set out as:

assets   equals   **capital**   plus   **liabilities**

It is in this form that we will see it used in the extended trial balance (Chapter 4, and later chapters).

Chapter Summary

- Accounting is used to record financial transactions.

- Financial accounts are used by the owner and managers of the business and also by other interested parties.

- The accounting system comprises a number of specific stages of recording and presenting business transactions:

  - financial documents

  - books of prime entry

  - the double-entry system of ledgers

  - the trial balance and extended trial balance

  - financial statements (final accounts)

- The statement of financial position uses the accounting equation:

  assets   *minus*   liabilities   *equals*   capital

- The extended trial balance uses the accounting equation:

  assets   *equals*   capital   *plus*   liabilities

Key Terms	In the course of this chapter a number of specific accounting terms have been introduced. You should now study this section closely to ensure that you are clear about these terms:

accounts — financial records, where business transactions are entered

ledger — the set of accounts of a business

assets — items owned by a business

liabilities — items owed by a business

capital/equity — the amount of the owner's/shareholders' stake in the business

trade receivables — individuals or businesses who owe money in respect of goods or services supplied by the business

trade payables — individuals or businesses to whom money is owed by the business

purchases — goods bought, either on credit or for cash, which are intended to be resold later

credit purchases — goods bought, with payment to be made at a later date

cash purchases — goods bought and paid for immediately

sales — the sale of goods, whether on credit or for cash, in which the business trades

credit sales — goods sold, with payment to be received at an agreed date in the future

cash sales — goods sold, with immediate payment received in cash, by cheque, by credit card, or by debit card

revenue — the total of sales, both cash and credit, for a particular time period

profit/loss — the profit/loss made by a business from selling goods or services during a particular time period

expenses — the costs of running the business, eg wages, rent, rates, telephone, etc

trial balance — list of the balances of all the double-entry accounts from the general ledger

Activities

1.1   Write out and complete the following sentences.

    (a)   The set of double-entry accounts of a business is called the ....

    (b)   A .... is a person who owes you money when you sell on credit.

    (c)   A .... is a person to whom you owe money when you buy on credit.

    (d)   The .... is a list of sales made, compiled from invoices issued.

    (e)   The business's record of bank account and amount of cash held is kept in the ....

    (f)   Accounts such as sales, purchases, expenses are kept in the ....

    (g)   The accounting equation is: .... minus .... equals ....

1.2   Distinguish between:

    (a)   assets and liabilities
    (b)   trade receivables and trade payables
    (c)   purchases and sales
    (d)   credit purchases and cash purchases

1.3   Show the dual aspect, as it affects the accounting equation (assets – liabilities = capital), of the following transactions (which follow one another) for a particular business (ignore VAT):

    (a)   owner starts in business with capital of £8,000 in the bank
    (b)   buys a computer for £4,000, paying by cheque
    (c)   obtains a loan of £3,000 by cheque from a friend
    (d)   buys a van for £6,000, paying by cheque

1.4   Fill in the missing figures:

	Assets £	Liabilities £	Capital £
(a)	20,000	0	....
(b)	15,000	5,000	....
(c)	16,400	....	8,850
(d)	....	3,850	10,250
(e)	25,380	....	6,950
(f)	....	7,910	13,250

1.5   The table below sets out account balances from the books of a business. The columns (a) to (f) show the account balances resulting from a series of transactions that have taken place over time. **You are to** compare each set of adjacent columns, ie (a) with (b), (b) with (c), and so on and state, with figures, what accounting transactions have taken place in each case. (Ignore VAT.)

	(a) £	(b) £	(c) £	(d) £	(e) £	(f) £
Assets						
Office equipment	–	2,000	2,000	2,000	2,000	2,000
Van	–	–	–	10,000	10,000	10,000
Bank	10,000	8,000	14,000	4,000	6,000	3,000
Liabilities						
Loan	–	–	6,000	6,000	6,000	3,000
Capital	10,000	10,000	10,000	10,000	12,000	12,000

2 Double-entry bookkeeping

this chapter covers...

We saw in Chapter 1 that bookkeeping is the basic recording of financial transactions. Before studying financial accounting in detail it is important to study the principles of double-entry bookkeeping, as these form the basis of all that we shall be doing in the rest of the book.

In Chapter 1 we looked briefly at the dual aspect of accounting – each time there is a financial transaction there are two effects on the accounting equation. This chapter shows how the dual aspect is used in the principles of bookkeeping. In particular, we shall be looking at accounts used when:

- *starting a business*
- *dealing with cash and bank transactions*
- *paying expenses and receiving income*
- *buying and selling goods*
- *dealing with returned goods, carriage costs and prompt payment discounts*
- *dealing with Value Added Tax*

DOUBLE-ENTRY ACCOUNTS

In this book we will use a simple account layout shown as follows:

Dr	Bank account		Cr
20-4	£	20-4	£
22 April Sales	1,450	23 April Wages	790

This layout is often known in accounting jargon as a 'T' account; it separates in a simple way the two sides of the account – debit (Dr) and credit (Cr). Note that each side records three items – the date, the nature of the transaction and the money amount.

debits and credits

The principle of double-entry bookkeeping is that for every business transaction:

■ one account is **debited** with the money amount of the transaction, and

■ one account is **credited** with the money amount of the transaction

Debit entries are on the left-hand side of the appropriate account, while credit entries are on the right. The rules for debits and credits are:

■ **debit entry** – the account which gains value, or records an asset, or an expense

■ **credit entry** – the account which gives value, or records a liability, or an income item

This is illustrated as follows:

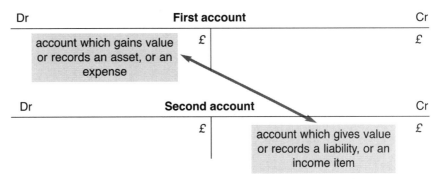

When one entry has been identified as a debit or credit, the other entry will be on the **opposite** side of the other account.

DOUBLE-ENTRY INVOLVING BANK ACCOUNT

In order to see how accounts are used, we will look at the business transactions undertaken by a new business which was set up by Jayne Hampson on 1 September 20-4 (and is not registered for VAT):

1 Sep	Started in business with capital of £5,000: a cheque from Jayne Hampson paid into the business bank account
4 Sep	Bought office equipment £2,500, paying by cheque
7 Sep	Paid rent of office £500, by cheque
10 Sep	Received commission of £100, by cheque
14 Sep	Withdrew £250 from the bank for own use (drawings)
16 Sep	Received a loan of £1,000 from James Henderson by cheque

All of these transactions involve the bank, and the business will enter them in its **bank account**. The bank account records money in the form of bank receipts and payments, ie cheques, standing orders, direct debits, BACS and Faster Payment transfers and debit card transactions. Note that most businesses also use a **cash account** to record transactions which involve money in the form of cash. These two accounts – bank account and cash account – are usually combined in a **cash book**.

In a cash book, the rules for debit and credit are:

■ **money in** is recorded on the debit side

■ **money out** is recorded on the credit side

Using these rules, the bank account of Jayne Hampson's business, after entering the transactions listed above, appears as:

Dr			Bank account			Cr
20-4		£	20-4			£
1 Sep	Capital	5,000	4 Sep	Office equipment		2,500
10 Sep	Commission	100	7 Sep	Rent paid		500
16 Sep	J Henderson: loan	1,000	14 Sep	Drawings		250
		Money in		Money out		

Note: the bank account shows the business's record of how much has been paid into, and drawn out of, the bank – it may not be exactly the same as the record of receipts and payments kept by the bank.

To complete the double-entry bookkeeping transactions we need to:

- identify on which side of the bank account the transaction is recorded – debit (money in), or credit (money out)

- record the other double-entry transaction on the opposite side of the appropriate account

- note that business transactions involving cash will be entered in the cash account

The other accounts involved can now be recorded, and we shall look at the principles involved for each transaction.

CAPITAL ACCOUNT

Capital is the amount of money invested in the business by the owner (or owners). The amount is **owed** by the business back to the owner, although it is unlikely to be repaid immediately as the business would cease to exist. A **capital account** is used to record the amount(s) paid into the business; the bookkeeping entries are:

- **capital introduced**
  - **debit** bank account, as in the case of Jayne Hampson, or cash account, or a non-current (fixed) asset account – see below – where these form part of the capital
  - **credit** capital account

example transaction

1 Sep 20-4   Started in business with capital of £5,000, a cheque paid into the bank.

Dr		Capital account		Cr
20-4	£	20-4		£
		1 Sep	Bank	5,000

Note: The dual aspect is that bank account has gained value and has been debited already (see page 18); capital account records a liability (to the owner) and is credited. Note that the business is a **separate entity** from the owner, and this bookkeeping entry looks at the transaction from the point of view of the business. The introduction of capital into a business is often the very first business transaction entered into the books of account.

NON-CURRENT ASSETS

Non-current assets are items purchased by a business for use on a semi-permanent basis. Examples are premises, vehicles, machinery and office equipment. All of these are bought by a business with the intention that they will be used for some time. Without non-current assets, it would be difficult to continue in business, eg without machinery it would prove difficult to run a factory; without delivery vans and lorries it would be difficult to transport the business's products to its customers.

When a business buys non-current assets, the expenditure is referred to as **capital expenditure**. This means that items have been bought for use in the business for some years to come. By contrast, **revenue expenditure** is where the items bought will be used by the business quite quickly. For example, the purchase of a car is capital expenditure, while the cost of repair of the car is revenue expenditure.

The importance of the difference between capital expenditure and revenue expenditure is covered in Chapter 9.

non-current assets and double-entry bookkeeping

When non-current assets are bought, a separate account for each type of non-current asset is used, eg premises account, vehicles account, machinery account, etc. The bookkeeping entries are:

- **purchase of a non-current asset**
    - **debit** non-current asset account (using the appropriate account)
    - **credit** bank account (or cash account)

example transaction

4 Sep 20-4   Bought office equipment £2,500, paying by cheque.

Dr		Office equipment account		Cr
20-4	£	20-4		£
4 Sep Bank	2,500			

The other part of the dual aspect of this transaction is a credit to bank account: this has been entered already (see account on page 18). Notice how the name of the other account involved in the double-entry transaction is always used in the details column as a description – this helps to cross-reference transactions.

EXPENSES

Businesses pay various running expenses, such as rent, wages, electricity, telephone, vehicle running expenses, etc. These day-to-day expenses of running the business are termed revenue expenditure. A separate account is used in the accounting system for each main class of revenue expenditure, eg rent paid account, wages account, etc.

The bookkeeping entries are:

■ **payment of an expense**

  –   **debit** expense account (using the appropriate account)

  –   **credit** bank account (or cash account)

---

example transaction

7 Sep 20-4   Paid rent of office £500, by cheque.

Dr		Rent paid account			Cr
20-4		£	20-4		£
7 Sep	Bank	500			

Note: The accounting rules followed are that we have debited the account which has gained value (rent – the business has had the use of the office for a certain time). The account which has given value (bank) has already been credited (see page 18).

INCOME

From time-to-time a business may receive amounts of income, such as rent received, commission received, or fees received. These are recorded in separate accounts for each category of income, eg rent received account, commission received account. The bookkeeping entries are:

■ **receipt of income**

– **debit** bank account (or cash account)

– **credit** income account (using the appropriate account)

---

example transaction

10 Sep 20-4   Received commission of £100, by cheque.

Dr	Commission received account		Cr
20-4	£	20-4	£
		10 Sep Bank	100

Note: We have already debited the account which has gained value (bank – see page 18) and credited the account which has given value (commission received).

OWNER'S DRAWINGS

Drawings is the term used when the owner takes money, in cash or by cheque (or sometimes goods), from the business for personal use. A drawings account is used to record such amounts; the bookkeeping entries for withdrawal of money are:

■ **owner's drawings**

– **debit** drawings account

– **credit** bank account (or cash account)

---

example transaction

14 Sep 20-4   Withdrew £250 from the bank for own use.

Dr	Drawings account		Cr
20-4	£	20-4	£
14 Sep Bank	250		

The other part of the dual aspect of this transaction is a credit to bank account: this entry has been made already (see page 18).

LOANS

When a business or organisation receives a loan, eg from a relative or from the bank, it is the cash account or bank account which gains value, while a loan account (in the name of the lender) records the liability.

◼ **loan received**
- **debit** bank account (or cash account)
- **credit** loan account (in name of the lender)

example transaction

16 Sep 20-4   Received a loan of £1,000 from James Henderson by cheque

Dr	James Henderson: loan account		Cr
20-4	£	20-4	£
		16 Sep Bank	1,000

The debit entry has already been made in bank account (see page 18).

FURTHER TRANSACTIONS

Using the accounts which we have seen already, here are some further transactions:

◼ **loan repayment**
- **debit** loan account
- **credit** bank account (or cash account)

◼ **sale of a non-current asset, or return of an unsuitable non-current asset**
- **debit** bank account (or cash account)
- **credit** non-current asset account

◼ **withdrawal of cash from the bank for use in the business**
- **debit** cash account
- **credit** bank account

◼ **payment of cash held by the business into the bank**
- **debit** bank account
- **credit** cash account

PURCHASES AND SALES

purchases account and sales account

Buying and selling goods or services are common business transactions. They are recorded in **purchases account** and **sales account** respectively. These two accounts are used to record the purchase and sale of the goods or services in which the business trades. For example, a shoe shop will buy shoes from the manufacturer and will record this in purchases account; as shoes are sold, the transactions will be recorded in sales account.

The normal entry on a purchases account is on the debit side – the account has gained value, ie the business has bought goods for resale. The normal entry on a sales account is on the credit side – the account has given value, ie the business has sold goods.

When a business buys an item for use in the business, eg a computer, this is debited to a separate account, because a non-current asset (see page 20) has been purchased. Likewise, when a non-current asset is sold, it is not entered in the sales account.

Case Study

TEMESIDE TRADERS: PURCHASES AND SALES

situation

To show the double-entry bookkeeping for purchases and sales, we will look at some financial transactions undertaken by Temeside Traders, a business which started trading on 1 October 20-6:

1 Oct	Started in business with capital of £7,000 paid into the bank
2 Oct	Bought goods for £5,000, paying by cheque
5 Oct	Sold some of the goods for £3,000, a cheque being received
6 Oct	Bought equipment for use in the business, £700, paying by cheque
12 Oct	Bought goods for £2,800, paying by cheque
13 Oct	Sold some of the goods for £5,000, a cheque being received
15 Oct	Paid rent £150, by cheque

Note: Temeside Traders is not yet registered for Value Added Tax.

solution

The entries into the bookkeeping system are shown on the next page.

Dr		Bank account			Cr
20-6		£	20-6		£
1 Oct	Capital	7,000	2 Oct	Purchases	5,000
5 Oct	Sales	3,000	6 Oct	Equipment	700
13 Oct	Sales	5,000	12 Oct	Purchases	2,800
			15 Oct	Rent paid	150

Dr		Capital account			Cr
20-6		£	20-6		£
			1 Oct	Bank	7,000

Dr		Purchases account			Cr
20-6		£	20-6		£
2 Oct	Bank	5,000			
12 Oct	Bank	2,800			

Dr		Sales account			Cr
20-6		£	20-6		£
			5 Oct	Bank	3,000
			13 Oct	Bank	5,000

Dr		Equipment account			Cr
20-6		£	20-6		£
6 Oct	Bank	700			

Dr		Rent paid account			Cr
20-6		£	20-6		£
15 Oct	Bank	150			

Notes:

- A purchases account and a sales account are used to record the two different movements of the goods or services in which a business trades.
- The equipment is a non-current asset, so its purchase is entered to a separate equipment account.
- The purchases and sales made in the transactions above are called cash purchases and cash sales, because payment is immediate.

CREDIT PURCHASES AND SALES

credit transactions

We have just looked at the bookkeeping for cash purchases and cash sales, ie where payment is made immediately. However, in business, many transactions for purchases and sales are made on credit, ie the goods or services are bought or sold now, with payment to be made at a later date. It is an important aspect of double-entry bookkeeping to record the credit transaction as a purchase or a sale, and then record the second entry in an account in the name of the trade payable or trade receivable, ie to record the amount owing by the business to a supplier, or to the business by a customer.

Businesses usually record credit transactions in appropriate books of prime entry:

■ credit purchases are entered in the purchases day book

■ credit sales are entered in the sales day book

At regular intervals – daily, weekly or monthly – the totals and amounts from the day books are transferred into the double-entry accounts.

credit purchases

Credit purchases are goods obtained from a supplier, with payment to take place at a later date. From the buyer's viewpoint, the supplier is a **trade payable**.

The bookkeeping entries are:

■ **credit purchase**
 – **debit** purchases account
 – **credit** trade payable's (supplier's) account

When payment is made to the supplier the bookkeeping entries are:

■ **payment made to trade payable**
 – **debit** trade payable's account
 – **credit** bank account or cash account

Many businesses keep their trade payables' accounts as subsidiary accounts in the purchases ledger and use a **purchases ledger control account** as part of the double-entry system. The use of control accounts is covered in Chapter 10.

credit sales

With credit sales, goods or services are sold to a customer who is allowed to settle the account at a later date. From the seller's viewpoint, the customer is a **trade receivable**.

The bookkeeping entries are:

■ **credit sale**

- **debit** trade receivable's (customer's) account
- **credit** sales account

When payment is received from the customer the bookkeeping entries are:

■ **payment received from trade receivable**

- **debit** bank account or cash account
- **credit** trade receivable's account

Many businesses keep their trade receivables' accounts as subsidiary accounts in the sales ledger and use a **sales ledger control account** as part of the double-entry system. The use of control accounts is covered in Chapter 10.

Case Study

WYVERN WHOLESALERS: CREDIT TRANSACTIONS

situation

A local business, Wyvern Wholesalers, has the following transactions:

20-7

18 Sep	Bought goods, £250, on credit from Malvern Manufacturing, with payment to be made in 30 days' time
21 Sep	Sold goods, £175, on credit to Strensham Stores, payment to be made in 30 days' time
16 Oct	Paid £250 by cheque to Malvern Manufacturing
20 Oct	Received a cheque for £175 from Strensham Stores

Notes:

• Wyvern Wholesalers is not registered for Value Added Tax

• day books are not used

solution

These transactions will be recorded in the bookkeeping system as follows (previous transactions on accounts, if there are any, are not shown here):

Dr	Purchases account		Cr
20-7	£	20-7	£
18 Sep Malvern Manufacturing	250		

Dr	Sales account		Cr
20-7	£	20-7	£
		21 Sep Strensham Stores	175

Dr		Malvern Manufacturing			Cr
20-7		£	20-7		£
16 Oct	Bank	250	18 Sep	Purchases	250

Dr		Strensham Stores			Cr
20-7		£	20-7		£
21 Sep	Sales	175	20 Oct	Bank	175

Dr		Bank account			Cr
20-7		£	20-7		£
20 Oct	Strensham Stores	175	16 Oct	Malvern Manufacturing	250

Note: the name of the other account involved has been used in the details column as a description.

balancing off accounts

In the Case Study above, after the transactions have been recorded in the books of Wyvern Wholesalers, the accounts of Malvern Manufacturing and Strensham Stores have the same amount entered on both debit and credit side. This means that nothing is owing to Wyvern Wholesalers, or is owed by it, ie the accounts have a 'nil' balance. In the course of trading, accounts will often **not** have a nil balance. We will explain in Chapter 3 how to 'balance' an account to show the 'total' of that account.

non-current assets bought on credit

Non-current assets are often purchased on credit terms. As with the purchase of goods for resale, an account is opened in the name of the supplier, as follows:

■ **purchase of a non-current asset on credit**

    –   **debit** non-current asset account

    –   **credit** trade payable's (supplier's) account

When payment is made to the supplier the bookkeeping entries are:

■ **payment made to trade payable**

    –   **debit** trade payable's account

    –   **credit** bank account or cash account

The book of prime entry for the purchase of non-current assets on credit is the journal – see Chapter 11.

PURCHASES RETURNS AND SALES RETURNS

From time-to-time goods bought or sold are returned, perhaps because the wrong items have been supplied (eg wrong type, size or colour), or because the goods are unsatisfactory. The bookkeeping entries for returned goods are explained below.

purchases returns

Purchases returns (or **returns out**) is where a business returns goods to a supplier.

The bookkeeping entries are:

– **debit** trade payable's (supplier's) account

– **credit** purchases returns (or returns outwards) account

Purchases returns are normally kept separate from purchases, ie they are entered in a separate purchases returns account rather than being credited to purchases account.

sales returns

Sales returns (or **returns in**) is where a customer returns goods to the business.

The bookkeeping entries are:

– **debit** sales returns (or returns in) account

– **credit** trade receivable's (customer's) account

Sales returns are normally kept separate from sales, ie they are entered in a separate sales returns account rather than being debited to sales account.

Businesses usually record returns transactions (of goods or services originally bought/sold on credit) in appropriate books of prime entry:

▨ purchases returns are entered in the purchases returns day book

▨ sales returns are entered in the sales returns day book

The totals and amounts from these day books are transferred into the double-entry accounts at regular intervals.

Now read the Case Study which follows on the next page. It shows how the double-entry bookkeeping for purchases and sales returns is carried out.

SUDBURY SUPPLIERS: PURCHASES RETURNS AND SALES RETURNS

situation

Sudbury Suppliers has the following transactions:

20-8

7 Oct   Bought goods, £280, on credit from B Lewis Limited

9 Oct   Returned unsatisfactory goods, £30, to B Lewis Limited

12 Oct   Sold goods, £125, on credit to A Holmes

19 Oct   A Holmes returned goods, £25

26 Oct   Paid the amount owing to B Lewis Limited by cheque

29 Oct   A Holmes paid the amount owing in cash

Notes:
* Sudbury Suppliers is not registered for Value Added Tax
* day books are not used

solution

The transactions will be recorded in the bookkeeping system (previous transactions on accounts, if any, not shown) as follows:

Dr		**Purchases account**			Cr
20-8		£	20-8		£
7 Oct	B Lewis Limited	280			

Dr		**B Lewis Limited**			Cr
20-8		£	20-8		£
9 Oct	Purchases returns	30	7 Oct	Purchases	280
26 Oct	Bank	250			

Dr		**Purchases returns account**			Cr
20-8		£	20-8		£
			9 Oct	B Lewis Limited	30

Dr		**Sales account**			Cr
20-8		£	20-8		£
			12 Oct	A Holmes	125

Dr		A Holmes		Cr
20-8	£	20-8		£
12 Oct Sales	125	19 Oct Sales returns		25
		29 Oct Cash		100

Dr		Sales returns account	Cr
20-8	£	20-8	£
19 Oct A Holmes	25		

Dr		Bank account		Cr
20-8	£	20-8		£
		26 Oct B Lewis Limited		250

Dr		Cash account	Cr
20-8	£	20-8	£
29 Oct A Holmes	100		

CARRIAGE IN AND CARRIAGE OUT

Carriage in (inwards) is where the buyer pays the carriage (transport) cost of purchases, eg an item is purchased by an internet order, and the buyer has to pay the additional cost of delivery (and possibly packing also).

Carriage out (outwards) is where the seller pays the carriage charge, eg an item is sold to the customer and described as 'post free'.

Both carriage in and carriage out are expenses and their cost should be debited to two separate expenses accounts, **carriage in account** and **carriage out account** respectively:

■ **carriage in**
- **debit** carriage in account (alternatively, purchases account could be debited)
- **credit** trade payable's account, or bank account/cash account

■ **carriage out**
- **debit** carriage out account
- **credit** bank account/cash account

> **Tutorial note:** the reason for using two separate expenses accounts is because they are dealt with differently in conventional format statements of profit or loss.

PROMPT PAYMENT DISCOUNT IN THE BOOKKEEPING SYSTEM

Prompt payment discount (PPD) is an allowance off the invoice amount for quick settlement, eg 2% discount for settlement within seven days. (Do not confuse prompt payment discount with **trade discount** – an amount sometimes allowed as a reduction in price when goods are supplied to other businesses, or with **bulk discount** – a reduction in price when large quantities of goods are supplied.) A business can be involved with prompt payment discount in two ways:

- discounts allowed to customers

- discounts received from suppliers

Case Study

R PATEL: DISCOUNTS ALLOWED AND RECEIVED

situation – discounts allowed

R Patel sells TV and computer equipment. When prompt payment discount is taken by one of his customers it is entered into the accounts as shown by the following transactions:

20-9

12 Oct   Sold goods, £100, on credit to P Henry, allowing a prompt payment discount of 2% for settlement within 7 days (note: the seller of the goods is not VAT-registered)

16 Oct   P Henry pays £98 by bank transfer

solution

Dr	Sales account		Cr
20-9	£	20-9	£
		12 Oct P Henry	100

Dr	P Henry		Cr
20-9	£	20-9	£
12 Oct Sales	100	16 Oct Bank	98
		16 Oct Discounts allowed	2
	100		100

Dr	Bank account		Cr
20-9	£	20-9	£
16 Oct P Henry	98		

Dr	Discounts allowed account		Cr
20-9	£	20-9	£
16 Oct P Henry	2		

Notes:

- The amount of the payment received from P Henry is debited to bank account and credited to trade receivable's account.
- The amount of the discount allowed – an expense to the business – is debited to discounts allowed account and credited to the trade receivable's account.

situation – discounts received

R Patel receives prompt payment discount from one of his suppliers. The following transactions show how discounts received is entered into the accounts.

20-9

20 Oct Bought goods, £200, on credit from H Singh Limited; 2.5% prompt payment discount is offered for settlement by the end of October (note: the seller of the goods is not registered for VAT)

30 Oct Paid H Singh Limited £195 by bank transfer

solution

Dr		Purchases account		Cr
20-9		£	20-9	£
20 Oct	H Singh Limited	200		

Dr		H Singh Limited		Cr
20-9		£	20-9	£
30 Oct	Bank	195	20 Oct Purchases	200
30 Oct	Discounts received	5		
		200		200

Dr		Bank account		Cr
20-9		£	20-9	£
			30 Oct H Singh Limited	195

Dr		Discounts received account		Cr
20-9		£	20-9	£
			30 Oct H Singh Limited	5

Notes:

- The business is receiving prompt payment discount from H Singh Limited, and the amount is entered as: debit trade payable's account, credit discounts received account.
- Discounts received account is an income account, because it represents a benefit given to the business by suppliers.

VAT AND DOUBLE-ENTRY ACCOUNTS

When a business is registered with HM Revenue & Customs for Value Added Tax, it is normally able to claim back VAT paid on purchases of goods, non-current assets and expenses – this is known as **input tax**. A VAT-registered business must also charge VAT – **output tax** – whenever it supplies goods and services (except for zero-rated and exempt goods and services). A separate account is opened for VAT.

When a VAT-registered business buys, for example, non-current assets, it will enter the amount of input VAT direct to the debit side of VAT account.

example transaction

On 16 April 20-1, Osborne Paints Limited, a company which is registered for Value Added Tax, buys a new computer at a cost of £1,000 + VAT of £200 (at 20%), paying £1,200 by bank transfer.

This is recorded in the double-entry accounts as:

Dr	Computer account		Cr
20-1	£	20-1	£
16 Apr Bank	1,000		

Dr	Value Added Tax account		Cr
20-1	£	20-1	£
16 Apr Bank	200		

Dr	Bank account		Cr
20-1	£	20-1	£
		16 Apr Computer	1,200

Similarly when Osborne Paints Limited sells its paints to a customer it will charge **output** VAT on the goods. For example, the entries for a sale of £720 (£600 + VAT at 20%) will be:

- **debit** customer's account £720 – this is the amount owed
- **credit** VAT account £120 – this is the VAT charged on the sale
- **credit** sales account £600 – this is the value of the goods sold

Chapter Summary

- Financial transactions are recorded in ledger accounts using double-entry bookkeeping principles.

- Each double-entry bookkeeping transaction involves a debit entry and a credit entry.

- Entries in the bank account and cash account are:
  - **debit** money in
  - **credit** money out

- Non-current assets are items purchased by a business for use on a semi-permanent basis, eg premises, vehicles, machinery and office equipment. The purchase of such items is called **capital expenditure**.

- Running expenses of a business, such as rent paid, wages, electricity, etc are called **revenue expenditure**.

- Other accounts are opened in the bookkeeping system for: capital, non-current assets, expenses, income, drawings and loans.

- Purchases account is used to record the purchase of goods in which the business trades: the normal entry is on the debit side.

- Sales account is used to record the sale of goods or services in which the business trades: the normal entry is on the credit side.

- The purchase of goods is recorded as:
  - **debit** purchases account
  - **credit** bank/cash account or, if bought on credit, trade payable's account

- The sale of goods or services is recorded as:
  - **debit** bank/cash account or, if sold on credit, trade receivable's account
  - **credit** sales account

- Purchases returns (or returns out) are recorded as:
  - **debit** trade payable's account
  - **credit** purchases returns account

- Sales returns (or returns in) are recorded as:
  - **debit** sales returns account
  - **credit** trade receivable's account

- 'Carriage' is the expense of transporting goods:
  - **carriage in (inwards)** is the cost of carriage paid on purchases
  - **carriage out (outwards)** is the cost of carriage paid on sales

- Prompt payment discount allowed is entered in the accounts as:
  - **debit** discounts allowed account
  - **credit** trade receivable's account

- Prompt payment discount received is entered as:
  - **debit** trade payable's account
  - **credit** discounts received account

- VAT account will record the amounts of input VAT (VAT on purchases and expenses) and output VAT (VAT on sales of goods and services).

Key Terms	**ledger accounts**	where double-entry bookkeeping transactions are recorded
	debit entry	the account which gains value, or records an asset or an expense
	credit entry	the account which gives value, or records a liability, or an income item
	capital	the amount of money invested in the business by the owner (or owners)
	non-current asset	item purchased by a business for use on a semi-permanent basis
	capital expenditure	the purchase of non-current assets for use by the business
	revenue expenditure	the expenses incurred in the day-to-day running of the business
	drawings	money taken from the business by the owner, in the form of cash or cheque (or sometimes goods) for personal use
	purchases account	used to record the purchase – whether on credit or for cash – of the goods in which the business trades
	sales account	used to record the sale – whether on credit or for cash – of the goods in which the business trades
	credit purchases	goods bought, with payment to be made at a later date
	credit sales	goods sold, with payment to be received at an agreed date in the future
	purchases returns	where a business returns goods to a supplier
	sales returns	where a customer returns goods to the business
	carriage in	the cost of carriage paid on purchases
	carriage out	the cost of carriage paid on sales
	prompt payment discount	an allowance off the invoice amount for quick payment
	discounts allowed	prompt payment discount allowed to customers
	discounts received	prompt payment discount received from suppliers

Activities

2.1 The payment of travel expenses in cash is recorded in the accounts as:

	Debit	Credit	
(a)	Travel expenses account	Drawings account	
(b)	Cash account	Travel expenses account	
(c)	Capital account	Travel expenses account	
(d)	Travel expenses account	Cash account	

2.2 A loan is received by cheque from John Box. This is recorded in the accounts as:

	Debit	Credit	
(a)	Bank account	Capital account	
(b)	Bank account	John Box: loan account	
(c)	Drawings account	John Box: loan account	
(d)	John Box: loan account	Bank account	

2.3 The owner of a business withdraws cash for her own use. This is recorded in the accounts as:

	Debit	Credit	
(a)	Drawings account	Bank account	
(b)	Bank account	Cash account	
(c)	Wages account	Cash account	
(d)	Drawings account	Cash account	

2.4 James Anderson has kept his bank account up-to-date, but has not got around to the other double-entry bookkeeping entries. Rule up the other accounts for him, and make the appropriate entries.

Dr				Bank account			Cr
20-4			£	20-4			£
2 Feb	Capital		7,500	6 Feb	Computer		2,000
13 Feb	Bank loan		2,500	9 Feb	Rent paid		750
20 Feb	Commission received		145	12 Feb	Wages		425
				23 Feb	Drawings		200
				25 Feb	Wages		380
				27 Feb	Van		6,000

Note: James Anderson is not registered for Value Added Tax

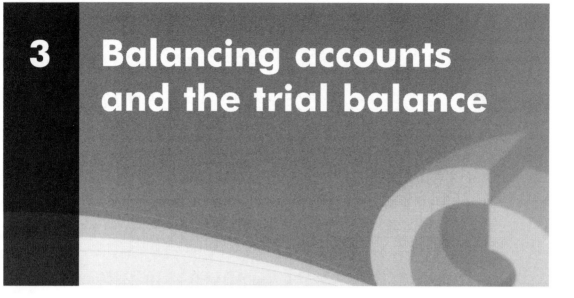

3 Balancing accounts and the trial balance

this chapter covers...

With the 'traditional' form of account (the 'T' account) that we have used so far, it is necessary to calculate the balance of each account from time-to-time, according to the needs of the business, and at the end of each financial year.

The balance of an account is the total of that account to date, eg the amount of wages paid, the amount of sales made. In this chapter we shall see how this balancing of accounts is carried out.

We shall then use the balances from each account in order to check the double-entry bookkeeping by extracting a trial balance, which is a list of the balances of all the general ledger accounts, including cash book (which contains bank account and cash account).

BALANCING THE ACCOUNTS

At regular intervals, often at the end of each month, 'T' accounts are balanced in order to show total amounts to date, for example:

- owing to each trade payable
- owing by each trade receivable
- cash and credit sales (referred to in total as 'revenue' or 'sales revenue')
- purchases
- sales returns (returns in)
- purchases returns (returns out)
- expenses incurred by the business
- non-current assets, eg premises, machinery, etc owned by the business
- bank and cash
- capital and drawings of the owner of the business
- liabilities, eg loans

The reason for balancing accounts is to enable the balances to be used in the trial balance (see page 43), which is a check on the accuracy of the double-entry bookkeeping and also the starting point for the preparation of year-end financial statements.

METHOD OF BALANCING ACCOUNTS

Set out below is an example of a traditional format double-entry account which has been balanced at the month-end:

Dr			Bank account			Cr
20-1		£	20-1			£
1 Sep	Capital	5,000	2 Sep	Computer		1,800
4 Sep	J Jackson: loan	2,500	7 Sep	Purchases		500
10 Sep	Sales	750	11 Sep	Drawings		100
			15 Sep	Wages		200
			30 Sep	Balance c/d		5,650
		8,250				8,250
1 Oct	Balance b/d	5,650				

The steps involved in balancing accounts are shown on the next page.

Step 1   The entries in the debit and credit money columns are totalled; these totals are not recorded in ink on the account at this stage, but can be written either as sub-totals in pencil on the account, or noted on a separate piece of paper. In the example on the previous page the debit side totals £8,250, while the credit side is £2,600.

Step 2   The difference between the two totals is the balance of the account and this is entered on the account:
- on the side of the smaller total
- on the next available line
- with the date of balancing (often the last day of the month)
- with the description 'balance c/d', or 'balance carried down'

In the example shown, the balance carried down is £8,250 – £2,600 = £5,650, entered in the credit column.

Step 3   Both sides of the account are now totalled, including the balance which has just been entered, and the totals (the same on both sides) are entered **on the same line** in the appropriate column, and double underlined. The double underline indicates that the account has been balanced at this point using the figures above the total: the figures above the underline should not be added in to anything below the underline.

In the example shown, the totals on each side of the account are £8,250.

Step 4   As we are using double-entry bookkeeping, there must be an opposite entry to the 'balance c/d' calculated in Step 2. The same money amount is entered **on the other side of the account** below the double underlined totals entered in Step 3. We have now completed both the debit and credit entry. The date is usually recorded as the next day after 'balance c/d', ie often the first day of the following month, and the description can be 'balance b/d' or 'balance brought down'.

In the example shown, the balance brought down on the bank account on 1 October 20-1 is £5,650 debit; this means that, according to the business's accounting records, there is £5,650 in the bank.

a practical point

When balancing accounts, use a pen and not a pencil (except for Step 1). If any errors are made, cross them through neatly with a single line, and write the corrected version on the line below. Avoid using correcting fluid – it may hide errors, but it can also conceal fraudulent transactions.

further examples of balancing accounts

Dr			Wages account			Cr
20-1			£	20-1		£
9 Apr	Bank		750	30 Apr	Balance c/d	2,250
16 Apr	Bank		800			
23 Apr	Bank		700			
			2,250			2,250
1 May	Balance b/d		2,250			

This wages account has transactions on one side only, but is still balanced in the same way. The account shows that the total amount paid for wages is £2,250.

Dr			B Lewis Limited			Cr
20-1			£	20-1		£
10 Apr	Purchases returns		30	7 Apr	Purchases	280
27 Apr	Bank		250			
			280			280

This trade payable's account has a 'nil' balance after the transactions for April have taken place. The two sides of the account are totalled and, as both debit and credit side are the same amount, there is nothing further to do, apart from entering the double underlined total.

Dr			A Holmes			Cr
20-1			£	20-1		£
1 Apr	Balance b/d		105	10 Apr	Bank	105
10 Apr	Sales		125	13 Apr	Sales returns	25
				30 Apr	Balance c/d	100
			230			230
1 May	Balance b/d		100			

This trade receivable's account has a debit balance at the start of the month of £105 brought down from March. After the various transactions for April, there remains a debit balance of £100 owing at 1 May.

Dr	Office equipment account		Cr
20-1	£	20-1	£
13 Apr Bank	2,000		

This account has just the one transaction and, in practice, there is no need to balance it. The account clearly has a debit balance of £2,000, which represents office equipment (a non-current asset).

Dr	Malvern Manufacturing Company		Cr
20-1	£	20-1	£
29 Apr Bank	250	17 Apr Purchases	250

This trade payable's account has a 'nil' balance, with just one transaction on each side. All that is needed here is to double underline the amount on both sides.

CONTROL ACCOUNTS

There is one further type of account to mention before looking at the accounts listed in the trial balance – a control account.

A control account is a summary account or master account, which records the totals of entries to a particular set of accounts.

Sales ledger control account shows the total of all the trade receivables' accounts in the sales ledger and tells the owner of the business how much in total is owing from trade receivables.

Purchases ledger control account shows the total of all the trade payables' accounts in the purchases ledger and tells the owner of the business how much in total is owing to trade payables.

Value Added Tax control account (also known as sales tax control account) brings together totals of VAT from books of prime entry, such as the day books and cash books, and tells the owner of the business how much in total is owing to (the usual situation for most businesses), or owing from, HM Revenue & Customs.

Payroll control account (also known as wages control account) brings together transactions from payroll accounts.

The use of control accounts is covered in more detail in Chapter 10.

control accounts and the trial balance

The trial balance (see next page) is the listing of all the account balances in two columns: debit balances on the left, credit balances on the right.

It is the balances of the control accounts which are taken to the trial balance rather than the individual trade receivables and trade payables account balances, which would clutter it up and make it very long. The description in the trial balance is 'sales ledger control account' (debit balance on the left) and 'purchases ledger control account' (credit balance on the right). This is illustrated in the following diagram.

EXTRACTING A TRIAL BALANCE

The purpose of a trial balance, which is taken from the accounting records – either manually or by generation of a computer report – is to:

■ check the accuracy of the double-entry bookkeeping, ie that the total of debit entries equals the total of the credit entries

■ form the basis for the preparation of the year-end financial statements of the business

A trial balance is a list of the balances of every account from the general ledger, (including cash book) setting out debit balances and credit balances in separate columns.

A trial balance is extracted at regular intervals – often at the end of each month. An example is shown on the next page.

Note the following points:

- The debit and credit columns have been totalled and are the same amount. Thus the trial balance proves that the accounting records are **arithmetically** correct – the total of the debits equals the total of the credits. (For types of errors, see page 47.)

- The heading for a trial balance gives the name of the business whose accounts have been listed and the date on which it was extracted.

- The balance for each account listed in the trial balance is the figure brought down after the accounts have been balanced.

- Most of the trial balances that you will see in Assessments are listed with the accounts in alphabetical order. There is no need for you to do this when preparing trial balances – unless, of course, you are instructed to do so, or are given an accounts list already in alphabetical order with the amounts to be filled in.

TARA SMITH, TRADING AS "THE FASHION SHOP" Trial balance as at 31 December 20-4		
	Dr £	Cr £
Opening inventory	12,500	
Purchases	105,000	
Sales revenue		155,000
Administration expenses	6,200	
Wages	23,500	
Rent paid	750	
Telephone	500	
Interest paid	4,500	
Travel expenses	550	
Premises	100,000	
Shop fittings	20,000	
Sales ledger control (trade receivables)	10,500	
Bank	5,450	
Cash	50	
Capital		75,000
Drawings	7,000	
Loan from bank		50,000
Purchases ledger control (trade payables)		14,500
Value Added Tax		2,000
	296,500	296,500

DEBIT AND CREDIT BALANCES – GUIDELINES

Certain accounts always have a debit balance, while others always have a credit balance. You should already know these, but the lists set out below will act as a revision guide, and will also help in your understanding of trial balances.

debit balances

- cash account
- purchases account
- sales returns account (returns in)
- non-current asset accounts, eg computers, vehicles, machinery, etc
- depreciation charges account (see Chapter 6)
- expenses accounts, eg wages, telephone, rent paid, discounts allowed, carriage in, carriage out, prepaid expenses; also income accrued (see Chapter 5)
- drawings account
- loan account, eg money lent by the business to another person or business
- sales ledger control account (the total of the trade receivables' accounts)

credit balances

- sales or sales revenue account
- purchases returns account (returns out)
- income accounts, eg rent received, discounts received, fees received, accrued expenses; also income prepaid (see Chapter 5)
- accumulated depreciation account (see Chapter 6)
- capital account
- loan account, eg money borrowed from a bank
- purchases ledger control account (the total of the trade payables' accounts)

Note that:

- **Bank account** can be either debit or credit – it will be debit when the business has money in the bank, and credit when it is overdrawn.
- **Value Added Tax account** (or sales tax account) can be either debit or credit – it will be debit when VAT is due to the business and credit when the business owes VAT to HM Revenue & Customs.
- Other account balances that can be either debit or credit include asset disposals (see Chapter 6), allowance for doubtful debts: adjustments, irrecoverable debts (see Chapter 7), and loan (noted above).

IF THE TRIAL BALANCE DOESN'T BALANCE . . .

If the trial balance fails to balance, ie the two totals are different, there is an error (or errors):

- **either** in the addition of the trial balance
- **and/or** in the double-entry bookkeeping

The procedure for finding the error(s) is as follows:

- check the addition of the trial balance

- check that the balance of each account has been correctly entered in the trial balance, and under the correct heading, ie debit or credit

- check that the balance of every account from the general ledger (including cash book) has been included in the trial balance

- check the calculation of the balance on each account

- calculate the amount that the trial balance is wrong, and then look in the accounts for a transaction for this amount: if one is found, check that the double-entry bookkeeping has been carried out correctly

- halve the amount by which the trial balance is wrong, and look for a transaction for this amount: if it is found, check the double-entry bookkeeping

- if the amount by which the trial balance is wrong is divisible by nine, then the error may be a reversal of figures, eg £65 entered as £56, or £45 entered as £54

- if the trial balance is wrong by a round amount, eg £10, £100, £1,000, the error is likely to be in the calculation of the account balances

- if the error(s) is still not found, it is necessary to check the bookkeeping transactions since the date of the last trial balance, by going back to the prime documents (invoices, cheques, etc) and the books of prime entry (day books and cash book)

- we will look at how to correct errors shown by the trial balance in Chapter 11, for example:
  - one-sided entry (ie only one of the two parts of a double-entry transaction has been recorded)
  - entry duplicated on one side, nothing on the other (ie two debits or two credits have been recorded for a transaction)
  - unequal entries (ie different amounts have been recorded for the debit and credit entries)
  - account balance incorrectly transferred to the trial balance

ERRORS NOT REVEALED BY A TRIAL BALANCE

As mentioned earlier, a trial balance does not prove the complete accuracy of the accounting records. The following are the main errors that are not revealed by a trial balance.

error of principle

This is when a transaction has been entered in the wrong type of account. For example, the cost of fuel for vehicles has been entered as a debit to vehicles account, and as a credit to bank account. The error is that vehicles account is a non-current asset and the transaction should have been debited to the vehicle expenses account. If not corrected, such an error of principle will show a false financial position for the business.

error of commission

Here, a transaction is entered to the wrong account. For example, a sale of goods on credit to A T Hughes entered as a debit to A J Hughes' account. The double-entry bookkeeping has been completed, but the error will be discovered when A J Hughes complains about the incorrect charge.

This error can also occur between other accounts, such as expenses or non-current assets.

error of original entry

Here, the correct accounts have been used, and the correct sides: what is wrong is that the amount has been entered incorrectly in **both** accounts. This could be caused by a 'bad figure' written on a financial document, eg an invoice, or it could be caused by a 'reversal of figures', eg an amount of £45 being entered in both accounts as £54. Note that where both debit and credit entries have been made incorrectly the trial balance will still balance; if one entry has been made incorrectly and the other is correct, then the error will be revealed.

error of omission

Here a transaction has been completely omitted from the accounting records, ie both the debit and credit entries have not been made.

reversal of entries

With this error, the debit and credit entries have been made in the accounts but on the wrong side of the two accounts concerned. For example, a cash sale has been entered wrongly as a debit to sales account, and as a credit to cash account. (This should have been entered as a debit to cash account, and a credit to sales account.)

Correction of errors is covered fully in Chapter 11.

IMPORTANCE OF THE TRIAL BALANCE

A business will extract a trial balance on a regular basis to check the arithmetical accuracy of the bookkeeping. More importantly, the trial balance is used as a basis for the preparation of the **financial statements** of a business. These financial statements, which are prepared once a year (often more frequently) comprise:

■ statement of profit or loss

■ statement of financial position

The financial statements show the owner(s) how profitable the business has been, what the business owns, and how the business is financed. The preparation of financial statements is an important aspect of accounting and one which we shall be developing further in this book.

In the next chapter we will see how the two-column trial balance is extended and the figures entered into further columns as a method of preparing the financial statements.

Chapter Summary

■ The traditional 'T' account needs to be balanced at regular intervals – often at the month-end.

■ When balancing accounts, the bookkeeper must adhere strictly to the rules of double-entry bookkeeping.

■ When each account in the ledger has been balanced, a trial balance can be extracted.

■ A trial balance does not prove the complete accuracy of the accounting records; errors not revealed by a trial balance are:
  – error of principle
  – error of commission
  – error of original entry
  – error of omission
  – reversal of entries

■ The trial balance is used as the starting point for the preparation of a business's financial statements.

Key Terms	balance of account	the total amount of the account to date
	control account	summary or master account which records the totals of entries to a particular set of accounts; examples are: – sales ledger control account – purchases ledger control account – Value Added Tax control account – payroll control account
	trial balance	list of the balances of every account forming the general ledger (including cash book), distinguishing between those accounts which have debit balances and those which have credit balances
	error of principle	transaction entered in the wrong type of account
	error of commission	transaction entered into the wrong account
	error of original entry	wrong amount entered incorrectly in accounts
	error of omission	business transaction completely omitted from the accounting records
	reversal of entries	debit and credit entries made on the wrong side of the accounts

Activities

3.1 A business's bank account is as follows:

Dr			Bank account			Cr
20-7		£	20-7			£
1 Jan	Capital	1,000	9 Jan	Computer		500
19 Jan	Sales	650	12 Jan	Purchases		400
			27 Jan	Purchases		350
			29 Jan	Electricity		75

At 31 January 20-7, the balance of the account is:

(a)	Credit £325	
(b)	Debit £1,650	
(c)	Debit £325	✓
(d)	Credit £1,325	

3.2   Which **one** of the following accounts normally has a debit balance?

(a) Capital account	
(b) Purchases account	✓
(c) Sales account	
(d) Purchases returns account	

3.3   Which **one** of the following accounts normally has a credit balance?

(a) Purchases account	
(b) Premises account	
(c) Capital account	✓
(d) Wages account	

3.4   The following are the business transactions of Andrew Johnstone, a retailer of computer software, for the months of January and February 20-4:

Transactions for January

1 Jan	Started in business with £10,000 in the bank
4 Jan	Paid rent on premises £500, by cheque
5 Jan	Bought shop fittings £1,500, by cheque
7 Jan	Bought stock of computer software £5,000, on credit from Comp Supplies Limited
11 Jan	Software sales £1,000 paid into bank
12 Jan	Software sales £1,250 paid into bank
16 Jan	Software sales £850 on credit to Rowcester College
20 Jan	Paid Comp Supplies Limited £5,000 by cheque
22 Jan	Software sales £1,450 paid into bank
25 Jan	Bought software £6,500 on credit from Comp Supplies Limited
27 Jan	Rowcester College returns software £100

Transactions for February

2 Feb	Paid rent on premises £500 by cheque
4 Feb	Software sales £1,550 paid into bank
5 Feb	Returned faulty software, £150 to Comp Supplies Limited
10 Feb	Software sales £1,300 paid into bank
12 Feb	Rowcester College pays the amount owing by cheque
15 Feb	Bought shop fittings £850 by cheque
19 Feb	Software sales £1,600 paid into bank
22 Feb	Paid Comp Supplies Limited the amount owing by cheque
24 Feb	Bought software £5,500 on credit from Comp Supplies Limited
25 Feb	Software sales £1,100 paid into bank
26 Feb	Software sales £1,050 on credit to Rowcester College

You are to:

(a) Record the January transactions in the double-entry accounts, and balance each account at 31 January 20-4

(b) Draw up a trial balance at 31 January 20-4

(c) Record the February transactions in the double-entry accounts, and balance each account at 28 February 20-4

(d) Draw up a trial balance at 28 February 20-4

Notes:
- Andrew Johnstone is not registered for Value Added Tax
- day books are not required
- Andrew Johnstone's accounting system does not use control accounts
- make sure that you leave plenty of space for each account – particularly sales, purchases and bank

3.5 Prepare the trial balance of Samantha Wilkes as at 31 March 20-4. **You are to** fill in the missing figure for her capital in order to balance the trial balance.

	£
Bank overdraft	2,750
Purchases	14,890
Sales revenue	35,680
Purchases returns	440
Purchases ledger control	2,360
Office equipment	8,000
Vehicle	14,000
Opening inventory	2,810
Sales returns	550
Sales ledger control	3,840
Administration expenses	12,060
Value Added Tax owing	1,420
Carriage out	740
Discount received	210
Capital	?

4 Financial statements – the extended trial balance

this chapter covers...

So far we have looked at the techniques of recording different types of financial transactions in the books of account. The financial accountant will use the information from the accounting system, summarised in the two-column trial balance, to produce the year-end financial statements of the business: statement of profit or loss and statement of financial position.

In this chapter we see how these financial statements (final accounts) can be produced using an extended trial balance (ETB). This sets out debit and credit columns for:

■ the ledger balances

■ adjustments to the figures

■ the financial statements where the figures are used: statement of profit or loss and statement of financial position

Later in the chapter we study the link between double-entry bookkeeping and the financial statements.

FINANCIAL STATEMENTS

At regular intervals the owner/owners of a business and other interested parties need to know how the business is progressing. To meet this need, financial statements (final accounts) are prepared which comprise:

- **statement of profit or loss** – showing the profitability and performance of the business during the accounting period
- **statement of financial position** – showing what the business is worth (in terms of assets, liabilities, and capital) at the end of the accounting period

In this chapter we will see how the figures for the financial statements are prepared by means of the **extended trial balance** which takes the figures from the two-column trial balance explained in the last chapter and sets them out in columns ready for the preparation of the statement of profit or loss and statement of financial position. To illustrate this process we will look at the accounts of a sole trader shop owner, Tara Smith.

In the three chapters which follow we will be developing the extended trial balance of Tara Smith to deal with accounting adjustments for accruals and prepayments, depreciation of non-current assets, irrecoverable debts and allowance for doubtful debts. Such adjustments are used to present a more realistic view of the business's financial statements.

ACCOUNTING PERIODS

There is a link between the financial statements: a statement of profit or loss covers a specific time period, and a statement of financial position shows the state of the business on the last day of that time period. For example:

- statement of profit or loss **for the year ended** 31 March 20-6
- statement of financial position **as at** 31 March 20-6

The time period covered by the statement of profit or loss is known as an **accounting period**. Generally, for each business, an accounting period covers the same length of time, for example the year ended 31 March 20-6, year ended 31 March 20-7, and so on. The last day of one accounting period is immediately followed by the first day of the next accounting period. While accounting periods can cover any length of time, the most common are:

- **monthly or quarterly** – used within a business to monitor activity and profitability in the accounting period, and the state of the business, in terms of assets and liabilities, at the end of the period

- **half-yearly** – often produced by public limited companies as information for their shareholders
- **annually** – the most common accounting period (but not always to fit the calendar year) used by virtually every business from sole traders and partnerships, through to the largest public limited companies

FINANCIAL STATEMENTS AND THE TRIAL BALANCE

As we have seen in earlier chapters, the bookkeeping system records day-to-day financial transactions. At regular intervals a trial balance is extracted to prove the arithmetical accuracy of the bookkeeping. It is the trial balance that provides the starting point in the preparation of financial statements. There are two trial balance formats:

- the two-column trial balance (shown opposite)
- the trial balance **extended** into a number of columns (see page 57)

Note that the statement of profit or loss is an 'account' in terms of double-entry bookkeeping. This means that an amount recorded in this account must be recorded elsewhere in the bookkeeping system, eg a debit to the statement of profit or loss is recorded as a credit to another account, in order to complete double-entry. By contrast, the statement of financial position is not an account, but is a list of account balances remaining after the statement of profit or loss has been prepared.

To understand the preparation of the extended trial balance you should now read the Tara Smith Case Study which follows.

Case Study

TARA SMITH: THE EXTENDED TRIAL BALANCE

situation

Tara Smith runs a designer clothes shop called 'The Fashion Shop'. Her bookkeeper has just extracted the year-end trial balance shown opposite. You will see that the trial balance includes the inventory value at the *start* of the year, while the end-of-year inventory valuation is noted *after* the trial balance. For the purposes of financial accounting, the inventory of goods for resale is valued by the business at the end of each financial year, and the valuation is subsequently entered into the bookkeeping system (see page 60).

We will go through the process of preparing the financial statements using an extended trial balance (ETB) – this is the next stage on from the two-column trial balance and is often presented in a spreadsheet format. We will go through this process before explaining adjustments for items such as accruals, prepayments, depreciation of non-current assets, irrecoverable debts, and allowance for doubtful debts (each of which will be dealt with in Chapters 5 to 7).

TARA SMITH, TRADING AS "THE FASHION SHOP"

	Dr £	Cr £
Opening inventory	12,500	
Purchases	105,000	
Sales revenue		155,000
Administration expenses	6,200	
Wages	23,500	
Rent paid	750	
Telephone	500	
Interest paid	4,500	
Travel expenses	550	
Premises at cost	100,000	
Shop fittings at cost	20,000	
Sales ledger control (trade receivables)	10,500	
Bank	5,450	
Cash	50	
Capital		75,000
Drawings	7,000	
Loan from bank		50,000
Purchases ledger control (trade payables)		14,500
Value Added Tax		2,000
	296,500	296,500

Note: closing inventory was valued at £10,500

The layout on page 57 shows how an extended trial balance uses columns and rows to prepare the financial statements of Tara Smith. The steps to complete the extended trial balance are as follows:

step 1 Enter the trial balance details into the account name and ledger balances columns. Total the debit and credit columns of ledger balances to show that the trial balance proves the arithmetical accuracy of the bookkeeping. Note that the blank lines after premises at cost and shop fittings at cost will be used for accumulated depreciation amounts – dealt with in Chapter 6.

step 2 Deal with adjustments – in this example, the only adjustment is for the valuation of closing inventory (at 31 December 20-4). In the adjustments columns the amount of closing inventory is credited to the statement of profit or loss and debited to the statement of financial position (see page 60 for the bookkeeping entries for closing inventory). Transfer the adjustment for closing inventory to:

- statement of profit or loss – credit column
- statement of financial position – debit column

Now total the debit and credit adjustment columns; note that the totals are the same, ie they balance. We shall be using the other adjustment items (eg accruals and prepayments) in the next few chapters.

step 3

Transfer to the statement of profit or loss columns the rows for:

- opening inventory at the start of the year
- purchases made by the business
- sales made by the business (together with small amounts of income, if any)
- expenses (revenue expenditure) of the business, such as administration expenses, wages, rent paid, interest paid, travel expenses

Ensure that debit balances from the trial balance rows are entered in the debit column of the statement of profit or loss; credit balances are entered in the credit column.

step 4

Transfer to the statement of financial position columns the remaining rows from the trial balance (keeping debit and credit figures in the correct columns). These figures represent:

- assets (amounts owned by the business) such as premises, shop fittings, sales ledger control, bank, cash
- liabilities (amounts owed by the business) such as bank overdraft, purchases ledger control, loans, Value Added Tax due to HM Revenue & Customs
- capital (the amount of the owner's finance in the business)
- drawings (the amount withdrawn from the business by the owner during the year)

step 5

In the statement of profit or loss columns, total the money amounts and then, just like balancing an account, enter the amount required to make both debit and credit sides equal: here it is £12,000. If the amount is entered on the debit side, it represents the profit of the business for the accounting period; if on the credit side, it is a loss. For Tara Smith, it is a profit of £12,000 for the financial year.

step 6

Enter the profit or loss for the year in the statement of financial position columns, but on the opposite side to that in the statement of profit or loss. For example, with Tara Smith's business, the amount of the profit row is £12,000, which is *debited* in the statement of profit or loss column and *credited* in the statement of financial position column.

Now total the debit and credit statement of financial position columns. They balance with the same total – here £153,500 – which proves that the statement of financial position balances.

points to note about the extended trial balance

Each account balance from the trial balance is entered into the financial statements once only – either to the statement of profit or loss (income and expenses), or to the statement of financial position (assets, liabilities, capital and drawings). The additional items of closing inventory and profit or loss for the year are entered into both financial statements – this ensures that the double-entry bookkeeping rules of one debit and one credit entry for each transaction are maintained.

There are blank rows below the items of premises and shop fittings. These are intentionally left blank and will eventually show accumulated depreciation amounts (see Chapter 6).

EXTENDED TRIAL BALANCE TARA SMITH TRADING AS "THE FASHION SHOP" **31 DECEMBER 20-4**

Account name	Ledger balances		Adjustments		Statement of profit or loss		Statement of financial position	
	Dr £	Cr £	Dr £	Cr £	Dr £	Cr £	Dr £	Cr £
Opening inventory	12,500				12,500			
Purchases	105,000				105,000			
Sales revenue		155,000				155,000		
Administration expenses	6,200				6,200			
Wages	23,500				23,500			
Rent paid	750				750			
Telephone	500				500			
Interest paid	4,500				4,500			
Travel expenses	550				550			
Premises at cost	100,000						100,000	
Shop fittings at cost	20,000						20,000	
Sales ledger control	10,500						10,500	
Bank	5,450						5,450	
Cash	50						50	
Capital		75,000						75,000
Drawings	7,000						7,000	
Loan from bank		50,000						50,000
Purchases ledger control		14,500						14,500
Value Added Tax		2,000						2,000
Closing inventory: statement of profit or loss				10,500		10,500		
Closing inventory: statement of financial position			10,500				10,500	
Accruals								
Prepayments								
Depreciation charges								
Irrecoverable debts								
Allowance for doubtful debts								
Allowance for doubtful debts: adjustment								
Profit/loss for the year					12,000			12,000
	296,500	296,500	10,500	10,500	165,500	165,500	153,500	153,500

Revenue expenditure (the payment of expenses) is shown in the statement of profit or loss, while **capital expenditure** (the cost of non-current assets, such as premises, vehicles and equipment) is shown in the statement of financial position. Note that if, for example, the cost of buying a new vehicle was wrongly recorded as an expense in the statement of profit or loss, then

- profit would be understated (or even a loss sustained)
- the statement of financial position would not show the value of a non-current asset owned by the business

This means that both financial statements would fail to show the correct state of the business's finances. Thus it is important to show revenue expenditure in the statement of profit or loss, and capital expenditure in the statement of financial position – we will look in more detail at these two types of expenditure in Chapter 8.

EXTENDED TRIAL BALANCE – LAYOUT

The extended trial balance gives an understanding of the principles of financial statements by showing:

- the profit or loss made by the business during the accounting period
- the assets, liabilities and capital of the business at the end of the accounting period

The extended trial balance format is often used by accountancy businesses as a step towards preparing year-end financial statements for their clients. When the adjustments have been completed, it provides a posting sheet for making transfers in the general ledger (see the bookkeeping entries in the section which follows).

To help with your practice of extended trial balances, a layout or pro forma is included in the Appendix. This may be photocopied (it is advisable to enlarge it up to A4 size); alternatively, the layout can be downloaded from www.osbornebooks.co.uk.

Note that the layout used for the extended trial balance includes space for a number of other adjustments (eg accruals and prepayments) – these will be covered in the later chapters.

DOUBLE-ENTRY BOOKKEEPING AND THE FINANCIAL STATEMENTS

We have already noted that the statement of profit or loss forms part of the double-entry bookkeeping system. Therefore, each amount recorded in this must have an opposite entry in the general ledger. In preparing the statement of profit or loss we are, in effect, emptying each account that has been storing up a record of transactions during the course of the financial year and transferring it to the statement of profit or loss.

> **Tutorial note:** Each of the transfers shown below requires a journal entry – see Chapter 11. This records the amount of the transfer in a book of prime entry and gives the bookkeeper the authority to record the transactions in the double-entry accounts.

purchases, sales and inventory

In the accounts of Tara Smith the balance of purchases account will be transferred to the statement of profit or loss as follows (**debit** statement of profit or loss; **credit** purchases account):

Dr			**Purchases account**		Cr
20-4		£	20-4		£
31 Dec	Balance b/d (ie total for year)	105,000	31 Dec	Statement of profit or loss*	105,000

*Note that, alternatively, this reference may be written as 'Profit or loss account'.

The account now has a nil balance and is ready to receive the transactions for next year.

The balances of sales account (and also, where used, sales returns and purchases returns accounts) will be cleared to nil in a similar way and the amounts transferred to the statement of profit or loss, as debits or credits as appropriate.

Inventory account, however, is dealt with differently. Inventory is valued for financial accounting purposes at the end of each year (it is also likely to be valued more regularly in order to provide management information). Only the annual inventory valuation is recorded on inventory account, and the account is not used at any other time. After the bookkeeper has extracted the trial balance, but **before** preparation of the statement of profit or loss, the inventory account appears as follows:

Dr			**Inventory account**		Cr
20-4		£	20-4		£
31 Dec	Balance b/d	12,500			

This balance, which is the opening inventory valuation for the year, is transferred to the statement of profit or loss to leave a nil balance, as follows (**debit** statement of profit or loss; **credit** inventory account), as follows:

Dr		Inventory account			Cr
20-4		£	20-4		£
31 Dec	Balance b/d	12,500	31 Dec	Statement of profit or loss	12,500

The *closing* inventory valuation for the year – for Tara Smith it is £10,500 – is now recorded on the account as an asset (**debit** inventory account; **credit** statement of profit or loss):

Dr		Inventory account			Cr
20-4		£	20-4		£
31 Dec	Balance b/d	12,500	31 Dec	Statement of profit or loss	12,500
31 Dec	Statement of profit or loss	10,500	31 Dec	Balance c/d	10,500
20-5			20-5		
1 Jan	Balance b/d	10,500			

The closing inventory figure is shown on the statement of financial position, and will be the opening inventory in next year's statement of profit or loss. In the extended trial balance the closing inventory figure is normally put through the adjustments columns; however, some trial balances in Activities and Assessments may already incorporate the closing inventory adjustments – see Activity 4.6 on page 65 for an example of this.

expenses

The expenses or overheads of running the business are transferred from the double-entry accounts to the statement of profit or loss. For example, the wages account of Tara Smith has been storing up information during the year and, at the end of the year, the total is transferred to the statement of profit or loss (**debit** statement of profit or loss; **credit** wages account):

Dr		Wages account			Cr
20-4		£	20-4		£
31 Dec	Balance b/d (ie total for year)	23,500	31 Dec	Statement of profit or loss	23,500

The wages account now has a nil balance and is ready to receive transactions for 20-5, the next financial year.

profit/loss for the year

After the statement of profit or loss has been completed, the amount of profit or loss for the year is transferred to the owner's capital account. The bookkeeping entries are:

- profit for the year
  - **debit** statement of profit or loss
  - **credit** capital account
- loss for the year
  - **debit** capital account
  - **credit** statement of profit or loss

Profit increases the owner's stake in the business by adding to capital account, while a loss decreases the owner's stake.

Note that profit for the year and loss for the year are often referred to as net profit and net loss.

At the same time the account for drawings, which has been storing up the amount of drawings during the year is also transferred to capital account:

- **debit** capital account
- **credit** drawings account

Thus the total of drawings for the year is debited to capital account.

When these transactions are completed, the capital account for Tara Smith appears as:

Dr			Capital account		Cr
20-4		£	20-4		£
31 Dec	Drawings for year	7,000	31 Dec	Balance b/d	75,000
31 Dec	Balance c/d	80,000	31 Dec	Statement of profit or loss (profit for year)	12,000
		87,000			87,000
20-5			20-5		
			1 Jan	Balance b/d	80,000

Note: Although the balance of capital account at the end of the year, £80,000, does not appear on the extended trial balance, the constituent figures are shown, ie capital £75,000, profit £12,000, drawings £7,000.

statement of financial position

Unlike the statement of profit or loss, the statement of financial position is not part of the double-entry accounts. The statement of financial position is made up of those accounts which remain with balances at the end of the financial year, after the statement of profit or loss transfers have been made. Thus it consists of asset and liability accounts, not forgetting the asset of closing inventory, together with the owner's capital and drawings.

Chapter Summary

■ The financial statements (final accounts) of a business comprise:
- – statement of profit or loss
- – statement of financial position

■ The extended trial balance method of preparing financial statements starts with the trial balance and then transfers each account balance to one of the financial statements.

■ Each account balance from the trial balance is entered into the financial statements once only; the additional items of closing inventory and profit or loss for the year are entered into both financial statements – this ensures that the double-entry rules of one debit and one credit entry for each transaction are maintained.

■ The statement of profit or loss forms part of the double-entry system; amounts entered must have the opposite entry recorded in the appropriate general ledger account.

■ The statement of financial position is not part of the double-entry system; it lists the balances of accounts for assets, liabilities and capital at a particular date.

■ The extended trial balance gives an understanding of the principles of financial statements. It is often used by accountancy businesses as a step towards preparing year-end financial statements for their clients.

Key Terms

financial statements	financial statements (final accounts), comprising statement of profit or loss and statement of financial position, produced at least once a year, which give information to the owner(s) and other interested parties on how the business is progressing
statement of profit or loss	shows the profit or loss of the business for the accounting period
statement of financial position	shows the assets, liabilities and capital of the business at the end of the accounting period
extended trial balance	a spreadsheet format used as a method of preparing the financial statements

Activities

Extended trial balance format: a blank photocopiable extended trial balance is included in the Appendix – it is advisable to enlarge it up to full A4 size. Alternatively you can set up a computer spreadsheet – but remember to allow for all the rows shown on the layout – they will be needed in later chapters. The layout can also be downloaded from www.osbornebooks.co.uk.

4.1 Which **one** of the following does not appear in the statement of profit or loss?

(a)	Salaries	
(b)	Vehicles	✓
(c)	Fuel for vehicles	
(d)	Profit for the year	

4.2 Profit for the year is:

(a)	Assets minus liabilities	
(b)	Sales revenue minus purchases	
(c)	Closing bank balance minus opening bank balance	
(d)	Income minus expenses	✓

4.3 **You are to** fill in the missing figures for the following businesses:

	Income	Expenses	Profit or loss*	Assets	Liabilities	Capital
	£	£	£	£	£	£
Business A	100,000	60,000	40,000	250,000	150,000	100,000
Business B	80,000	70,000	10,000	200,000	100,000	100,000
Business C	70,000	50,000	20,000	90,000	40,000	50,000
Business D	60,000	75,000	(15,000)	130,000	60,000	70,000
Business E	90,000	100,000	(10,000)	100,000	60,000	40,000

*Note: loss is indicated by brackets

4.4 Complete the table below for each item (a) to (g) indicating with a tick:

• whether the item would normally appear in the debit or credit column of the trial balance

• in which financial statement the item would appear at the end of the accounting period and whether as a debit or credit in the extended trial balance

| | | Trial balance | | FINANCIAL STATEMENTS | | | |
| | | | | Statement of profit or loss | | Statement of financial position | |
		Debit	Credit	Debit	Credit	Debit	Credit
(a)	Salaries	✓		✓			
(b)	Purchases	✓		✓			
(c)	Sales ledger control	✓				✓	
(d)	Sales returns	✓		✓			
(e)	Discounts received		✓		✓		
(f)	Vehicle	✓				✓	
(g)	Capital		✓				✓

4.5 The following trial balance has been extracted by Nick Johnson on 31 December 20-3:

	Dr £	Cr £
Opening inventory	25,000	
Purchases	210,000	
Sales revenue		310,000
Administration expenses	12,400	
Wages	41,000	
Rent paid	7,500	
Telephone	1,000	
Interest paid	9,000	
Travel expenses	1,100	
Premises at cost	200,000	
Machinery at cost	40,000	
Sales ledger control (trade receivables)	31,000	
Bank	900	
Cash	100	
Capital		150,000
Drawings	14,000	
Loan from bank		100,000
Purchases ledger control (trade payables)		29,000
Value Added Tax		4,000
	593,000	593,000

Note: closing inventory was valued at £21,000

You are to prepare the extended trial balance of Nick Johnson for the year ended 31 December 20-3.

4.6 The following trial balance has been extracted by the bookkeeper of Alan Harris at 30 June 20-4:

	Dr	Cr
	£	£
Opening inventory	13,250	
Capital		70,000
Premises at cost	65,000	
Vehicle at cost	5,250	
Purchases	55,000	
Sales revenue		85,500
Administration expenses	850	
Wages	9,220	
Rent paid	1,200	
Telephone	680	
Interest paid	120	
Travel expenses	330	
Sales ledger control (trade receivables)	1,350	
Purchases ledger control (trade payables)		6,400
Value Added Tax		1,150
Bank	2,100	
Cash	600	
Drawings	8,100	
Closing inventory – statement of profit or loss		18,100
Closing inventory – statement of financial position	18,100	
	181,150	181,150

Tutorial note: this trial balance already incorporates the closing inventory adjustments

You are to prepare the extended trial balance of Alan Harris for the year ended 30 June 20-4.

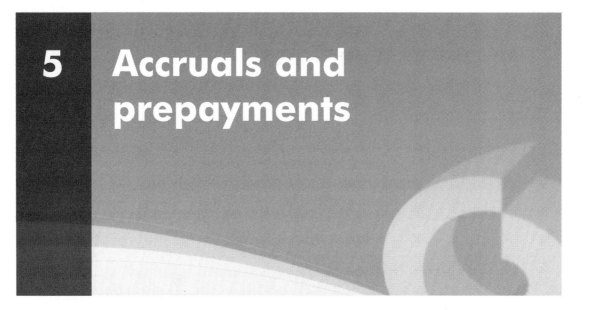

5 Accruals and prepayments

this chapter covers...

In the previous chapter we have looked at the preparation of financial statements – or final accounts – using the extended trial balance, or spreadsheet, approach.

There are a number of adjustments which are made to the financial statements at the year-end in order to show a more realistic view of the state of the business. This chapter is concerned with the adjustments to be made for accruals and prepayments of expenses and income.

To illustrate the effect of adjustments for accruals and prepayments on financial statements we shall be referring to the extended trial balance of Tara Smith seen in the previous chapter.

ACCRUAL OF EXPENSES

An accrual is an amount due, or the calculation of an amount due (eg a pro-rata amount for part of a year), in an accounting period which is unpaid at the end of that period, eg an insurance premium or an electricity bill not yet paid.

In the financial statements, accrued expenses are:

■ added to the expense account (eg insurance account, electricity account) shown in the trial balance, before it is listed in the statement of profit or loss

■ shown as a liability in the year-end statement of financial position

The reason for dealing with accruals in this way is to ensure that the statement of profit or loss records the expense that has been incurred for the year, instead of simply the amount that has been paid. In other words, the expense is adjusted to relate to the time period covered by the statement of profit or loss. The year-end statement of financial position shows a liability for the amount that is due, but unpaid.

journal entry

A journal entry – see Chapter 11 – is made at the end of the financial year for accruals of expenses. The journal entry records the amounts of accruals in a book of prime entry and gives the bookkeeper the authority to record the transactions in the double-entry accounts.

Case Study

TARA SMITH: ACCRUAL OF AN EXPENSE

The trial balance of Tara Smith at 31 December 20-4 (see page 55) shows a debit balance for telephone expenses of £500. Before preparing the financial statements, a telephone bill for £100 is received on 4 January 20-5, ie early in the new financial year. An examination of the bill shows that it is for costs incurred in 20-4, therefore an adjustment needs to be made to the financial statements for 20-4 to record this accrued expense.

accruals – the extended trial balance

The accrual is shown in the extended trial balance as follows:

• in the adjustments columns

  – record £100 on the debit side of the telephone row

  – record £100 on the credit side of the accruals row

• on the debit side of the statement of profit or loss column the total cost of the telephone row is now £600 (ie £500 from the trial balance, plus £100 accrual)

• on the credit side of the statement of financial position column £100 from the accruals row is shown as a liability of the business

This adjustment is shown on Tara Smith's extended trial balance (page 72): the figures affected by the accrual (and also the prepayment – see below) are shaded for ease of reference.

accruals – the double-entry bookkeeping

In the double-entry accounts, the amount of the accrual and the transfer of the year's expense to the statement of profit or loss are shown. The telephone account in the records of Tara Smith will appear as follows:

Dr		Telephone account		Cr
20-4		£	20-4	£
31 Dec	Balance b/d	500	31 Dec Statement of profit or loss	600
31 Dec	Accrued expenses	100		
		600		600

Dr		Accrued expenses account		Cr
20-4		£	20-4	£
31 Dec	Balance c/d	100	31 Dec Telephone	100
20-5		£	20-5	£
1 Jan	Telephone	100	1 Jan Balance b/d	100

Notes:

- The bookkeeper's trial balance showed the debit side balance brought down of £500 on the telephone account
- As £100 is owing for telephone expenses at the end of the year, the transfer to the statement of profit or loss is the expense that has been incurred for the year of £600
- The amount of the accrual is transferred to the credit side of the accrued expenses account; it is listed on the statement of financial position at 31 December 20-4 as a liability
- At the beginning of the new financial year, amounts held in accrued expenses account are reversed to the expenses accounts. For telephone, the transfer is debit accrued expenses, credit telephone

Later on, for example on 15 January 20-5, the telephone bill is paid from the bank and the telephone account now appears as:

Dr		Telephone account		Cr
20-5		£	20-5	£
15 Jan	Bank	100	1 Jan Accrued expenses (reversal)	100

The effect of the payment on 15 January is that telephone account now has a 'nil' balance and the bill received on 4 January will not be recorded as an expense in the statement of profit or loss drawn up at the end of 20-5.

PREPAYMENT OF EXPENSES

A prepayment is a payment made in advance, or the calculation of an amount paid in advance (eg a pro-rata amount for part of a year), of the accounting period to which it relates.

A prepayment is, therefore, the opposite of an accrual: with a prepayment of expenses, some part of the expense has been paid in advance.

In the financial statements, prepaid expenses are:

■ deducted from the expense account shown in the trial balance before it is listed in the statement of profit or loss

■ shown as an asset in the year-end statement of financial position

As with accruals, the reason for dealing with prepaid expenses in this way is to ensure that the statement of profit or loss records the cost incurred for the year, and not the amount that has been paid – the expense relates to the time period covered by the statement of profit or loss. The year-end statement of financial position shows an asset for the amount that has been prepaid.

journal entry

A journal entry – see Chapter 11 – is made at the end of the financial year for prepayments of expenses. The journal entry records the amounts of prepayments in a book of prime entry and gives the bookkeeper the authority to record the transactions in the double-entry accounts.

Case Study

TARA SMITH: PREPAID EXPENSES

Tara Smith tells you that the trial balance figure for rent paid – for a storage unit – of £750 includes £75 of rent for January 20-5 paid in advance. An adjustment needs to be made to the financial statements for 20-4 to record this prepaid expense.

prepayments – the extended trial balance

The prepayment is shown in the extended trial balance as follows:

• in the adjustments columns

　– record £75 on the credit side of the rent paid row

　– record £75 on the debit side of the prepayments row

• on the debit side of the statement of profit or loss column the total cost of rent paid is now £675 (ie £750 from the trial balance, less £75 prepaid)

• on the debit side of the statement of financial position column £75 from the prepayments row is shown as an asset of the business

The prepayment adjustment is shown on Tara Smith's extended trial balance (page 72), together with the accrual we have just dealt with – both are shaded for ease of reference.

prepayments – the double-entry bookkeeping

In the double-entry accounts, the amount of the prepayment and the transfer of the year's expense to the statement of profit or loss are shown.

The rent paid account in the records of Tara Smith will appear as follows:

Dr			**Rent paid account**		Cr
20-4		£	20-4		£
31 Dec	Balance b/d	750	31 Dec	Statement of profit or loss	675
			31 Dec	Prepaid expenses	75
		750			750
20-5		£	20-5		£
1 Jan	Prepaid expenses (reversal)	75			

Dr			**Prepaid expenses account**		Cr
20-4		£	20-4		£
31 Dec	Rent paid account	75	31 Dec	Balance c/d	75
20-5		£	20-5		£
1 Jan	Balance b/d	75	1 Jan	Rent paid account	75

Notes:

- The trial balance total for rent paid is £750

- As £75 is prepaid at the end of the year, the transfer to the statement of profit or loss is the expense that has been incurred for the year of £675

- The amount of the prepayment is transferred to the debit side of prepaid expenses account; it is listed on the statement of financial position at 31 December 20-4 as an asset

- At the beginning of the new financial year, amounts held in prepaid expenses account are reversed to the expenses accounts. For rent prepaid, the transfer is debit rent paid, credit prepaid expenses

- This now gives the rent paid account a debit balance of £75 which will be included in the expense for rent paid for the year and will be transferred to the statement of profit or loss on 31 December 20-5

TARA SMITH: ACCRUALS AND PREPAYMENTS IN THE FINANCIAL STATEMENTS

We will now focus on how the adjustments for accruals and prepayments are shown in the statement of profit or loss and statement of financial position of Tara Smith. Remember that we are taking note of the following items at 31 December 20-4:

- telephone accrued £100
- rent prepaid £75

extended trial balance

The layout for the extended trial balance – see next page – includes rows for accruals and prepayments. The columns which are affected are adjustments, statement of profit or loss and statement of financial position – the altered figures are shaded for illustrative purposes. Note that:

- the statement of profit or loss columns show the net figure for each expense after allowing for the accrual or prepayment
- the statement of financial position columns show the accrual as a liability and the prepayment as an asset

The effect of taking note of accruals and prepayments is to alter profit for the year from that shown by the extended trial balance for Tara Smith, seen earlier (page 57):

	£
Profit for the year before adjustments	12,000
Less telephone accrued	100
	11,900
Add rent prepaid	75
Profit for the year after adjustments	11,975

EXTENDED TRIAL BALANCE   TARA SMITH TRADING AS "THE FASHION SHOP"   31 DECEMBER 20-4

Account name	Ledger balances Dr £	Ledger balances Cr £	Adjustments Dr £	Adjustments Cr £	Statement of profit or loss Dr £	Statement of profit or loss Cr £	Statement of financial position Dr £	Statement of financial position Cr £
Opening inventory	12,500				12,500			
Purchases	105,000				105,000			
Sales revenue		155,000				155,000		
Administration expenses	6,200				6,200			
Wages	23,500				23,500			
Rent paid	750			75	675			
Telephone	500		100		600			
Interest paid	4,500				4,500			
Travel expenses	550				550			
Premises at cost	100,000						100,000	
Shop fittings at cost	20,000						20,000	
Sales ledger control	10,500						10,500	
Bank	5,450						5,450	
Cash	50						50	
Capital		75,000						75,000
Drawings	7,000						7,000	
Loan from bank		50,000						50,000
Purchases ledger control		14,500						14,500
Value Added Tax		2,000						2,000
Closing inventory: statement of profit or loss				10,500		10,500		
Closing inventory: statement of financial position			10,500				10,500	
Accruals				100				100
Prepayments			75				75	
Depreciation charges								
Irrecoverable debts								
Allowance for doubtful debts								
Allowance for doubtful debts: adjustment								
Profit/loss for the year					11,975			11,975
	296,500	296,500	10,675	10,675	165,500	165,500	153,575	153,575

ACCRUALS AND PREPAYMENTS OF INCOME

Just as expenses can be accrued or prepaid at the end of a financial year, income amounts can also be accrued or prepaid.

accrual of income

Here, income of a business is due but unpaid at the end of the financial year. For example, commission might have been earned, but the payment is received after the end of the financial year to which it relates. In the extended trial balance and financial statements, accrual of income is:

■ added to the income amount in the trial balance before it is listed in the statement of profit or loss

■ shown as an asset in the year-end statement of financial position

A journal entry – see Chapter 11 – is made at the end of the financial year for accruals of income, which shows the entries to be made in the accounts.

prepayment of income

Here, the income of a business has been paid in advance by the payer. For example, the rent received account for this financial year could include an advance payment received from a tenant in respect of the next financial year. In the extended trial balance and financial statements, prepayment of income is:

■ deducted from the income amount in the trial balance before it is listed in the statement of profit or loss

■ shown as a liability in the year-end statement of financial position

As with expenses, the objective of taking note of accruals and prepayments of income is to ensure that the money amounts relate to the period covered by the statement of profit or loss.

A journal entry – see Chapter 11 – is made at the end of the financial year for prepayments of income, which shows the entries to be made in the accounts.

> **Tutorial note:** do not net off accruals of income and expenditure or prepayments of income and expenditure – it is not good accounting practice and each should be shown separately in the statement of financial position.

PRIVATE EXPENSES AND GOODS FOR OWN USE

Adjustments also have to be made in the financial statements for the amount of any business facilities that are used by the owner for private purposes. These adjustments are for private expenses and goods for own use.

private expenses

Sometimes the owner of a business uses business facilities for private purposes, eg telephone, or car. The owner will agree that part of the expense shall be charged to him or her as drawings, while the other part represents a business expense.

For example, the balance of the telephone account is £600 at the year-end, and the owner agrees that this should be split as one-quarter private use, and three-quarters to the business. The bookkeeping entries to record such adjustments are:

- – **debit** drawings account
- – **credit** telephone account
- – **debit** statement of profit or loss
- – **credit** telephone account

The telephone account will be completed at the end of the year as follows:

Dr		Telephone account		Cr
20-4		£	20-4	£
31 Dec	Balance b/d	600	31 Dec Drawings	150
			31 Dec Statement of profit or loss	450
		600		600

When using a trial balance to produce the financial statements, private expenses should be adjusted by deducting from the expense account and adding to drawings.

A journal entry – see Chapter 11 – is made at the end of the financial year for private expenses.

goods for own use

When the owner of a business takes some of the goods in which the business trades for his or her own use, the double-entry bookkeeping is:

- – **debit** drawings account
- – **credit** purchases account

Note that:

- ▨ Where a business is VAT-registered, VAT must be accounted for on goods taken by the owner.
- ▨ An alternative method of accounting for goods for own use is:
  - – **debit** drawings account
  - – **credit** sales account

This method is preferred by HM Revenue & Customs for tax purposes; however, either is acceptable for the purpose of financial accounting – which method is used will depend on the custom and practice of the business.

When using a trial balance to produce the financial statements, goods for own use should be adjusted by adding to drawings and deducting from purchases (or adding to sales).

A journal entry – see Chapter 11 – is made at the end of the financial year for goods for own use.

INCOME AND EXPENDITURE ACCOUNTING

In this chapter we have made adjustments for accruals and prepayments to ensure that the statement of profit or loss shows the correct amount of income and expenses for the financial year, ie what should have been paid, instead of what has actually been paid. In doing this we are adopting the principle of **income and expenditure accounting**. If we simply used the trial balance figures, we would be following the principle of **receipts and payments accounting**, ie comparing money coming in, with money going out: this will usually give a false view of the profit for the year.

The principle of income and expenditure accounting is applied in the same way to purchases and sales, although no adjustments are needed because of the way in which these two are handled in the accounting records. For purchases, the amount is entered into the accounts when the supplier's invoice is received, although the agreement to buy will be contained in the legal contract which exists between buyer and seller. From the accounting viewpoint, it is receipt of the supplier's invoice that causes an accounting entry to be made; the subsequent payment is handled as a different accounting transaction. A business could have bought goods, not paid for them yet, but will have a purchases figure to enter into the statement of profit or loss – the suppliers will soon be wanting payment!

Sales are recorded in a similar way – when the invoice for the goods is sent, rather than when payment is made. This applies the principle of income and expenditure accounting. In this way, a business could have made a large amount of sales, which will be entered in the statement of profit or loss, but may not yet have received any payments.

accruals principle of accounting

The way in which financial statements are adjusted to take note of accruals and prepayments is recognised in the **accruals principle** of accounting – this is discussed in more detail in Chapter 8.

Chapter Summary

- Financial statements are prepared on the income and expenditure basis, rather than the receipts and payments basis.

- Adjustments should be made at the end of the financial year in respect of accruals and prepayments.

- In the financial statements, accrued expenses are:
  - added to the expense of the trial balance
  - shown as a liability in the statement of financial position

- Prepaid expenses are:
  - deducted from the expense of the trial balance
  - shown as an asset in the statement of financial position

- An accrual of income is:
  - added to the income amount of the trial balance
  - shown as an asset in the statement of financial position

- A prepayment of income is:
  - deducted from the income amount of the trial balance
  - shown as a liability in the statement of financial position

- Adjustments also need to be made in the financial statements for:
  - private expenses
  - goods for own use

- A journal entry – see Chapter 11 – must be made for all adjustments for accruals and prepayments and for private expenses and goods for own use. The journal entry records the amounts in a book of prime entry and gives the bookkeeper the authority to record the transactions in the double-entry accounts.

- Accruals and prepayments are an application of the accruals principle of accounting – see Chapter 8.

Key Terms		
	accrual of expenses	an amount due, or the calculation of an amount due (pro-rata), in an accounting period which is unpaid at the end of that period
	prepayment of expenses	a payment made in advance, or the calculation of an amount paid in advance (pro-rata), of the accounting period to which it relates
	accrual of income	income of a business due in an accounting period which is unpaid at the end of that period
	prepayment of income	income of a business which has been paid in advance of the accounting period to which it relates
	pro-rata	the amount of accrual or prepayment calculated for part of a year
	goods for own use	where the owner of a business takes some of the goods in which the business trades for his/her own use
	income and expenditure accounting	recording the amounts that should have been received and paid during an accounting period
	receipts and payments accounting	recording the actual amounts that have been received and paid during an accounting period, without taking note of accruals and prepayments

Activities

> **Extended trial balance format:** a blank photocopiable pro forma of the extended trial balance is included in the Appendix – it is advisable to enlarge it up to full A4 size. The layout can also be downloaded from www.osbornebooks.co.uk.

5.1 Wages accrued are shown as:

(a)	An asset on the statement of financial position	
(b)	A debit balance in accrued expenses account	
(c)	Income on the statement of profit or loss	
(d)	A credit balance in accrued expenses account	✓

5.2   Rates prepaid are shown as:

(a) A liability on the statement of financial position	
(b) An expense on the statement of profit or loss	
(c) A debit balance in prepaid expenses account	✓
(d) A credit balance in prepaid expenses account	

5.3   John Harrington runs an import/export business. At the end of his financial year, on 31 December 20-7, the vehicle expenses account is as follows:

Dr		Vehicle expenses account		Cr
20-7		£	20-7	£
31 Dec Balance b/d		1,680		

John Harrington tells you that 25 per cent of vehicle expenses represents his private motoring expenses. He asks you to transfer the amount to his drawings account, before transferring the remainder to the statement of profit or loss. Show the vehicle expenses account after these transactions have been entered.

5.4   Explain how the following would be dealt with in the statement of profit or loss, and statement of financial position of a business with a financial year-end of 31 December 20-1:

(a)   Wages and salaries paid to 31 December 20-1 amount to £55,640. However, at that date £1,120 is owing: this amount is paid on 4 January 20-2.

(b)   Rates totalling £3,565 have been paid to cover the period 1 January 20-1 to 31 March 20-2.

(c)   A computer is rented at a cost of £150 per month. The rental for January 20-2 was paid in December 20-1 and is included in the total payments during 20-1 which amount to £1,950.

5.5   This Activity is about accounting for accruals and prepayments and preparing a trial balance.

You are working on the accounts of a business for the year ended 31 March 20-7. In this Activity you can ignore VAT.

You have the following information:

Balances as at:	1 April 20-6
	£
Accrual for rent paid	750
Prepayment for administration expenses	250

The bank summary for the year shows payments for rent of £11,250. Included in this figure is £2,250 for the quarter ended 31 May 20-7.

(a) **You are to** prepare the rent paid account for the year ended 31 March 20-7 and close it off by showing the transfer to the statement of profit or loss. Dates are not required.

Rent paid

	£		£

The bank summary for the year shows payments for administration expenses of £10,400. In April 20-7, £175 was paid for administration expenses incurred in March 20-7.

(b) **You are to** prepare the administration expenses account for the year ended 31 March 20-7 and close it off by showing the transfer to the statement of profit or loss. Include dates.

Administration expenses

		£			£

You have the following extract of balances from the general ledger.

(c) **Using your answers** to (a) and (b), and the figures given below, enter amounts in the appropriate debit or credit column for the accounts shown. Do not enter zeros in unused column cells.

Extract from trial balance as at 31 March 20-7

Account	£	Dr £	Cr £
Accrued expenses			
Capital	75,000		
Discounts received	680		
Drawings	10,000		
Interest received	200		
Machinery at cost	20,000		
Prepaid expenses			
Sales revenue	115,000		

5.6 This Activity is about accounting for accruals and prepayments and preparing a trial balance.

You are working on the accounts of a business for the year ended 30 June 20-3. In this Activity you can ignore VAT.

You have the following information:

Balances as at:	1 July 20-2 £
Prepayment for rent received	450
Accrual for vehicle expenses	220

The bank summary for the year shows rent received of £5,850. Included in this figure is £1,350 for the three months ended 31 August 20-3.

(a) **You are to** prepare the rent received account for the year ended 30 June 20-3 and close it off by showing the transfer to the statement of profit or loss. Dates are not required.

Rent received

	£		£

The bank summary for the year shows payments for vehicle expenses of £6,450. In July 20-3, £380 was paid for vehicle expenses incurred in June 20-3.

(b) **You are to** prepare the vehicle expenses account for the year ended 30 June 20-3 and close it off by showing the transfer to the statement of profit or loss. Include dates.

Vehicle expenses

		£			£

You have the following extract of balances from the general ledger.

(c) **Using your answers** to (a) and (b), and the figures given below, enter amounts in the appropriate debit or credit column for the accounts shown. Do not enter zeros in unused column cells.

Extract from trial balance as at 30 June 20-3

Account	£	Dr £	Cr £
Accrued expenses			
Capital	30,000		
Cash	250		
Discounts allowed	600		
Prepaid income			
Purchases	15,500		
Sales returns	850		
Vehicles at cost	12,000		

5.7 The following trial balance has been extracted by the bookkeeper of Don Smith, who runs a wholesale stationery business, at 31 December 20-2:

	Dr £	Cr £
Sales ledger control	24,325	
Purchases ledger control		15,408
Value Added Tax		4,276
Capital		30,000
Bank		1,083
Rent and rates	10,862	
Electricity	2,054	
Telephone	1,695	
Salaries	55,891	
Vehicles at cost	22,250	
Office equipment at cost	7,500	
Vehicle expenses	10,855	
Drawings	15,275	
Discounts allowed	478	
Discounts received		591
Purchases	138,960	
Sales revenue		257,258
Opening inventory	18,471	
	308,616	308,616

Notes at 31 December 20-2:

- closing inventory was valued at £14,075
- rates prepaid £250
- electricity accrued £110
- salaries accrued £365

You are to prepare the extended trial balance of Don Smith for the year ended 31 December 20-2.

5.8 The following trial balance has been extracted by the bookkeeper of John Barclay at 30 June 20-3:

	Dr	Cr
	£	£
Sales revenue		864,321
Purchases	600,128	
Sales returns	2,746	
Purchases returns		3,894
Office expenses	33,947	
Salaries	122,611	
Vehicle expenses	36,894	
Discounts allowed	3,187	
Discounts received		4,951
Sales and purchases ledger control	74,328	52,919
Value Added Tax		10,497
Opening inventory	63,084	
Vehicles at cost	83,500	
Office equipment at cost	23,250	
Land and buildings at cost	100,000	
Bank loan		75,000
Bank	1,197	
Capital		155,000
Drawings	21,710	
	1,166,582	1,166,582

Notes at 30 June 20-3:

- closing inventory was valued at £66,941
- vehicle expenses accrued £1,250
- office expenses prepaid £346
- goods costing £250 were taken by John Barclay for his own use

You are to prepare the extended trial balance of John Barclay for the year ended 30 June 20-3.

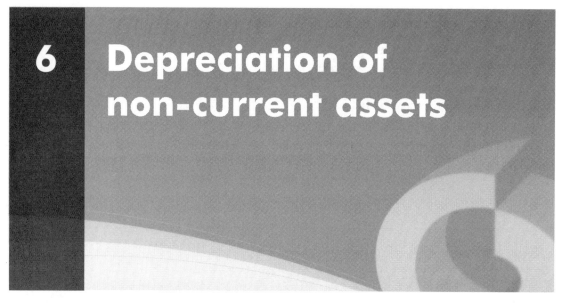

6 # Depreciation of non-current assets

this chapter covers...

Non-current assets, such as machinery and vehicles, lose value as time goes by, largely as a result of wear and tear. This loss in value is known as depreciation. In financial accounting it is necessary to record an estimate of depreciation in the accounting records. In this chapter we will:

■ *define depreciation and understand its purpose*

■ *consider common methods of calculating depreciation*

■ *study the bookkeeping entries for depreciation*

■ *apply depreciation to the extended trial balance*

■ *investigate the bookkeeping entries involved when a non-current asset is sold*

WHAT IS DEPRECIATION?

Depreciation is the estimate of the amount of the loss in value of a non-current asset over its useful life.

The purpose of depreciation is to spread the cost of a non-current asset over its useful life. Most non-current assets lose value over time and it is necessary, in order to present a realistic view of the business, to record the amount of the loss in value. This is done by:

- showing an expense – depreciation charge – in the statement of profit or loss
- showing the non-current asset at carrying amount – cost price less accumulated depreciation – in the statement of financial position

Depreciation – which is linked to the cost price of the asset – **estimates** the loss in value and the time period over which the loss occurs.

The main factors which cause non-current assets to depreciate are:

- **wear and tear through use**, eg vehicles, machinery, etc
- **passage of time**, eg the lease on a building
- **depletion**, eg extraction of stone from a quarry
- **economic reasons**
    - obsolescence, eg a new design of machine which does the job better and faster, making the old machine obsolete
    - inadequacy, eg a machine such as a photocopier no longer has the volume capacity to meet the needs of the business

Non-current assets – including buildings – are depreciated over their useful life. The only exception is freehold land, which is a non-wasting asset that does not normally depreciate (unless it is a quarry or a mine, when it will have a known useful economic life).

Depreciation links directly to the non-current asset register (see Chapter 9) where a business keeps records of all the non-current assets it owns, together with the cost price of each, depreciation charge, and accumulated depreciation.

CALCULATING DEPRECIATION

There are several different ways in which we can allow for the loss in value of non-current assets. All of these are **estimates**, and it is only when disposal of the asset takes place that we will know the accuracy of the estimate. A business can use any acceptable depreciation method; however, once selected, the method would not be changed from one year to the next without good reason.

Common methods of calculating depreciation are:

- straight-line method
- diminishing balance method (also called reducing balance method)
- units of production method – see page 89

To calculate the annual depreciation charge, we will use the following data:

DATA FOR DEPRECIATION OF MACHINE

Cost price (net of VAT)	£2,000
Useful life	4 years
Estimated production:	
Year 1	60,000 units
Year 2	50,000 units
Year 3	25,000 units
Year 4	25,000 units
Total	160,000 units
Estimated residual value at end of four years	£400

---

straight-line method of depreciation

With this method, a fixed percentage or fraction is written off the **original cost** of the asset each year. For this example, 25 per cent or one-quarter will be written off each year by the straight-line method. The depreciation charge for **each year** is:

$$£2,000 \quad \times \quad 25\% \quad = \quad £500 \text{ per year}$$

The depreciation percentage or fraction will be decided by a business on the basis of what it considers to be the useful life of the asset. Thus, 25 per cent each year gives a useful life of four years (assuming a nil residual value at the end of its life).

Different classes of non-current assets are often depreciated at different rates, eg vehicles may be depreciated at a different rate to office equipment. It is important that, once a particular method and rate of depreciation has been selected, depreciation should be applied consistently, ie methods and rates are not changed from year-to-year without good reason.

When an asset has a residual value at the end of its useful life, depreciation is calculated on the **depreciable amount**, ie cost, less residual value as follows:

$$\frac{\text{cost of asset} - \text{estimated residual (scrap or salvage) sale proceeds}}{\text{useful life of asset}}$$

For example, the machine above is expected to have a residual (scrap or salvage) value of £400 (net of VAT) at the end of four years. This means that the depreciation charge will be:

$$\frac{£2,000 - £400}{4 \text{ years}} = £400 \text{ per year (ie 20\% per annum on cost)}$$

diminishing (reducing) balance method

With this method, a fixed percentage is written off the diminished balance – referred to as the 'carrying amount' – of the asset each year. The diminished – or reduced – balance is the cost of the asset less the accumulated depreciation. For example, the machine is to be depreciated by 33.3% recurring (one-third) each year, using the diminishing balance method. The depreciation charges for the four years of ownership are:

	£
Original cost	2,000
Year 1 depreciation: 33.3% recurring of £2,000	667
Carrying amount at end of year 1	1,333
Year 2 depreciation: 33.3% of £1,333	444
Carrying amount at end of year 2	889
Year 3 depreciation: 33.3% of £889	296
Carrying amount at end of year 3	593
Year 4 depreciation: 33.3% of £593	193
Carrying amount at end of year 4 (residual value)	400

Note: the figures have been rounded to the nearest £, and year 4 depreciation has been adjusted by £5 to leave a residual value of £400.

As a matter of interest, the formula to calculate the percentage of diminishing balance depreciation is:

$$r = 1 - \sqrt[n]{\frac{s}{c}}$$

where:

r = percentage rate of depreciation

n = number of years

s = scrap or salvage (residual) value

c = cost of asset

In the example on the previous page the 33.3% is calculated as:

$$r = 1 - \sqrt[4]{\frac{400}{2,000}}$$

$$r = 1 - \sqrt[4]{0.2}$$ (to find the fourth root press the square root key on the calculator twice)

$$r = 1 - 0.669$$

r = 0.331 or 33.1% (which is close to the 33.3% used above)

Note: you will not need to use this formula in AAT Assessments.

straight-line and diminishing balance methods compared

The following tables use the depreciation amounts calculated on the previous page, assuming a residual value of £400.

Straight-line depreciation				
	1	**2**	**3**	**4**
Year	**Original cost**	**Depreciation charges**	**Accumulated depreciation**	**Carrying amount* (ie column 1-3)**
	£	£	£	£
1	2,000	400	400	1,600
2	2,000	400	800	1,200
3	2,000	400	1,200	800
4	2,000	400	1,600	400
*Note: Carrying amount is cost price less accumulated depreciation, ie column 1, less column 3.				

Diminishing (reducing) balance depreciation				
	1	**2**	**3**	**4**
Year	**Original cost**	**Depreciation charges**	**Accumulated depreciation**	**Carrying amount (ie column 1-3)**
	£	£	£	£
1	2,000	667	667	1,333
2	2,000	444	1,111	889
3	2,000	296	1,407	593
4	2,000	193	1,600	400

Using these tables, we will now see how the two methods compare:

	Straight-line method	**Diminishing balance method**
Depreciation charges	Same money amount each year – see chart below	Different money amounts each year: more than straight-line in early years, less in later years – see chart below
Depreciation percentage or fraction	Lower depreciation percentage or fraction required to achieve same residual value	Higher depreciation percentage or fraction required to achieve same residual value – but can never reach a nil value
Suitability	Best used for non-current assets likely to be kept for the whole of their useful lives, eg machinery, office equipment, fixtures and fittings	Best used for non-current assets which depreciate more in early years and which are not kept for the whole of their useful lives, eg vehicles

The year-by-year depreciation charges of the machine in the example are shown on the following bar chart:

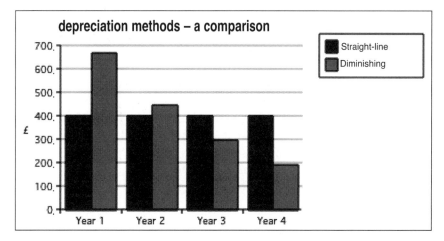

units of production method

This method estimates:

- the number of units to be produced by a machine, or
- the number of hours of operation of a machine, or
- the number of miles expected from a vehicle

over its expected life. Depreciation for a given year is calculated by reference to the number of units/hours/miles for that year.

For example, the machine referred to earlier is to be depreciated by £1,600 (ie £2,000 – £400 residual value). As the total number of units to be produced by the machine is expected to be 160,000, then each year's depreciation will be calculated at £100 for every 10,000 units produced (£1,600 ÷ 160,000 units).

Depreciation amounts will be:

Year 1	£600	depreciation for year
Year 2	£500	depreciation for year
Year 3	£250	depreciation for year
Year 4	£250	depreciation for year
	£1,600	total depreciation

This method has the benefit of linking usage (ie units/hours/miles) to the depreciation amount. In years of high usage, depreciation is higher than in years of low usage. As the asset gets older, so the usage may be lower, but repair costs may be increasing: in this way the total expense (depreciation + repair costs) will probably be a similar amount from year-to-year.

BOOKKEEPING ENTRIES FOR DEPRECIATION

Once the depreciation charges have been calculated using the methods described in the previous section, they can be recorded in the non-current asset register (see Chapter 9) and in the bookkeeping system. It is usual to separate out the main classes of non-current assets – premises, vehicles, machinery, computers, office equipment – and to record separately the financial information for each.

journal entry

A journal entry – see Chapter 11 – is made at the end of the financial year for the depreciation charge for each class of non-current asset. The journal entry records amounts of depreciation charges in a book of prime entry and gives the bookkeeper the authority to record the transactions in the double-entry accounts.

bookkeeping accounts

In bookkeeping, the usual procedure is to have three accounts in the general ledger:

- **non-current asset at cost account** for each class of asset – eg machinery at cost – which records the cost price of the asset (note that the value of the asset can include certain other capital costs, eg installation costs – see page 143)
- **depreciation charges account**, which records the amount of depreciation for the asset for the year

■ **accumulated depreciation account** for each class of asset – eg machinery accumulated depreciation account – which records the amount of depreciation to date

BOOKKEEPING ENTRIES FOR DEPRECIATION

A machine is purchased for £2,000 net of VAT on 1 January 20-4. It is decided to depreciate it at twenty per cent each year, using the straight-line method. The business's financial year runs from 1 January to 31 December. The general ledger accounting records for the first four years will be:

Dr		**Machinery at cost account**		Cr
20-4		£	20-4	£
1 Jan	Bank	2,000		

This account remains with the balance of £2,000, which is the cost price of the machine. (The other transactions on 1 January 20-4 are to bank account and VAT account – these have not been shown.)

> **Note that**, if the business in this Case Study was not registered for VAT, the full cost of the non-current asset, ie £2,400, would be recorded in the machinery at cost account. Depreciation would then be calculated on £2,400 x 20 per cent = £480 per year.

Dr		**Depreciation charges account**			Cr
20-4		£	20-4		£
31 Dec	Machinery: accumulated depreciation	400	31 Dec	Statement of profit or loss	400
20-5			20-5		
31 Dec	Machinery: accumulated depreciation	400	31 Dec	Statement of profit or loss	400
20-6			20-6		
31 Dec	Machinery: accumulated depreciation	400	31 Dec	Statement of profit or loss	400
20-7			20-7		
31 Dec	Machinery: accumulated depreciation	400	31 Dec	Statement of profit or loss	400

The depreciation charges account acts as a 'holding' account for the year's depreciation. The amount is:

• credited to depreciation charges account, and debited to the statement of profit or loss

• debited to depreciation charges account, and credited to accumulated depreciation account

Note that depreciation charges account may be credited with depreciation amounts for various classes of non-current assets (eg buildings, machinery, vehicles); the amounts are then debited out and credited to the accumulated depreciation account for each class of non-current asset.

Dr			**Machinery: accumulated depreciation account**		Cr
20-4		£	20-4		£
31 Dec	Balance c/d	400	31 Dec	Depreciation charges	400
20-5			20-5		
31 Dec	Balance c/d	800	1 Jan	Balance b/d	400
			31 Dec	Depreciation charges	400
		800			800
20-6			20-6		
31 Dec	Balance c/d	1,200	1 Jan	Balance b/d	800
			31 Dec	Depreciation charges	400
		1,200			1,200
20-7			20-7		
31 Dec	Balance c/d	1,600	1 Jan	Balance b/d	1,200
			31 Dec	Depreciation charges	400
		1,600			1,600
20-8			20-8		
			1 Jan	Balance b/d	1,600

The accumulated depreciation account – which is specific to each class of non-current asset – stores up the amounts of the depreciation charges year by year. Notice that, while the asset account of machinery has a debit balance, accumulated depreciation account has a credit balance. The difference between the two balances at any time will tell us the carrying amount of the asset, ie what it is worth according to our accounting records. For example, at 31 December 20-6, the carrying amount of the machine is £800 (£2,000 cost, less £1,200 accumulated depreciation).

When a business owns several non-current assets of the same class, eg several machines, it is usual practice to maintain only one asset at cost account and one accumulated depreciation account for that class. This does mean that the calculation of amounts of depreciation can become quite complex – particularly when assets are bought and sold during the year. It is good practice to calculate the separate depreciation amount for each machine, or asset, before amalgamating the figures as the year's depreciation charges. These amounts will be shown separately for each asset held in the non-current asset register – see Chapter 9.

DEPRECIATION AND FINANCIAL STATEMENTS

accruals principle of accounting

The way in which financial statements are adjusted to take note of depreciation of non-current assets is recognised in the **accruals principle** of accounting – discussed in more detail in Chapter 8.

statement of profit or loss

The depreciation amount calculated for each class of non-current asset is listed amongst the expenses in the statement of profit or loss. For example, to consider the machine depreciated in the previous sections, the statement of profit or loss will show 'depreciation charges: machinery £400' amongst the expenses. The double-entry bookkeeping records the annual amount for depreciation as follows:

– **debit** statement of profit or loss
– **credit** depreciation charges account

As we have seen earlier, amounts held in depreciation charges account are then debited out and credited to the appropriate accumulated depreciation accounts.

statement of financial position

Each class of non-current asset is shown:

– at cost price in the debit column
– with accumulated depreciation (often on the line below cost price – see page 95) in the credit column

Note that the net amount of these two shows the carrying amount of the asset at the date of the statement of financial position.

The table below shows how the depreciation on the machine in the Case Study (bookkeeping entries on page 91) will be shown in the extended trial balances.

Year	Statement of profit or loss		Statement of financial position	
	Dr	Cr	Dr	Cr
	Expense	**Income**	**Cost**	**Accumulated depreciation**
	£	£	£	£
20-4	400	–	2,000	400
20-5	400	–	2,000	800
20-6	400	–	2,000	1,200
20-7	400	–	2,000	1,600

depreciation policies of a business

In Activities and Assessments, information will be given – where it is needed – on the accounting policy for depreciation of the business whose accounts are being prepared. In particular, information will be given on what to do when a non-current asset is bought part of the way through a business's financial year. The choices here will be to depreciate for the part of the year that it is owned; alternatively the business may choose to depreciate for the whole year on assets held at the end of the year.

Note: In AAT Assessments you may be required to make pro-rata calculations for part of a year for the straight-line depreciation method only (not the diminishing balance method). For example, if the machine from the Case Study had been bought on 1 April 20-4 (rather than 1 January 20-4) the business might decide to calculate depreciation on its ownership of nine months. The pro-rata depreciation will then be £300 (ie £400/12months x 9 months) for the first year.

Case Study

TARA SMITH:
DEPRECIATION IN THE FINANCIAL STATEMENTS

We will now focus on how the depreciation amounts are shown in the statement of profit or loss and the statement of financial position. We will continue with the trial balance of Tara Smith and include depreciation adjustments for the year of:

- premises: 2 per cent straight-line, ie £2,000
- shop fittings: 25 per cent diminishing balance, ie £5,000

extended trial balance

The layout for the extended trial balance – see opposite – includes a pre-printed row for depreciation. Study the extended trial balance on the next page and read the notes that follow.

The depreciation is shown in the extended trial balance as follows:

- in the account name column:
  - on the blank line below premises write in 'premises: accumulated depreciation'
  - on the blank line below shop fittings write in 'shop fittings: accumulated depreciation'
- in the adjustments columns:
  - record £7,000 (ie £2,000 + £5,000) on the debit side of the depreciation charges row
  - record £2,000 on the credit side of the premises: accumulated depreciation row
  - record £5,000 on the credit side of the shop fittings: accumulated depreciation row

EXTENDED TRIAL BALANCE — TARA SMITH TRADING AS "THE FASHION SHOP" — 31 DECEMBER 20-4

Account name	Ledger balances Dr £	Ledger balances Cr £	Adjustments Dr £	Adjustments Cr £	Statement of profit or loss Dr £	Statement of profit or loss Cr £	Statement of financial position Dr £	Statement of financial position Cr £
Opening inventory	12,500				12,500			
Purchases	105,000				105,000			
Sales revenue		155,000				155,000		
Administration expenses	6,200				6,200			
Wages	23,500				23,500			
Rent paid	750			75	675			
Telephone	500		100		600			
Interest paid	4,500				4,500			
Travel expenses	550				550			
Premises at cost	100,000						100,000	
Premises: accumulated depreciation				2,000				2,000
Shop fittings at cost	20,000						20,000	
Shop fittings: accumulated depreciation				5,000				5,000
Sales ledger control	10,500						10,500	
Bank	5,450						5,450	
Cash	50						50	
Capital		75,000						75,000
Drawings	7,000						7,000	
Loan from bank		50,000						50,000
Purchases ledger control		14,500						14,500
Value Added Tax		2,000						2,000
Closing inventory: statement of profit or loss				10,500		10,500		
Closing inventory: statement of financial position			10,500				10,500	
Accruals				100				100
Prepayments			75				75	
Depreciation charges			7,000		7,000			
Irrecoverable debts								
Allowance for doubtful debts								
Allowance for doubtful debts: adjustment								
Profit/loss for the year					4,975			4,975
	296,500	296,500	17,675	17,675	165,500	165,500	153,575	153,575

- on the debit side of the statement of profit or loss column record the depreciation charges for the year of £7,000

- on the credit side of the statement of financial position column record the £2,000 and £5,000 accumulated depreciation on the two classes of assets

Remember that:

- depreciation charges is the annual amount of depreciation

- accumulated depreciation is the total depreciation to date for each class of non-current asset

As this is the first year that Tara Smith has recorded depreciation, both depreciation charges and accumulated depreciation amounts are the same. The figures for depreciation are shaded for ease of reference (note that the extended trial balance already incorporates adjustments for accruals and prepayments of expenses). As a result of the depreciation charges, profit for the year is reduced by £7,000 (ie £2,000 + £5,000) to £4,975.

DEPRECIATION: A NON-CASH EXPENSE

It is very important to realise that depreciation is a non-cash expense: unlike the other expenses in the statement of profit or loss, no payment is made for depreciation. In cash terms, depreciation causes no outflow of money. Nevertheless, it is correct, in the financial statements of a business, to show an allowance for depreciation in the statement of profit or loss, and the accumulated depreciation in the statement of financial position. This is because the business has had the use of the asset, and needs to record the fall in value as an expense to present a true picture of its financial state. Thus we are led back to the definition of depreciation as 'the estimate of the amount of the loss in value of a non-current asset over its useful life', ie it is an accounting adjustment.

As depreciation is a non-cash expense, it should be noted that depreciation is not a method of providing a fund of cash which can be used to replace the asset at the end of its life. In order to do this, it is necessary to create a separate fund into which cash is transferred at regular intervals. This technique is often known as a sinking fund, and it needs to be represented by a separate bank account, eg a deposit account, which can be drawn against when the new non-current asset is to be purchased.

DISPOSAL OF NON-CURRENT ASSETS

When a non-current asset is sold or disposed, it is necessary to bring together:

■ the original cost of the asset

■ accumulated depreciation over the life of the asset

■ disposal proceeds

In the non-current asset register (see Chapter 9) it is necessary to identify the correct asset which is being disposed and to remove it from the non-current asset register. At the same time, amounts for original cost, accumulated depreciation and disposal proceeds are transferred from the appropriate accounts in the general ledger of the double-entry system to an asset disposal account. The **disposals account** will enable us to calculate the gain or loss on disposal of the asset caused by over or under depreciation (over depreciation = gain on disposal; under depreciation = loss on disposal).

The double-entry transactions are:

■ original cost of the asset

– **debit** asset disposals account

– **credit** non-current asset account

■ depreciation to date

– **debit** accumulated depreciation account

– **credit** asset disposals account

Note:

The depreciation charge for the current accounting period may need to be calculated, eg if disposal takes place part of the way through a financial year and the business's policy is to charge for part-years.

■ disposal proceeds

– **debit** bank/cash account

– **credit** asset disposals account

■ loss on disposal

– **debit** statement of profit or loss

– **credit** asset disposals account

■ gain on disposal

– **debit** asset disposals account

– **credit** statement of profit or loss

Small adjustments for gains or losses on disposals – caused by over or under depreciation respectively – will usually be needed because it is impossible, at the start of an asset's life, to predict exactly what it will sell for in a number of years' time.

journal entries

A journal entry – see Chapter 11 – is made to record all general ledger transfers in connection with the disposal of non-current assets. This journal entry records in a book of prime entry:

– the original cost of the asset being debited to asset disposals account

– the accumulated depreciation being credited to asset disposals account

– the disposal proceeds being credited to asset disposals account

– the amount of over or under depreciation being credited or debited to the statement of profit or loss

The journal entry gives the bookkeeper the authority to record the transactions in the double-entry accounts.

We will see the journal entries for the following Case Study when we study journals in detail in Chapter 11.

Case Study

DISPOSAL OF NON-CURRENT ASSETS

To illustrate the transactions to record the disposal of non-current assets, we will use the machine purchased for £2,000 (net of VAT) on 1 January 20-4, which is depreciated at 20 per cent each year, using the straight-line depreciation method. On 31 December 20-6, the machine is sold for £600 (net of VAT) received into the bank; the company's accounting policy is to depreciate assets in the year of sale. The calculations are:

	£
cost price of machine (net of VAT)	2,000
less accumulated depreciation to date	1,200
carrying amount at date of sale	800
disposal price (net of VAT)	600
loss on disposal	200

The bookkeeping entries (excluding bank account and VAT account) are:

Dr		Machinery at cost account		Cr
20-4		£	20-6	£
1 Jan	Bank	2,000	31 Dec Disposals	2,000

Dr				Machinery: accumulated depreciation account			Cr
20-4			£	**20-4**			£
31 Dec	Balance c/d		400	31 Dec	Depreciation charge		400
20-5				**20-5**			
31 Dec	Balance c/d		800	1 Jan	Balance b/d		400
				31 Dec	Depreciation charge		400
			800				800
20-6				**20-6**			
31 Dec	Disposals		1,200	1 Jan	Balance b/d		800
				31 Dec	Depreciation charge		400
			1,200				1,200

Dr		Machinery: disposals account			Cr
20-6		£	**20-6**		£
31 Dec	Machinery at cost	2,000	31 Dec	Accumulated depreciation	1,200
			31 Dec	Bank	600
			31 Dec	Statement of profit or loss	
				(loss on disposal)	200
		2,000			2,000

Statement of profit or loss for the year ended 31 December 20-6		
	Dr	Cr
	Expense	**Income**
	£	£
Depreciation charge*: machinery	400	–
Loss on disposal of machinery	200	–
*depreciation charges account is on page 91		

> **Note that** if the business in this Case Study was not registered for VAT, it would not charge VAT on disposal of the machinery. The loss on disposal would be £360, ie cost £2,400 − (£480 depreciation x 3 years) = carrying amount* £960 − sale proceeds £600 = £360 loss.
>
> *cost less accumulated depreciation

Notes:

- In the machinery account, which is always kept 'at cost', the original price of the asset is transferred at the date of disposal to disposals account. In this example, a nil balance remains on machinery account; however it is quite likely that the machinery account includes several machines, only one of which is being sold – in this case, there would be a balance on machinery account comprising the cost prices of the remaining machines.

- In accumulated depreciation account, the amount of depreciation relating to the machine disposed is transferred to disposals account. In this example, as only one machine is owned, the whole balance is transferred. However, if there were machines remaining, only part of the balance would be transferred – the amount left on the account comprising the accumulated depreciation of the remaining machines.

- Disposals account would balance without the need for a statement of profit or loss transfer if the depreciation rate used reflected exactly the fall in value of the machine. In practice, this is unlikely to happen, so a transfer to the statement of profit or loss must be made. In this example, it is an under-depreciation (loss on disposal), and the statement of profit or loss lists an extra expense. If there had been an over-depreciation (gain on disposal), an item of additional income would be shown in the statement of profit or loss.

- In an extended trial balance the disposal of a non-current asset will show as either a debit balance (loss on disposal) or a credit balance (gain on disposal). In this Case Study it will be a debit balance of £200. All that has to be done in the ETB is to transfer the disposal amount to the same – debit or credit – column of the statement of profit or loss.

- At the end of the accounting period after assets have been disposed of, they will have a carrying amount of zero in the statement of financial position.

The journal entries for the accounting entries in this Case Study are shown on page 218.

PART-EXCHANGE OF NON-CURRENT ASSETS

Instead of disposing of an old non-current asset for cash, it is quite common to part-exchange it for a new asset. This is exactly the same as if a person trades in their old car for a new (or newer) one.

Once the part-exchange allowance has been agreed, the bookkeeping entries for disposal are as detailed earlier except that, instead of disposal proceeds, there will be:

– **debit** non-current asset account with the amount of the part-exchange allowance

– **credit** asset disposals account with the amount of the part-exchange allowance

The remainder of the purchase cost of the new non-current asset paid from the bank is debited to non-current asset account and credited to bank account in the usual way. For a VAT-registered business there will also be amounts to record on the VAT account.

For example, the machine referred to earlier in this section is part-exchanged on 31 December 20-6 at an agreed value of £600 (net of VAT) for a new machine costing £2,500 (net of VAT). The balance is paid from the bank.

Machinery at cost account is now shown as:

Dr			Machinery at cost account			Cr
20-4			£	20-6		£
1 Jan	Bank		2,000	31 Dec	Disposals	2,000
20-6						
31 Dec	Disposals (part-exchange allowance)		600	31 Dec	Balance c/d	2,500
31 Dec	Bank (balance paid)		1,900			
			2,500			2,500
20-7						
1 Jan	Balance b/d		2,500			

Notes:

■ This gives two debits (£600 and £1,900) in machinery account for a single machine.

■ Disposals account is unchanged, except that the description for the credit transaction of £600 is machinery at cost account, instead of bank. The account is as follows:

Dr		Machinery: disposals account			Cr
20-6		£	20-6		£
31 Dec	Machinery at cost	2,000	31 Dec	Accumulated depreciation	1,200
			31 Dec	Machinery at cost	600
			31 Dec	Statement of profit or loss	
				(loss on disposal)	200
		2,000			2,000

IAS 16: PROPERTY, PLANT AND EQUIPMENT

International Accounting Standard (IAS) No 16, entitled *Property, Plant and Equipment,* is the accounting standard (see also Chapters 8 and 9) which includes the rules for dealing with depreciation in financial statements.

IAS 16 states that:

- all non-current assets having a known useful life are to be depreciated
- depreciation methods that can be used include straight-line and diminishing (reducing) balance
- depreciation amounts are normally based on the cost of the non-current assets (where assets are revalued, depreciation is based on the revalued amount)

Chapter Summary

- Non-current assets lose value – depreciation – as time goes by as a result of:
  - wear and tear
  - passage of time
  - depletion
  - economic reasons, such as obsolescence and inadequacy

- The purpose of depreciation is to spread the cost of a non-current asset over its useful life.

- Common methods of calculating depreciation are the straight-line method, the diminishing balance method, and the units of production method.

- In terms of bookkeeping, the accounts used to record depreciation are:
  - depreciation charges account, which records the amount of depreciation for the asset for the year
  - non-current asset accumulated depreciation account, which records the amount of depreciation to date

- The depreciation charges for each class of non-current asset is included amongst the expenses in the statement of profit or loss, while the cost of the asset is shown in the statement of financial position together with accumulated depreciation.

- Depreciation is a non-cash expense.

- When a non-current asset is disposed, it is necessary to make an adjustment in respect of any under depreciation (loss on disposal) or over depreciation (gain on disposal) during the life of the asset. The amount is calculated by means of a disposals account, and is then transferred to the statement of profit or loss.

- Journal entries – see Chapter 11 – must be made for all year-end depreciation charges and for all accounting transactions relating to the disposal of non-current assets. The journal entries record amounts in a book of prime entry and give the bookkeeper the authority to record the transactions in the double-entry accounts.

- IAS 16, *Property, Plant and Equipment*, is the international accounting standard which includes depreciation.

Key Terms	depreciation	the estimate of the amount of the loss in value of a non-current asset over its useful life
	carrying amount	cost price of non-current asset, less accumulated depreciation
	straight-line depreciation	a fixed percentage or fraction is written off the original cost (less any residual or scrap value) of the asset each year
	diminishing (reducing) balance depreciation	a fixed percentage is written off the diminished balance of the asset each year
	units of production depreciation	depreciation calculated by reference to output (units/hours/miles)
	pro-rata depreciation	the amount of depreciation calculated for part of a year
	depreciation charges account	used to record the annual depreciation charge, which is debited to the statement of profit or loss, for one or more classes of non-current assets
	non-current asset accumulated depreciation account	used to record the amount of accumulated depreciation for an asset or class of non-current asset
	depreciation policy	the method and rate of depreciation used by a business for each class of non-current asset
	asset disposal account	used to calculate any gain or loss on disposal of non-current assets

Activities

6.1 A machine costs £5,000 net of VAT and is expected to last for five years. At the end of this time, it is estimated that it will have a residual (scrap) value of £500 net of VAT. The annual depreciation charges for a VAT-registered business which uses the straight-line method will be:

(a) £900	
(b) £1,000	
(c) £1,100	
(d) £1,250	

6.2 The business for which you work depreciates its delivery vans on the diminishing balance method. Why do you think this method is used?

6.3 A machine cost £32,000 and has an expected total output of 56,000 units and residual value of £4,000.

Calculate the depreciation charge each year for the first three years of its useful life, based on the following production output.

	Output	Depreciation charge
Year 1	14,000 units	
Year 2	12,000 units	
Year 3	10,000 units	

6.4 On 1 January 20-2, Martin Jackson bought a car for £12,000. In his financial statements, which have a year-end of 31 December, he has been depreciating it at 25 per cent per annum using the diminishing balance method. On 31 December 20-4, he sells the car for £5,500 (cheque received); his accounting policy is to depreciate assets in the year of sale.

You are to show:

(a)   the car accumulated depreciation account for 20-2, 20-3 and 20-4

(b)   the statement of financial position extract, showing cost and accumulated depreciation, at 31 December 20-2 and 20-3

(c)   the asset disposals account

Round your answers down to whole £s where appropriate.

6.5 This Activity is about recording non-current asset information in the general ledger.

- You are working on the accounts of a business that is registered for VAT.
- A new machine has been acquired. VAT can be reclaimed on this machine.
- The cost excluding VAT was £8,000; this was paid from the bank.
- The residual value is expected to be £3,000 excluding VAT.
- The depreciation policy for machines is that they are depreciated on a straight-line basis over four years.
- Depreciation has already been entered into the accounts for the existing machines.

You are to make entries to account for:

- the purchase of the new machine
- the depreciation on the new machine

On each account, show clearly the balance carried down or transferred to the statement of profit or loss. (Note that dates are not required in the accounts.)

Machinery at cost

Balance b/d	£20,000		

Machinery: accumulated depreciation

		Balance b/d	£6,000

Machinery: depreciation charges

Balance b/d	£2,000		

6.6 This Activity is about recording non-current asset information in the general ledger.

· You are working on the accounts of a business that is registered for VAT.

· During the year an old vehicle was disposed.

· The vehicle had been bought for £12,000 plus VAT (the VAT was reclaimed), as already shown in the vehicle at cost account.

· Two years' depreciation has been applied.

· Depreciation is provided at 25 per cent per year on a diminishing balance basis.

· The vehicle was sold for £7,000 plus VAT (at 20%), with payment being received into the bank.

You are to:

(a) Calculate the accumulated depreciation on the vehicle now sold:

Year 1	£
Year 2	£
Total	£

(b) Make entries in the accounts which follow to record the disposal of the vehicle, showing clearly any balance carried down or transferred to the statement of profit or loss (note that dates are not required in the accounts).

Vehicle at cost

Balance b/d	£12,000		

Vehicle: disposals

Bank/cash

(c)   Tick the relevant box to show whether there is a gain or loss on disposal of the vehicle.

Gain	
Loss	

6.7   This Activity is about recording non-current asset information in the general ledger.

- You are working on the accounts of a business that is registered for VAT.
- The business has part-exchanged a machine during the year, but no entries have been made in the general ledger for this transaction.
- The original cost of the machine that was part-exchanged was £4,200 plus VAT (the VAT was reclaimed).
- The accumulated depreciation on the machine that was part-exchanged was £3,150.
- A part-exchange allowance of £1,200 plus VAT (which can be reclaimed) was given against the new machine.
- The £4,800, plus VAT, balance owing for the new machine was paid from the bank during the year. The VAT can be reclaimed.
- A full year's depreciation charges needs to be made on the new machine on a 25 per cent straight-line basis. It is assumed that there will be no residual value. No other depreciation charges need to be made.

You are to make entries to account for:

- the disposal of the old machine
- the purchase of the new machine
- the depreciation on the new machine

On each account, show clearly the balance carried down or transferred to the statement of profit or loss. (Note that dates are not required in the accounts.)

Machinery at cost

Balance b/d	£4,200		

Machinery: accumulated depreciation

		Balance b/d	£3,150

Machinery: depreciation charges

Machinery: disposals

6.8   You are given the following extract of balances from the general ledger of a business.

You are to enter the amounts in the appropriate column for the accounts shown. Do not enter zeros in unused column cells.

Extract from trial balance as at 31 December 20-4

Account	£	Dr £	Cr £
Accrued expenses	680		
Capital	25,000		
Depreciation charges	1,200		
Drawings	8,000		
Interest received	200		
Machinery at cost	6,500		
Machinery: accumulated depreciation	2,400		
Prepaid expenses	210		

6.9   The following list of balances has been extracted from the books of John Henson at 31 December 20-1:

	£
Purchases	71,600
Sales revenue	121,750
Opening inventory	6,250
Vehicle running expenses	1,480
Rent and rates	5,650
Office expenses	2,220
Discounts received	285
Wages and salaries	18,950
Office equipment at cost	10,000
Vehicle at cost	12,000
Sales ledger control	5,225
Purchases ledger control	3,190
Value Added Tax (owing to HMRC)	1,720
Capital	20,000
Drawings for the year	13,095
Bank	725
Gain on disposal of non-current asset	250

Notes at 31 December 20-1:

- inventory was valued at £8,500
- depreciation charges for office equipment for the year £1,000
- depreciation charges for vehicle for the year £3,000

You are to prepare the extended trial balance of John Henson for the year ended 31 December 20-1.

6.10   A friend of yours has recently started in business: knowing that you are studying financial accounting, she seeks your assistance. She has just bought a machine at a cost of £1,000 net of VAT and asks you to advise on depreciation methods. The machine is expected to last for five years after which it will be valueless. She tells you that, if there is a choice of depreciation methods, she would like to use the one 'that gives the larger net profit in the early years because the business could make good use of the extra cash'. Advise your friend by means of a letter.

6.11   The following trial balance has been extracted by the bookkeeper of Hazel Harris at 31 December 20-8:

	Dr	Cr
	£	£
Bank loan		75,000
Capital		125,000
Purchases and sales revenue	465,000	614,000
Building repairs	8,480	
Vehicle at cost	12,000	
Vehicles: accumulated depreciation		2,400
Vehicle expenses	2,680	
Premises at cost	100,000	
Premises: accumulated depreciation		4,000
Bank overdraft		2,000
Furniture at cost	25,000	
Furniture: accumulated depreciation		2,500
Wages and salaries	86,060	
Discounts	10,610	8,140
Drawings	24,000	
Rates and insurance	6,070	
Sales and purchases ledger control	52,130	32,600
Value Added Tax		5,250
Administration expenses	15,460	
Opening inventory	63,000	
Disposal of non-current asset	400	
	870,890	870,890

Notes at 31 December 20-8:

- inventory was valued at £88,000
- wages and salaries outstanding: £3,180
- rates and insurance paid in advance: £450
- depreciate premises at 2 per cent using the straight-line method
- depreciate the vehicle at 20 per cent using the diminishing balance method
- depreciate furniture at 10 per cent using the straight-line method

You are to prepare the extended trial balance of Hazel Harris for the year ended 31 December 20-8.

7 Irrecoverable debts and allowance for doubtful debts

this chapter covers...

Most businesses selling their goods and services to other businesses do not receive payment immediately. Instead, they often have to allow a period of credit and, until the payment is received, they have an asset of trade receivables (in sales ledger control account).

Unfortunately, it is likely that not all trade receivables will eventually settle the amounts they owe, ie the amounts are irrecoverable debts which have to be written off.

At the same time a business needs to make an allowance for doubtful debts, which allows for trade receivables who may not pay.

In this chapter we will:

- *distinguish between irrecoverable debts and allowance for doubtful debts*

- *prepare the accounting entries for irrecoverable debts, and consider the effect on the financial statements*

- *prepare the accounting entries to make an allowance for doubtful debts, and consider the effect on the financial statements*

IRRECOVERABLE DEBTS AND ALLOWANCE FOR DOUBTFUL DEBTS

irrecoverable debts

Irrecoverable debts (sometimes called bad debts) are debts owing to a business which it considers will never be paid.

Let us consider a business with trade receivables of £10,000, made up of a number of customers' accounts. At any one time, a few of these accounts will be irrecoverable, and therefore the amount is uncollectable: they need to be written off as irrecoverable debts, ie the business will give up trying to collect the debt and will accept the loss.

allowance for doubtful debts

Allowance for doubtful debts (sometimes called provision for bad debts) is the estimate by a business of the likely percentage of its trade receivables which may become irrecoverable during any one accounting period.

There are likely to be some trade receivables accounts which, although they are not yet irrecoverable, may be giving some concern as to their ability to pay: An allowance for doubtful debts needs to be made in respect of these. The one thing the business with trade receivables of £10,000 cannot do is to show this amount as an asset in the statement of financial position: to do so would be to imply that the full £10,000 is recoverable. Instead, this trade receivables figure might be reduced in two stages, for example:

- trade receivables accounts totalling £200 are to be written off as **irrecoverable debts**
- an **allowance for doubtful debts** is to be made amounting to 2% of remaining trade receivables after the £200 has been written off

The trade receivables figure then becomes:	£
Gross trade receivables	10,000
Less: irrecoverable debts written off	200
	9,800
Less: allowance for doubtful debts at 2%	196
Net trade receivables	9,604

Note: the level of percentage is likely to reflect the level of risk of the doubtful debt

general and specific allowances

A **general allowance** for doubtful debts is an allowance applied (as in the above example) to the total trade receivables after writing off irrecoverable debts.

A **specific allowance** is an allowance applied to one or more specific doubtful debts where the risk of default is thought to be higher.

accruals principle of accounting

Allowance for doubtful debts is an application of the accrual basis of accounting. By reducing the trade receivables figure, a more accurate figure is shown in the statement of financial position of the amount that the business can expect to receive. The accrual basis is discussed in more detail in Chapter 8.

TREATMENT OF IRRECOVERABLE DEBTS

Irrecoverable debts are written off when they become uncollectable. This means that all reasonable efforts to recover the amount owing have been exhausted, ie statements, letters and emails have been sent to the customer requesting payment and legal action, where appropriate, or the threat of legal action has failed to obtain payment.

In writing off a trade receivable's account as irrecoverable, the business is bearing the cost of the amount due. The account is closed and the amount (or amounts, where a number of accounts are dealt with in this way) is debited to **irrecoverable debts** account in the general ledger. This account stores up the amounts of account balances written off during the year (in much the same way as an expense account). At the end of the financial year, the balance of the account is transferred to the statement of profit or loss as an expense, where it is described as **irrecoverable debts**.

In terms of double-entry bookkeeping, the transactions are:

– **debit** irrecoverable debts

– **credit** trade receivable's account

At the end of the financial year, irrecoverable debts account is transferred to the statement of profit or loss as an expense:

– **debit** statement of profit or loss

– **credit** irrecoverable debts

For example, the following customer's account is in the sales ledger:

Dr			T Hughes		Cr
20-7		£	20-7		£
5 Jan	Sales	55	8 May	Bank	25
			6 Jul	Cash	5

It is now 15 December 20-7 and you are reviewing the customers' accounts before the end of the financial year on 31 December. Your business has sent statements and 'chaser' letters to T Hughes – the last letter was dated 30 September, and was returned marked 'gone away, not known at this address'. Nothing further has been heard from T Hughes. You take the decision to write off this account as an irrecoverable debt – ignore VAT. The account will be closed off as shown below:

Dr			**T Hughes**		Cr
20-7		£	20-7		£
5 Jan	Sales	55	8 May	Bank	25
			6 Jul	Cash	5
			15 Dec	Irrecoverable debts	25
		55			55

The balance is transferred to the 'holding' account, **irrecoverable debts**, together with other accounts written off. At the end of the financial year, the total of this account is transferred to the statement of profit or loss:

Dr			**Irrecoverable debts account**		Cr
20-7		£	20-7		£
15 Dec	Sales ledger control (T Hughes)	25	31 Dec	Statement of profit or loss	200
15 Dec	Sales ledger control (Lane & Co)	85			
15 Dec	Sales ledger control (A Harvey)	90			
		200			200

> **Tutorial note:** irrecoverable debts must be recorded in sales ledger control account – see Chapter 10.

In financial statements, the effect of writing off debts as irrecoverable is to reduce the previously reported profit for the year – in the example above, by £200.

Notes:

- If you are preparing financial statements and the figure for irrecoverable debts is shown in the trial balance (debit side), simply record the amount as an expense in the statement of profit or loss – the trade receivables (sales ledger control) figure has been reduced already.

- If the irrecoverable debts figure is not already shown in the trial balance, and a note tells you to write off a particular account as bad, you need to list the amount as an expense in the statement of profit or loss and reduce the trade receivables (sales ledger control) figure for the statement of financial position. In an extended trial balance, use the adjustments columns, debit irrecoverable debts, and credit the sales ledger control figure (in the statement of financial position columns show a net amount for sales ledger control, ie less adjustment).

■ In sales ledger control account (see Chapter 10) the amount of irrecoverable debts must be recorded on the credit side of the control account.

journal entries

A journal entry – see Chapter 11 – must be made for all irrecoverable debts which are written off. The journal entry records the amounts being written off in a book of prime entry and gives the bookkeeper the authority to record the transactions in the double-entry accounts.

RECOVERY OF A DEBT

Recovery of a debt is when a former trade receivable, whose account has been written off as irrecoverable, makes a payment – either voluntarily, or as a result of debt collection procedures. For such a recovery the bookkeeping transactions are:

■ debit cash/bank account (with the amount of the recovery)

■ credit irrecoverable debts account

Recovery of a debt paid after being previously written off should be a rare event because a debt should not be treated as irrecoverable unless certain. Having recovered payment from a former trade receivable, if the customer now wishes to buy goods or services, it is prudent to insist on cash payment for some time to come!

At the end of the financial year the net balance of irrecoverable debts account is transferred to the statement of profit or loss:

■ when the amount of debts written off is more than debts recovered, irrecoverable debts account will have a debit balance, which will be recorded in the debit column of the statement of profit or loss

■ when the amount of debts written off is less than debts recovered, irrecoverable debts account will have a credit balance, which will be recorded in the credit column of the statement of profit or loss

From the above, note that irrecoverable debts account could have either a debit or a credit balance – simply take the balance to the relevant column of the statement of profit or loss.

Case Study

CASE STUDY: RECOVERY OF A DEBT

T Hughes is a customer – the balance of £25 on his account was written off as an irrecoverable debt on 15 December 20-7.

Today, on 15 April 20-8, T Hughes wishes to pay off the amount of the debt – with a cheque for £25.

The bookkeeping entries to record the debt recovered on 15 April 20-8 are as follows:

Dr		**Bank Account**		Cr
20-8	£	20-8		£
15 Apr Irrecoverable debts	25			

Dr		**Irrecoverable Debts Account**		Cr
20-8	£	20-8		£
		15 Apr Bank (T Hughes)		25

If there are no other transactions on irrecoverable debts account, at the end of the financial year the total of the account will be transferred to the credit column of the statement of profit or loss:

Dr		**Irrecoverable Debts Account**		Cr
20-8	£	20-8		£
31 Dec Statement of profit or loss	25	15 Apr Bank (T Hughes)		25

In financial statements, the effect of recovering a debt is to increase the previously reported profit for the year – by £25 in this case.

Note that debts recovered must not be recorded in sales ledger control account – see Chapter 10 – as there is no longer an account in sales ledger for the former customer.

Tutorial note:

Some businesses may have an accounting policy of crediting debt recoveries to a separate debts recovered account – instead of using irrecoverable debts account. If you should see a trial balance with a credit balance for debts recovered, simply show the amount in the statement of profit or loss credit column: this will have the effect of increasing profit for the year.

TREATMENT OF ALLOWANCE FOR DOUBTFUL DEBTS

Allowance for doubtful debts is different from writing off an irrecoverable debt because there is only the possibility – not the certainty – of future irrecoverable debts. The trade receivables figure (after writing off irrecoverable debts) is reduced either by totalling the balances of the accounts that may not pay or, more likely, by applying a percentage to the total figure for trade receivables. The percentage chosen is based on past experience and varies from business to business – for example, a hire purchase company may well use a higher percentage than a bank.

The usual procedure is to have two accounts in the general ledger:

▪ **allowance for doubtful debts: adjustment account**, which records the amount to create, increase or decrease the allowance each year

▪ **allowance for doubtful debts account**, which records the accumulated total of the allowance

initial creation of an allowance for doubtful debts

Making an allowance for doubtful debts comes **after** writing off irrecoverable debts (if any). The steps are:

step 1   A business, at the end of its financial year in 20-1, estimates the percentage of its trade receivables which are doubtful and may become irrecoverable, at say two per cent.

step 2   The allowance is calculated (eg £9,800 x 2% = £196)

step 3   The allowance is recorded in the double-entry system:

– **debit** allowance for doubtful debts: adjustment

– **credit** allowance for doubtful debts

– **debit** statement of profit or loss (as an expense)

– **credit** allowance for doubtful debts: adjustment

The allowance for doubtful debts: adjustment account acts as a 'holding' account, through which transfers to and from the statement of profit or loss are made. The allowance for doubtful debts account holds the accumulated total of the allowance, which is shown on the opposite side from sales ledger control in the statement of financial position (see below).

step 4   In financial statements, the amount of the allowance for doubtful debts is shown as:

▪ a debit in the statement of profit or loss columns

▪ a credit in the statement of financial position columns

The amounts are as follows:

Year	Statement of profit or loss		Statement of financial position	
	Dr **Expense**	Cr **Income**	Dr **Sales ledger control**	Cr **Allowance for doubtful debts**
20-1	£ 196	£ –	£ 9,800	£ 196

Note that the business, in creating an allowance for doubtful debts, is presenting a more accurate estimate of its trade receivables.

adjustments to allowance for doubtful debts

Once an allowance for doubtful debts has been created, the only adjustments that need to be made are as a result of:

■ a **policy change** in the allowance, eg an increase in the fixed percentage from 2% to 5%

■ an **arithmetical adjustment** in the allowance as a result of a change in the total of trade receivables, eg increase in trade receivables of £5,000 will require a proportionally higher allowance

If, or when, either of these two situations arises, the adjustment to the existing allowance will be:

■ either **upwards** (increase in allowance percentage, or increase in trade receivables figure)

■ or **downwards** (decrease in allowance percentage, or decrease in trade receivables figure)

increasing the allowance

The **increase in the allowance** is recorded in the double-entry system as follows:

– **debit** allowance for doubtful debts: adjustment account

– **credit** allowance for doubtful debts account

– **debit** statement of profit or loss (as an expense)

– **credit** allowance for doubtful debts: adjustment account

For the statement of financial position, the balance of allowance for doubtful debts account is shown on the opposite side to sales ledger control.

decreasing the allowance

The **decrease in the allowance** is recorded as:

– **debit** allowance for doubtful debts account

– **credit** allowance for doubtful debts: adjustment account

– **debit** allowance for doubtful debts: adjustment account

– **credit** statement of profit or loss (ie income)

Again, the statement of financial position shows the balance of allowance for doubtful debts account in the credit column.

Note that allowance for doubtful debts and irrecoverable debts are completely separate adjustments: the two should not be confused. It is quite usual to see, in a statement of profit or loss, entries for both irrecoverable debts and allowance for doubtful debts.

journal entries

A journal entry – see Chapter 11 – must be made for the creation of, and any subsequent adjustments to, the allowance for doubtful debts. The journal entry records the amount in a book of prime entry and gives the bookkeeper the authority to record the transaction in the double-entry accounts.

Case Study

BOOKKEEPING FOR ALLOWANCE FOR DOUBTFUL DEBTS

A business decides to create an allowance for doubtful debts of five per cent of its trade receivables. After writing off irrecoverable debts, the trade receivables figures at the end of each of three years are:

20-6   £10,000

20-7   £15,000

20-8   £12,000

bookkeeping entries

creating the allowance (year 20-6):
£10,000 x 5% = £500

– **debit** allowance for doubtful debts: adjustment

– **credit** allowance for doubtful debts

– **debit** statement of profit or loss

– **credit** allowance for doubtful debts: adjustment

increasing the allowance (year 20-7):
£5,000 (increase in trade receivables) x 5% = £250

– **debit** allowance for doubtful debts: adjustment

– **credit** allowance for doubtful debts

– **debit** statement of profit or loss

– **credit** allowance for doubtful debts: adjustment

decreasing the allowance (year 20-8):
£3,000 (decrease in trade receivables) x 5% = £150

– **debit** allowance for doubtful debts

– **credit** allowance for doubtful debts: adjustment

– **debit** allowance for doubtful debts: adjustment

– **credit** statement of profit or loss

The bookkeeping entries in the general ledger for

• allowance for doubtful debts: adjustment

• allowance for doubtful debts

are as follows:

Dr			**Allowance for doubtful debts account**		Cr
20-6		£	20-6		£
31 Dec	Balance c/d	500	31 Dec	Allowance for doubtful debts: adjustment	500
20-7			20-7		
31 Dec	Balance c/d	750	1 Jan	Balance b/d	500
			31 Dec	Allowance for doubtful debts: adjustment (increase in allowance)	250
		750			750
20-8			20-8		
31 Dec	Allowance for doubtful debts: adjustment (decrease in allowance)	150	1 Jan	Balance b/d	750
31 Dec	Balance c/d	600			
		750			750
20-9			20-9		
			1 Jan	Balance b/d	600

Dr		Allowance for doubtful debts: adjustment account		Cr
20-6	£	20-6		£
31 Dec Allowance for doubtful debts	500	31 Dec Statement of profit or loss		500
20-7		20-7		
31 Dec Allowance for doubtful debts	250	31 Dec Statement of profit or loss		250
20-8		20-8		
31 Dec Statement of profit or loss	150	31 Dec Allowance for doubtful debts		150

the financial statements

The effect of the above transactions on the financial statements is shown as follows:

Year	Statement of profit or loss		Statement of financial position	
	Dr	Cr	Dr	Cr
	Expense	**Income**	**Sales ledger control**	**Allowance for doubtful debts**
	£	£	£	£
20-6	500	–	10,000	500
20-7	250	–	15,000	750
20-8	–	150	12,000	600

Note:

When preparing financial statements in Activities and Assessments, there will be a note to the trial balance telling you to make an adjustment to the allowance for doubtful debts. Sometimes you will be told a percentage figure, eg 'allowance for doubtful debts is to be maintained at five per cent of trade receivables'; alternatively, you may be told the new allowance figure (be careful of the wording – distinguish between 'increase the allowance to £750' and 'increase the allowance by £750').

IRRECOVERABLE DEBTS AND ALLOWANCE FOR DOUBTFUL DEBTS IN THE EXTENDED TRIAL BALANCE

irrecoverable debts

If irrecoverable debts already appear in the trial balance, simply show the amount in the debit column of the statement of profit or loss: this will have the effect of reducing profit for the year. Do not alter the figure for sales ledger control, as it will have been reduced already by the amount written off.

If a note to the trial balance tells you to write off, say, £100 of irrecoverable debts, then you will need to include a row in the extended trial balance for irrecoverable debts. In the adjustments column, show £100 as a debit to this row, and credit the sales ledger control row. This will give an expense of £100 for the statement of profit or loss, and will reduce sales ledger control for the statement of financial position by £100 (show a net figure for sales ledger control in the statement of financial position column).

recovery of a debt

If a trial balance shows a credit balance for either irrecoverable debts account or debts recovered account, simply show the amount in the statement of profit or loss credit column: this will have the effect of increasing profit for the year.

allowance for doubtful debts

In the extended trial balance layout you will see that, towards the bottom, a row is preprinted for allowance for doubtful debts: adjustment. Use this as the 'holding' account to create, or increase, or decrease the allowance.

For example, to increase an existing allowance of £500 (which will be shown in the trial balance) by, say, £250, record the following in the extended trial balance:

- in the adjustments column:

    - **debit** allowance for doubtful debts: adjustment

    - **credit** allowance for doubtful debts

- in the statement of profit or loss column record the £250 amount of the allowance for doubtful debts: adjustment as an expense in the debit column

- in the statement of financial position column record the allowance for doubtful debts as £750, ie the trial balance figure of £500 and the amount of £250 shown in the adjustments column

Where a new allowance is to be created the above principles are followed; to reduce an existing allowance, then the reverse of the above will be followed.

Remember that, in the extended trial balance:

- allowance for doubtful debts: adjustment is shown in the statement of profit or loss and records the amount to create, increase or decrease the allowance each year

- allowance for doubtful debts is shown in the credit column of the statement of financial position and is the accumulated total of the allowance

TARA SMITH:
IRRECOVERABLE DEBTS AND ALLOWANCE FOR DOUBTFUL DEBTS

We will now focus on how the irrecoverable debt and allowance for doubtful debts amounts are shown in the statement of profit or loss and statement of financial position. We will continue with the trial balance of Tara Smith and include adjustments for the year for:

- irrecoverable debts of £100 written off (ignore VAT)

- allowance for doubtful debts of £250 created (note that there is no existing allowance)

extended trial balance (see next page)

The columns which are affected are adjustments, statement of profit or loss, and statement of financial position – the altered figures are shaded for illustrative purposes.

EXTENDED TRIAL BALANCE   TARA SMITH TRADING AS "THE FASHION SHOP"   31 DECEMBER 20-4

Account name	Ledger balances		Adjustments		Statement of profit or loss		Statement of financial position	
	Dr £	Cr £	Dr £	Cr £	Dr £	Cr £	Dr £	Cr £
Opening inventory	12,500				12,500			
Purchases	105,000				105,000			
Sales revenue		155,000				155,000		
Administration expenses	6,200				6,200			
Wages	23,500				23,500			
Rent paid	750			75	675			
Telephone	500		100		600			
Interest paid	4,500				4,500			
Travel expenses	550				550			
Premises	100,000						100,000	
Premises: accumulated depreciation				2,000				2,000
Shop fittings	20,000						20,000	
Shop fittings: accumulated depreciation				5,000				5,000
Sales ledger control	10,500			100			10,400	
Bank	5,450						5,450	
Cash	50						50	
Capital		75,000						75,000
Drawings	7,000						7,000	
Loan from bank		50,000						50,000
Purchases ledger control		14,500						14,500
Value Added Tax		2,000						2,000
Closing inventory: statement of profit or loss				10,500		10,500		
Closing inventory: statement of financial position			10,500				10,500	
Accruals				100				100
Prepayments			75				75	
Depreciation charges			7,000		7,000			
Irrecoverable debts			100		100			
Allowance for doubtful debts				250				250
Allowance for doubtful debts: adjustment			250		250			
Profit/loss for the year					4,625			4,625
	296,500	296,500	18,025	18,025	165,500	165,500	153,475	153,475

- Not all trade receivables of a business will eventually settle the amounts they owe: such amounts are **irrecoverable debts** which have to be written off.

- An **allowance for doubtful debts** is made for trade receivables who may not pay.

- This sequence should be followed:
  - write off irrecoverable debts (if any)
  - create (or adjust) allowance for doubtful debts

- To write off an irrecoverable debt:
  - **debit** irrecoverable debts account
  - **credit** trade receivables account

  At the end of the financial year irrecoverable debts account is transferred, as an expense, to the debit column of the statement of profit or loss.

- An allowance for doubtful debts is often based on a fixed percentage of trade receivables at the year-end.

- For bookkeeping purposes, two accounts are used to create, increase or decrease an allowance for doubtful debts:

  - allowance for doubtful debts: adjustment account, to record the annual change
  - allowance for doubtful debts account, to record the accumulated total

- Having created an allowance for doubtful debts, it will usually be adjusted either upwards or downwards in subsequent years in line with the change in the level of receivables.

- A journal entry – see Chapter 11 – must be made for all irrecoverable debts which are written off and for the creation of, and any subsequent adjustments to, the allowance for doubtful debts. The journal entries record the amounts in a book of prime entry and give the bookkeeper the authority to record the transactions in the double-entry accounts.

irrecoverable debts	debts owing to a business which it considers will never be paid
irrecoverable debts account	the account to which the amounts of account balances written off as irrecoverable are debited
allowance for doubtful debts	an estimate by a business of the likely percentage of its trade receivables which are doubtful and may become irrecoverable during any one accounting period
allowance for doubtful debts: adjustment account	used to record the annual change in the allowance for doubtful debts
allowance for doubtful debts account	used to record the accumulated total of the allowance for doubtful debts

Activities

7.1 Ken Shah, a customer of the business where you work, is unable to pay the amount owing and the accounts supervisor has decided to write off his account as irrecoverable. How will this be recorded in the double-entry accounts (assume that the business does not use control accounts)?

	Debit	**Credit**	
(a)	Irrecoverable debts	K Shah's account	
(b)	K Shah's account	Irrecoverable debts	
(c)	Cash account	K Shah's account	
(d)	Sales revenue account	K Shah's account	

(Ignore VAT)

7.2 A trial balance shows trade receivables of £48,000 and an allowance for doubtful debts of £2,200. It is decided to make the allowance for doubtful debts equal to five per cent of trade receivables. What bookkeeping entry will be made on the allowance for doubtful debts account?

(a)	Debit £200	
(b)	Debit £2,400	
(c)	Credit £200	
(d)	Credit £2,200	

7.3 You are the bookkeeper at Waterston Plant Hire. At 31 December 20-2, the end of the financial year, the business has trade receivables of £20,210. The owner decides to:

(a) write off, as irrecoverable debts (ignore VAT), the accounts of:

P Ross	£55
J Ball	£105
L Jones	£50

(b) make an allowance for doubtful debts of 2.5% of trade receivables (after writing off the above debts)

You are to explain how these transactions will be recorded in the financial statements at the end of the year.

7.4 Ross Engineering has an existing allowance for doubtful debts of £300, based on five per cent of trade receivables. After writing off irrecoverable debts, the amounts of trade receivables at the end of the next two financial years are found to be:

       31 December 20-5   £8,000

       31 December 20-6   £7,000

The business continues to keep the allowance for doubtful debts equal to five per cent of trade receivables.

As an Accounts Assistant at Ross Engineering, you are to show how the allowance for doubtful debts account will be adjusted at the end of the financial years ended 31 December 20-5 and 31 December 20-6, and how it will be recorded in the appropriate financial statements.

7.5 This Activity is about accounting for irrecoverable debts and allowance for doubtful debts and preparing a trial balance.

You are working on the financial statements of a business for the year ended 31 December 20-8. In this task you can ignore VAT.

You have the following information:

Irrecoverable debts to be written off:	£
Thompson & Co	110
T Aziz	65
Wyvern Traders	80
Allowance for doubtful debts at 1 January 20-8	600

The balance of trade receivables (sales ledger control account) before irrecoverable debts are written off is £28,255. The allowance for doubtful debts is to be 2.5% of trade receivables after irrecoverable debts.

(a) **You are to** prepare the irrecoverable debts account for the year ended 31 December 20-8 and close it off by showing the transfer to the statement of profit or loss. Dates are not required.

Irrecoverable debts

	£		£

(b) **You are to** prepare the allowance for doubtful debts account for the year ended 31 December 20-8 and to show clearly the balance carried down. Include dates.

Allowance for doubtful debts

		£			£

You have the following extract of balances from the general ledger.

(c) **Using your answers** from (a) and (b), record the adjustments on the extract from the extended trial balance. Do not enter zeros in unused column cells.

Extract from trial balance as at 31 December 20-8

Account	Ledger balances		Adjustments	
	Dr £	Cr £	Dr £	Cr £
Allowance for doubtful debts		600		
Allowance for doubtful debts: adjustment				
Irrecoverable debts				
Loan interest	790			
Sales ledger control	28,255			
Vehicles at cost	12,000			
Vehicles: accumulated depreciation		6,400		
Wages	35,470			

7.6 The following trial balance has been extracted by the bookkeeper of Paul Sanders, who runs an office supplies business, as at 31 December 20-4:

	Dr £	Cr £
Purchases and sales revenue	51,225	81,762
Sales and purchases returns	186	254
Opening inventory	6,031	
Discounts allowed and received	324	238
Vehicle expenses	1,086	
Wages and salaries	20,379	
Electricity	876	
Telephone	1,241	
Rent and rates	4,565	
Sundry expenses	732	
Irrecoverable debts	219	
Sales and purchases ledger control	1,040	7,671
Value Added Tax		1,301
Bank	3,501	
Cash	21	
Vehicles at cost	15,000	
Vehicles: accumulated depreciation		3,000
Office equipment at cost	10,000	
Office equipment: accumulated depreciation		5,000
Capital		25,000
Drawings	8,000	
Disposal of non-current asset		200
	124,426	124,426

Notes at 31 December 20-4:

- inventory was valued at £8,210
- electricity owing £102
- rent prepaid £251
- depreciate vehicles at 20 per cent and office equipment at 10 per cent per annum, using the straight-line method
- create an allowance for doubtful debts of 5 per cent of trade receivables

You are to prepare the extended trial balance of Paul Sanders for the year ended 31 December 20-4.

7.7   The following trial balance has been extracted by the bookkeeper of James Jenkins, who owns a patisserie and coffee lounge, as at 30 June 20-5:

	Dr	Cr
	£	£
Capital		36,175
Drawings	19,050	
Purchases and sales revenue	105,240	168,432
Opening inventory	9,427	
Sales and purchases ledger control	3,840	5,294
Value Added Tax		1,492
Sales and purchases returns	975	1,237
Discounts allowed and received	127	643
Wages and salaries	30,841	
Vehicle expenses	1,021	
Rent and rates	8,796	
Heating and lighting	1,840	
Telephone	355	
General expenses	1,752	
Irrecoverable debts	85	
Vehicle at cost	8,000	
Vehicle: accumulated depreciation		3,500
Shop fittings at cost	6,000	
Shop fittings: accumulated depreciation		2,000
Allowance for doubtful debts		150
Cash	155	
Bank	21,419	
	218,923	218,923

Notes at 30 June 20-5:
- inventory was valued at £11,517
- vehicle expenses owing £55
- rent prepaid £275
- depreciate the vehicle at 25 per cent per annum, using the diminishing balance method
- depreciate shop fittings at 10 per cent per annum, using the straight-line method
- the allowance for doubtful debts is to be equal to 2.5 per cent of trade receivables

You are to prepare the extended trial balance of James Jenkins for the year ended 30 June 20-5.

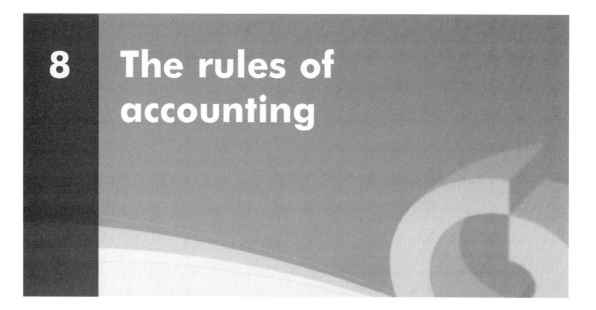

8 The rules of accounting

this chapter covers...

In this chapter we will explain the rules of accounting to be followed when preparing financial statements. These rules take the form of:

- *accounting principles (or concepts)*
- *accounting policies and fundamental accounting characteristics*
- *ethical principles*
- *accounting standards*

If the same rules have been followed, then broad comparisons can be made between the financial statements of different businesses.

We will see the accounting rules relating to:

- *the accounting treatment for non-current assets, including depreciation (IAS 16, Property, plant and equipment)*
- *the valuation of inventory (IAS 2, Inventories)*

Later in the chapter we focus on the importance of the distinction between capital expenditure and revenue expenditure.

ACCOUNTING PRINCIPLES

Accounting principles (or concepts) underlie the maintaining of financial records and the preparation of financial statements. Accounting principles help to ensure that the records and statements we prepare are relevant and reliable to users, and that they are comparable and understandable. In particular, principles help to ensure that records and statements are fit to be used for:

- **internal control** – within the business to ensure that financial records are accurate and that financial statements show the true position of the business

- **measuring business performance** – both internally and externally – so that financial reports and statements can be compared

- **obtaining credit/financing** – providing lenders with the current financial position of the business

- **statutory requirements** – providing information for tax and other purposes when required to do so by law

The diagram below illustrates the main accounting principles – described in more detail over the next few pages.

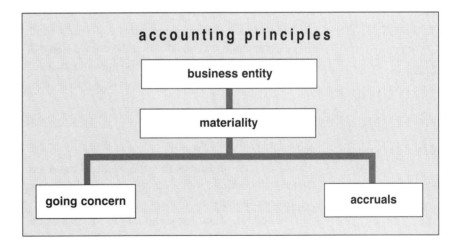

business entity

This refers to the fact that financial statements record and report on the activities of one particular business. They do not include the assets and liabilities of those who play a part in owning or running the business. Thus the personal assets and liabilities of the owner/owners are kept separate from those of the business: the main links between the business and the personal funds of the owner/owners are capital and drawings.

materiality

Some items in accounts are of such low value that it is not worthwhile recording them separately, ie they are not 'material'.

Examples include:

- small expense items, such as donations to charities, the purchase of plants for the office, window cleaning, etc, do not justify their own separate expense account; instead they are grouped together in a sundry expenses account

- end-of-year unused office stationery, eg paper clips, staples, photocopying paper, etc, is often not valued for the purpose of financial statements, because the amount is not material and does not justify the time and effort involved. This does mean, however, that the cost of all stationery purchased during the year is charged as an expense to the statement of profit or loss – technically wrong, but not material enough to affect the financial statements

- low-cost non-current assets are often charged as an expense in the statement of profit or loss, instead of being classed as capital expenditure, eg a stapler, waste-paper basket, etc. Strictly, these should be treated as non-current assets and depreciated each year over their useful life; in practice, because the amounts involved are not material, they are treated as expenses in the statement of profit or loss

Materiality depends very much on the size of the business. For example, a large company may consider that the cost of items of less than £1,000 are not material; by contrast, a small business may use a much lower amount, perhaps £100. It is for a business to set a policy as to what amount is material and what is not.

going concern

Going concern presumes that the business to which the financial statements relate will continue to trade in the foreseeable future. The statement of profit or loss and statement of financial position are prepared on the basis that there is no intention to reduce significantly the size of the business or to liquidate the business. If the business is no longer a going concern, assets will have very different values, and the statement of financial position will be affected considerably. For example, a large, purpose-built factory has considerable value to a going concern business but, if the factory had to be sold, it is likely to have a limited use for other industries, and therefore will have a lower market value. Values based on liquidation amounts are the opposite of the going concern and require extra depreciation to be charged as an expense to the statement of profit or loss to allow for the reduced value of non-current assets. In a similar way, inventory that is to be sold in a clearance sale will be reduced in value.

accruals

This means that income and expenses are matched so that they relate to the same goods or services and the same accounting period. This means that the statement of profit or loss shows the amount of the expense that should have been incurred, and the amount of income that should have been received. This is the principle of income and expenditure accounting, rather than using receipts and payments as and when they fall due. Examples of the use of accruals in accounting are:

- accruals
- prepayments
- depreciation charges
- allowance for doubtful debts
- cost of inventory

ETHICAL PRINCIPLES

As well as accounting principles, policies and characteristics, accountants must apply ethical principles when recording financial transactions. Such work requires a high level of ethics so that users can be assured that it has been prepared to the highest professional standards.

The fundamental ethical principles, as set out in AAT's Code of Professional Ethics, are:

- integrity
- objectivity
- professional competence and due care
- confidentiality
- professional behaviour

The meaning and application of these ethical principles to the recording of financial transactions is now explained.

Integrity means being straightforward and honest in all professional and business relationships. When recording transactions, the bookkeeper should identify whether transactions are genuine and valid for inclusion in the records of the business. For example, a bookkeeper who records an inflated or bogus expenses claim submitted by a member of staff would not be following the principle of integrity.

Objectivity means not allowing bias, conflict of interest or the undue influence of others to override professional or business judgements. In addition the bookkeeper must appreciate the importance of:

- transparency, being confident of showing to others decisions made

- fairness, being certain that decisions made will be considered fair by those affected by them

Professional competence and due care means maintaining professional knowledge and skill at the level required to provide a competent professional service to an employer or client. For example, a bookkeeper who has not studied taxation and has never completed a tax return but, nevertheless, advertises a tax advice service, would not be following the principle of professional competence and due care.

Confidentiality means that information acquired as a result of professional or business relationships should not be disclosed to third parties, except when there is a legal or professional right to disclose. For example, a bookkeeper who tells a friend about the losses made by a client would not be following the principle of confidentiality.

Professional behaviour means complying with relevant laws and regulations and avoiding bringing the accountancy profession into disrepute. This includes dealing with the pressures, whether actual or perceived, of familiarity and authority. Familiarity means that the bookkeeper must not, because of a close or personal relationship, become too sympathetic to the interests of others. Authority means that the bookkeeper must not be deterred from acting professionally despite pressure from managers, business owners or others at a supervisory level.

ACCOUNTING STANDARDS

Accounting standards – which form part of the rules of accounting – have been developed to provide a framework for accounting and to reduce the variety of accounting treatments used in financial statements.

Accounting standards take the form of:

- International Accounting Standards (IASs)
- International Financial Reporting Standards (IFRSs)

International standards are widely used in the UK.

There are two accounting standards relevant to your studies from this book – one deals with inventories, and the other with property, plant and equipment, ie non-current assets.

IAS 2 Inventories

The purpose of this standard is to set out the accounting techniques to be used when valuing inventories. The broad rule is that inventories are to be valued at the lower of cost and net realisable value – see the following section.

IAS 16 Property, plant and equipment

This standard sets out the accounting treatment for property, plant and equipment, ie non-current assets – such as land and buildings, machinery, office equipment, shop fittings and vehicles.

It is important to know what can be included in the **cost** of a non-current asset – and what cannot be included. This distinction between capital expenditure and revenue expenditure is explained fully on page 143 of this chapter.

A key feature of the IAS is depreciation and, as we have already seen in Chapter 6, most non-current assets lose value over time. Therefore it is necessary, in order to present a realistic view of the business, to record the amount of the loss in value. The standard defines the following terms:

■ **cost** – the amount paid to acquire an asset at the time of its acquisition

■ **useful life** – the length of time, or the number of units of production, for which an asset is expected to be used

■ **residual value** – the net amount the business expects to obtain for an asset at the end of its useful life after deducting the expected costs of disposal

■ **depreciable amount** – the cost of an asset, less any residual value

■ **carrying amount** – the amount at which an asset is shown in the statement of financial position, after deducting accumulated depreciation

The purpose of depreciation is to spread the cost of a non-current asset over its useful life. This is an application of the accruals principle – seen earlier in this chapter – where the depreciation charge is matched to the accounting periods over which it is used.

IAS 16 requires that depreciation is to be charged on all non-current assets, with the exception of freehold land. Depreciation methods to be used include the straight-line and diminishing (reducing) balance methods (see Chapter 6):

■ straight-line depreciation results in a constant depreciation charge over the asset's useful life

■ diminishing balance depreciation results in a decreasing depreciation charge over the useful life (ie the depreciation charge in the early years is greater than in later years)

A business chooses the depreciation method which best reflects the way in which the benefits of the asset are used. IAS 16 requires that the depreciation method used should be reviewed at least annually in order to consider if the method used is still the most appropriate one.

IAS 2: VALUATION OF INVENTORIES

The control and valuation of inventory is an important aspect in the efficient management of a business. Manual or computer records are used to keep a note of the amount of inventory held and its value at any time during the year. However, at the end of the financial year it is essential for a business to make a physical **inventory-take** for use in the financial statements. This involves inventory control personnel going into the stores, the shop, or the warehouse and counting each item. The counted inventory is then valued as follows:

number of items held x inventory valuation per item = inventory value

The auditors of a business may make random checks to ensure that the inventory value is correct.

The value of inventory at the beginning and end of the financial year is used as an adjustment to the financial statements – see Chapter 4. Therefore, the inventory value has an effect on profit for the year.

IAS 2 applies to all types of inventories – raw materials, work-in-progress (partly manufactured goods), finished goods, products bought in for resale by a retailer and service items, such as stationery, bought for use within a business.

The overriding principle of inventory valuation, as set out in IAS 2, is that inventories are to be valued at **'the lower of cost and net realisable value'**. This means that two different inventory values are compared:

■ **cost**, which is
  –   the cost of purchase
  –   delivery costs
  –   costs of conversion, ie to manufacture the product including direct labour costs

  (note that the cost of storage of finished goods and selling costs cannot be included in the cost of inventory)

■ **net realisable value**, which is
  –   the estimated selling price, less the estimated costs to get the product into the condition necessary to complete the sale

This inventory valuation – the lower of cost and net realisable value – is illustrated as follows:

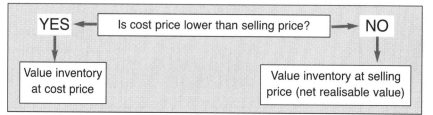

As the diagram shows, the lower of cost and net realisable value is taken; note that **different items or groups of inventory are compared separately**. The principles are illustrated in the two Case Studies which follow.

THE CLOTHING STORE: INVENTORY VALUATION

situation

The Clothing Store bought in a range of 'designer' beachwear in the spring, with each item costing £15 and retailing for £30. Most of the goods sell well but, by autumn, ten items remain unsold. These are put on the 'bargain rail' at £18 each. On 31 December, at the end of the store's financial year, five items remain unsold. At what price will they be included in the year-end inventory valuation?

Twelve months later, three items still remain unsold and have been reduced further to £10 each. At what price will they now be valued in the year-end inventory valuation?

solution

- At 31 December, the five items will be valued at a cost of £15 each, ie 5 x £15 = £75.

- Twelve months later, the three items remaining unsold will be valued at a net realisable value of £10 each, ie 3 x £10 = £30.

Important note: Inventory is **never** valued at selling price when selling price is above cost price. The reason for this is that selling price includes profit, and to value inventory in this way would bring the profit into the financial statements before it has been earned.

PAINT AND WALLPAPER SUPPLIES: INVENTORY VALUATION

situation

The year-end valuations for the two main groups of inventory held by the business 'Paint and Wallpaper Supplies' are found to be:

	Cost	Net Realisable Value
	£	£
Paints	2,500	2,300
Wallpapers	5,000	7,500
	7,500	9,800

Which of the following inventory valuations do you think is correct?

(a)   £7,500

(b)   £9,800

(c)   £7,300

(d)   £10,000

solution

Inventory valuation (c) is correct, because it has taken the 'lower of cost and net realisable value' for each **group** of inventory, ie

Paints (at net realisable value)	£2,300
Wallpapers (at cost)	£5,000
	£7,300

You will also note that this valuation is the lowest of the four possible choices.

inventory valuation methods

IAS 2 allows two different methods to be used to calculate the cost price of inventories.

- **FIFO** (first in, first out) – this method assumes that the first items received are the first to be used, so that the valuation of inventory on hand at any time consists of the most recently acquired items.

- **AVCO** (average cost), or **weighted average cost** – here the average cost of items held at the beginning of the period is calculated; as new inventory is received a new average cost is calculated (usually based on a weighted average, using the number of units bought as the weighting).

A further method of inventory valuation but which cannot be used under IAS 2 is:

- **LIFO** (last in, first out) – this method assumes that the last items received are the first to be used, so that the inventory on hand is made up of earlier purchases.

LIFO is sometimes used by businesses for their internal purposes – such as working out the cost of a product to the customer. However, for financial accounting, it cannot be used in financial statements.

The use of a particular method does not necessarily correspond with the method of physical distribution adopted in a business's stores. For example, in a car factory one car battery of type X is the same as another, and no-one will be concerned if the storekeeper issues one from the latest batch received, even if the FIFO method has been adopted. However, perishable goods are always physically handled on the basis of first in, first out, even if the accounting inventory records use the AVCO method.

Having chosen a suitable inventory valuation method, a business would continue to use that method unless there were good reasons for making the change.

effect on profit

The cost of inventory is recognised in the statement of profit or loss when the goods are sold – this follows the **accruals principle**. At the same time the statement of profit or loss is affected by the opening and closing inventory valuations – the different methods will have an effect on profit. In times of rising prices, FIFO gives the highest profit (because the closing inventory is higher, being based on the latest prices); LIFO gives the lowest profit (closing inventory is lower, being based on older prices); AVCO is in between. In times of falling prices, the reverse will be true. However, over the life of a business, total profit is the same in total, whichever method is chosen: the profit is allocated to different years depending on which method is selected.

The 'rules' to remember for closing inventory are:

■ higher closing inventory = higher profit

■ lower closing inventory = lower profit

For opening inventory, the 'rules' are:

■ higher opening inventory = lower profit

■ lower opening inventory = higher profit

calculating inventory at cost

It is quite common for a business to record its inventory at selling prices – eg a shop will often total its inventory by recording the selling prices of the goods on its shelves. It is then necessary to convert this selling price to cost price by taking off the sales margin. In a similar way inventory which includes VAT needs – for a VAT-registered business – to be converted to a cost price which excludes VAT.

The following two examples show how to calculate the cost price of inventory from selling price and from a VAT-inclusive value.

example 1: from selling price

■ inventory at selling price is £150,000

■ the sales margin is 30%

Cost of inventory is:

$$£150,000 \quad x \quad \frac{(100-30^*)}{100} \quad = \quad £105,000 \text{ cost of inventory}$$

*sales margin of 30%

example 2: from a VAT-inclusive value

■ inventory, including VAT, is £90,000

■ VAT is 20%

Cost of inventory, excluding VAT, is:

$$\text{£90,000} \quad \text{x} \quad \frac{100}{(100 + 20^*)} \quad = \quad \text{£75,000 cost of inventory}$$

*VAT at 20%

Note that example 1 is a **margin** (based on the selling price) while example 2 is where there has been a **mark-up** – or addition – of VAT (based on the purchase cost).

CAPITAL EXPENDITURE AND REVENUE EXPENDITURE

When preparing financial statements it is important to distinguish between **capital expenditure** and **revenue expenditure**.

capital expenditure

Capital expenditure is expenditure incurred on the purchase, alteration or improvement of non-current assets.

Included in capital expenditure are directly attributable costs, such as:

■ delivery of non-current assets

■ installation of non-current assets

■ improvement (but not repair) of non-current assets

■ legal costs of buying property

An example of capital expenditure is the purchase of a car for use in the business.

Note that we use the word 'capitalised' to mean that an item has been treated as capital expenditure.

Capital expenditure is always subject to the application of the **materiality principle** – when items have a low monetary value and/or a very short useful life it is not worth recording them separately, and they will be included in revenue expenditure.

revenue expenditure

Revenue expenditure is expenditure incurred on running expenses.

Included in revenue expenditure are the costs of:

■ repair, maintenance and servicing of non-current assets

■ administration and general overheads of the business

■ selling and distributing the goods or products in which the business trades

An example of revenue expenditure is the cost of petrol or diesel for the car (above) used in the business.

capital and revenue expenditure – the differences

Capital expenditure is shown on the statement of financial position, while revenue expenditure is an expense in the statement of profit or loss. It is important to classify these types of expenditure correctly in the accounting system. For example, if the cost of the car was shown as an expense in the statement of profit or loss, then profit for the year would be reduced considerably, or a loss recorded; meanwhile, the statement of financial position would not show the car as a non-current asset – clearly this is incorrect as the business owns the asset. Note, however, that there is a link between capital expenditure and the statement of profit or loss: as non-current assets are depreciated, the depreciation charge is shown as an expense in the statement of profit or loss. This is an application of the **accruals principle**, ie the depreciation charge relates to the useful life of the asset.

A business will always have a policy as to the value at which non-current assets are capitalised. A large business may consider that £1,000 (or higher) is the value; a small business may use a lower figure.

In some circumstances we must take care to distinguish between capital and revenue expenditure. For example:

■ *cost of building an extension to the factory £30,000, which includes £1,000 for repairs to the existing factory*
  – capital expenditure, £29,000
  – revenue expenditure, £1,000 (because it is for repairs to an existing non-current asset)

■ *a plot of land has been bought for £20,000, the legal costs are £750*
  – capital expenditure £20,750 (the legal costs are included in the capital expenditure, because they are the cost of acquiring the non-current asset, ie the legal costs are capitalised)

■ *the business's own employees are used to install a new air conditioning system: wages £1,000, materials £1,500*
  – capital expenditure £2,500 (an addition to the property). Note that, in cases such as this, revenue expenditure, ie wages and materials purchases, will need to be reduced to allow for the transfer to capital expenditure

■ *own employees used to repair and redecorate the premises: wages £500, materials £750*
  – revenue expenditure £1,250 (repairs and redecoration are running expenses)

■ *purchase of a new machine £10,000, payment for installation and setting up £250*

- capital expenditure £10,250 (costs of installation of a non-current asset are capitalised)

Only by allocating capital expenditure and revenue expenditure correctly between the statement of financial position and the statement of profit or loss can the financial statements provide a realistic view of the business. The chart below shows the main items of capital expenditure and revenue expenditure associated with the major classes of non-current assets – premises, vehicles, machinery, computers and office equipment.

Classes of non-current assets	Capital expenditure	Revenue expenditure
Premises	• cost of building/construction • cost of extension • delivery costs of raw materials used • professional fees, eg legal • labour cost of own employees used on building/construction • installation of utilities, eg gas, water, electricity	• insurance of building • general maintenance • repairs • redecoration • depreciation charge
Vehicles	• cost of vehicle, including any optional extras • delivery costs • number plates • changes to the vehicle	• fuel • road fund licence • extended warranty • painting company logo • insurance • servicing and repairs • depreciation charge
Machinery/ computers/ office equipment	• cost of asset • delivery costs • installation and testing • modifications to meet specific needs of business • installation of special wiring, etc • computer programs (but can be classified as revenue expenditure if cost is low and will have little impact on financial statements – the accounting principle of materiality)	• insurance of asset • servicing and repairs • consumables – such as paper, ink, cartridges, etc • computer programs (or can be classified as capital expenditure if cost is high and will have a large impact on financial statements) • depreciation charge

Note that, when accounting for capital transactions, you should know the implications of VAT (or sales tax). A business that is registered for VAT will enter the amount of VAT in its VAT account and the net amount of the transaction in its non-current asset account. By contrast, a business that is not registered for VAT will record the gross amount of the capital transaction in its non-current asset account.

Chapter Summary

■ The accounting principles (or concepts) of business entity, materiality, going concern and accruals are fundamental to the relevance and reliability of financial records and statements.

■ Accountants apply ethical principles when recording financial transactions. This assures users that such work has been prepared to the highest professional standards.

■ Accounting standards comprise IASs and IFRSs. International standards are widely used in the UK.

■ IAS 16, *Property, plant and equipment*, sets out the accounting treatment for non-current assets; a key feature of the IAS is depreciation.

■ The purpose of depreciation is to spread the cost of a non-current asset over its useful life.

■ The usual valuation for inventory is at the lower of cost and net realisable value – IAS 2, *Inventories*.

■ Inventory valuation methods include:
  – FIFO (first in, first out)
  – LIFO (last in, first out)
  – AVCO (average cost, based on a weighted average)

■ Having chosen one inventory valuation method, a business should apply it consistently.

■ Inventory at cost may need to be calculated from selling prices or VAT-inclusive values.

■ It is important to allocate capital expenditure and revenue expenditure correctly between the statement of financial position and statement of profit or loss so that the financial statements provide a realistic view of the business.

■ For capital expenditure transactions, VAT (or sales tax) should be treated currently, dependent on the registration status of the business.

Key Terms		
	accounting principles	part of the rules of accounting
	business entity principle	financial statements record and report on the activities of one particular business
	materiality principle	items with a low value are not worthwhile recording in the accounts separately
	going concern principle	the presumption that the business to which the financial statements relate will continue to trade in the foreseeable future
	accruals principle	income and expenses are matched so that they relate to the same goods or services and the same accounting period
	fundamental ethical principles	– integrity – objectivity – professional competence and due care – confidentiality – professional behaviour
	accounting standards	provide a framework for accounting and reduce the variety of accounting treatments used in financial statements
	inventory valuation	inventory is valued 'at the lower of cost and net realisable value' (IAS 2)
	capital expenditure	expenditure incurred on the purchase, alteration or improvement of non-current assets
	revenue expenditure	expenditure incurred on running expenses

Activities

8.1 The cost of inventory is recognised in the statement of profit or loss when the goods are sold. This follows the principle of:

(a) Materiality	
(b) Going concern	
(c) Business entity	
(d) Accruals	

8.2 A discussion is taking place between Jane Smith, a sole trader, who owns a furniture shop, and her husband, John, who solely owns an engineering business. The following points are made:

(a) John says that he has bought a new machine for use in his business at a cost of £10,000. He tells Jane that he plans to show the full amount as an expense in his statement of profit or loss for the year. He says this will give him a lower profit, which means he will pay less income tax.

(b) John's car is owned by his business but he keeps referring to it as 'my car'. Jane reminds him that it does not belong to him, but to the business. He replies that of course it belongs to him and, furthermore, if the business went bankrupt, he would be able to keep the car.

(c) On the last day of her financial year, Jane sold a large order of furniture, totalling £3,000, to a local hotel. The furniture was invoiced and delivered that day, before the year-end inventory-take commenced. The payment was received early in the new financial year and Jane now asks John if she will be able to put this sale through the accounts for the new year, instead of the old, but without altering the figures for purchases and closing inventory for the old year.

(d) John says that his accountant talks of preparing his financial statements on a going concern basis. He asks Jane if she knows of any other basis that can be used, and which it is usual to follow.

You are to take each of the points and state the correct accounting treatment, referring to appropriate accounting principles (concepts).

8.3 Write in the accounting principle (concept) which relates to each of the statements below.

Statement	Accounting principle
Some items are of such low value that it is not worthwhile recording them separately.	
The financial statements record and report on the activities of one particular business.	
Income and expenses are matched so that they relate to the same goods or services and the same accounting period.	
The presumption is that the business to which the financial statements relate will continue to trade in the foreseeable future.	

8.4 You are the bookkeeper at JC Trading. A sales executive passes to you an expenses claim for car miles to visit a client. You know that the executive travelled in another colleague's car when they both visited the client.

Indicate the **two** ethical principles that are at issue.

(a)	Integrity	
(b)	Objectivity	
(c)	Professional competence and due care	
(d)	Confidentiality	
(e)	Professional behaviour	

8.5 Indicate the ethical principle at issue for each of the following.

(a)	No compromise of professional judgement	
(b)	Transactions are genuine and valid for inclusion in the records of the business	
(c)	Compliance with relevant laws and regulations	
(d)	Non-disclosure of information to third parties	
(e)	Knowledge and skill is maintained at the level required to provide a competent professional service	

Choose from the following list:

- Integrity
- Objectivity
- Professional competence and due care
- Confidentiality
- Professional behaviour

8.6 **(a)** Explain briefly the purpose of depreciation of non-current assets.

(b) A business is going to buy some office furniture. The furniture is expected to be of equal use to the business for each of the next four years, at the end of which it will have no value.

Which method of depreciation do you recommend them to use?

(a) 20% diminishing balance method	
(b) 20% straight-line method	
(c) 25% diminishing balance method	
(d) 25% straight-line method	

8.7 Inventory is valued at:

(a) Cost price	
(b) Net realisable value	
(c) Lower of cost and net realisable value	
(d) Selling price	

8.8 A garden supplies shop has the following valuations for each group of inventory at the end of its financial year:

	cost	selling price
	£	£
Seeds	1,550	1,450
Fertilisers and insecticides	2,270	3,560
Tools	4,390	6,920

What valuation for closing inventory will be used in its financial statements?

8.9 A business has, in error, overvalued its closing inventory by £1,000. Before the error is corrected, what is the effect:

(a)   on this year's profit?

(b)   on next year's profit?

8.10 **(a)** Describe the basis of inventory valuation according to IAS 2, *Inventories*.

(b) You are an accounts assistant at Canley Cakes, a business that bakes and sells speciality cakes for birthdays, Christmas and Easter. The financial year-end is 30 June.

The policy of the business is that if cakes are unsold after five days from baking they are reduced to half of the normal selling price.

You are helping with the inventory-take at 30 June 20-4 and have the following information:

	number of cakes	220
of which:	up to 5 days old	160
	over 5 days old	60
	normal selling price	£10
	cost price	£6

What is the inventory valuation for the 220 cakes held at 30 June 20-4?

(a) £1,100	
(b) £1,260	
(c) £1,320	
(d) £2,200	

(c) An error in the date stamping of cakes has been found and this means that, of the 220 cakes, 100 cakes are now found to be over five days old. By how much will the inventory valuation change?

(a) £500 decrease	
(b) £400 decrease	
(c) £40 increase	
(d) £40 decrease	

(d) Will the change in inventory valuation from (c) cause the profit for the year to 30 June 20-4 to increase, decrease or stay the same? Tick one box.

☐ increase

☐ decrease

☐ stay the same

8.11 A business has bought an accounting program for its computer system. The cost of the software is £99. Will this be treated as capital expenditure or revenue expenditure? Give reasons for your answer.

8.12 Capital expenditure is money spent on non-current assets. As these are recorded on the statement of financial position, then it is true to say that capital expenditure has no effect on the statement of profit or loss.

Discuss this statement, saying whether or not you agree with it and giving reasons for your answer.

8.13 Classify the following costs (tick the appropriate column):

	Capital expenditure	Revenue expenditure
(a) Purchase of machinery		
(b) Installation of machinery		
(c) Depreciation of machinery		
(d) Purchase of property		
(e) Legal fees relating to the purchase of property		
(f) Repairs to property		
(g) Insurance of property		
(h) Labour costs of own employees used to build extension to property		
(i) Repainting and redecoration of property		

8.14   **You are to** calculate the cost price of inventory from the information given.

    (a)   •   inventory at selling price is £240,000

          •   the sales margin is 40%

          The cost price of inventory is £ ⬚

    (b)   •   inventory, including VAT, is £105,000

          •   VAT is 20%

          The cost of inventory, excluding VAT, is £ ⬚

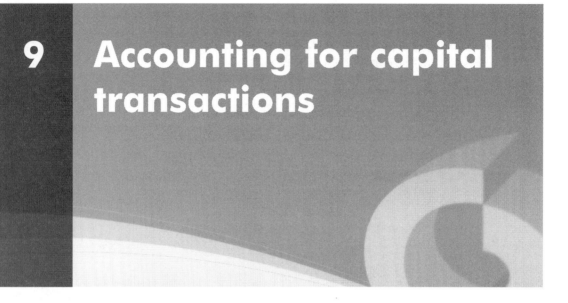

9 Accounting for capital transactions

this chapter covers...

Capital transactions concern all aspects of the acquisition and disposal of non-current assets. Because of the nature of capital transactions – their high cost and long-term use within the business – management keeps careful control over them.

In this chapter we will examine:

- *accounting entries to record acquisition, depreciation, and disposal of non-current assets*

- *the importance of distinguishing between capital expenditure and revenue expenditure*

- *acquisition and control of non-current assets, including the use of a non-current asset register*

- *methods of funding capital expenditure; cash purchase, part-exchange, borrowing (loans, hire purchase and finance leases)*

When accounting for capital transactions be aware of the implications of VAT (or sales tax). A business that is registered for VAT will be able to enter amounts of tax in its VAT account and only the net amount of the capital transaction will be recorded. By contrast, a business that is not registered for VAT will record the gross amount of the capital transaction.

CAPITAL TRANSACTIONS

Capital transactions concern all aspects of non-current assets – through purchasing, control and final disposal.

Non-current assets are usually tangible items that are:

■ held for use in the production or supply of goods or services

■ expected to have a life span of more than one year

Examples of non-current assets include land, premises, vehicles, machinery, computers and office equipment. Tangible non-current assets have a physical existence, ie they can be touched and felt. By contrast, assets which have no physical form are intangible – for example, goodwill which is often paid by the purchaser when buying an existing business.

Because of the nature of non-current assets – their high cost and long-term use within the business – management will keep careful control over capital transactions. For example, the purchase of a new computer system costing £500,000 will be authorised by a meeting of senior management; by contrast the purchase of new wastepaper baskets for the office at a cost of £50 will be authorised by the office supervisor.

Before we study the procedures for authorising the purchase, control and final disposal of non-current assets, we will look at a Case Study which shows the accounting entries to record the life of a non-current asset.

<table>
<tr><td>Case
Study</td><td></td></tr>
</table>

ACCOUNTING FOR NON-CURRENT ASSETS

situation

Eveshore Growers Limited is a co-operative venture which sells fruit, vegetables and flowers grown by its members in the Vale of Eveshore. The company's financial year end is 31 December.

On 4 January 20-1 the company buys a Supra XL computer for use in the administration office. The cost is £2,000 + VAT at 20% (Eveshore Growers Limited is registered for VAT); the amount is paid from the bank.

The computer is depreciated using the straight-line method at a rate of 25 per cent of cost each year. It is company policy to charge a full year's depreciation in the year of purchase, but none in the year of sale.

By mid-20-4 the computer is beginning to show its age and it is decided to replace it by a more up-to-date model. The old computer is sold on 12 July 20-4 for £400 + VAT at 20%, a payment being received into the bank.

Show the journal and accounting entries to record:

• acquisition of the computer

• depreciation

• disposal

solution

ACQUISITION

The cost of the non-current asset is £2,000 + VAT (at 20%) of £400. This is entered in the journal (see Chapter 11) as the book of prime entry and then recorded in the double-entry accounts:

Journal

Date	Details	Reference	Dr	Cr
20-1			£	£
4 Jan	Computer	GL	2,000	
	VAT	GL	400	
	Bank	CB		2,400
			2,400	2,400
	Purchase of Supra XL computer			
	for use in the administration office;			
	capital expenditure authorisation			
	number 015/20-1			

Tutorial note: the journal is a book of prime entry which is used to list transactions before they are entered in the double-entry accounts; its use will be discussed in Chapter 11.

Dr	**Computer at cost account**			Cr
20-1		£	20-1	£
4 Jan	Bank	2,000		

Dr	**Value Added Tax account**			Cr
20-1		£	20-1	£
4 Jan	Bank	400		

Cash book (payments)

		Cash	Bank	VAT	Trade payables	Other expenses
20-1		£	£	£	£	£
4 Jan	Computer		2,400	400		2,000

Note that, as Eveshore Growers Limited is registered for VAT, it will debit its VAT account with the tax. The amount is then included with VAT paid on inputs (purchases and expenses) and set-off against VAT charged on outputs (sales and services).

DEPRECIATION

Depreciation at 25 per cent straight-line per year, based on the cost price, is as follows:

year ended 31 December 20-1	£500	(full year's depreciation)
year ended 31 December 20-2	£500	
year ended 31 December 20-3	£500	

Note that, following company policy, no depreciation is charged in 20-4, being the year of disposal.

Depreciation charges are recorded in the journal (first year only shown) and in the depreciation charges account, machinery: accumulated depreciation and statement of profit or loss as follows:

Journal

Date	Details	Reference	Dr	Cr
20-1			£	£
31 Dec	Depreciation charges	GL	500	
	Computer: accumulated depreciation	GL		500
	Depreciation charges for year on			
	Supra XL computer			
31 Dec	Statement of profit or loss	GL	500	
	Depreciation charges	GL		500
	Transfer to the statement of profit or			
	loss of Supra XL computer			

Dr				Depreciation charges account		Cr
20-1		£		20-1		£
31 Dec	Computer: accumulated depreciation	500		31 Dec	Statement of profit or loss	500
20-2				20-2		
31 Dec	Computer: accumulated depreciation	500		31 Dec	Statement of profit or loss	500
20-3				20-3		
31 Dec	Computer: accumulated depreciation	500		31 Dec	Statement of profit or loss	500

Dr			**Computer: accumulated depreciation account**		Cr
20-1		£	20-1		£
31 Dec	Balance c/d	500	31 Dec	Depreciation charges	500
20-2			20-2		
31 Dec	Balance c/d	1,000	1 Jan	Balance b/d	500
			31 Dec	Depreciation charges	500
		1,000			1,000
20-3			20-3		
31 Dec	Balance c/d	1,500	1 Jan	Balance b/d	1,000
			31 Dec	Depreciation charges	500
		1,500			1,500
			20-4		
			1 Jan	Balance b/d	1,500

The extended trial balance shows the following amounts for the statement of profit or loss and the statement of financial position.

Year	Statement of profit or loss		Statement of financial position	
	Dr	Cr	Dr	Cr
	Expense	Income	Cost	Accumulated depreciation
	£	£	£	£
20-1	500	–	2,000	500
20-2	500	–	2,000	1,000
20-3	500	–	2,000	1,500

Note that, if Eveshore Growers Limited had not been registered for VAT, the full cost of the non-current asset, ie £2,400, would be recorded in the computer at cost account. Depreciation would then be calculated on £2,400 x 25 per cent = £600 per year.

DISPOSAL

The accounting entries to deal with the disposal of non-current assets have been described in Chapter 6 (pages 97-100). The asset disposal account brings together

- the original cost of the computer
- accumulated depreciation over the asset's life
- disposal proceeds

The computer is sold for £400 + VAT at 20%; payment is received from the buyer. The transaction is recorded in the journal as the book of prime entry, and in the double-entry accounts as follows:

Journal

Date	Details	Reference	Dr	Cr
20-4			£	£
12 Jul	Disposals	GL	2,000	
	Computer at cost	GL		2,000
	Computer: accumulated depreciation	GL	1,500	
	Disposals	GL		1,500
	Bank	CB	480	
	Disposals	GL		400
	VAT	GL		80
	Statement of profit or loss	GL	100	
	Disposals	GL		100
			4,080	4,080
	Sale of Supra XL computer; loss on disposal of £100 transferred to statement of profit or loss			

Dr		**Computer disposals account**			Cr
20-4		£	20-4		£
12 Jul	Computer at cost	2,000	12 Jul	Computer: accumulated depreciation	1,500
			12 Jul	Bank	400
			12 Jul	Statement of profit or loss (loss on disposal)	100
		2,000			2,000

Dr		**Computer at cost account**			Cr
20-4		£	20-4		£
1 Jan	Balance b/d	2,000	12 Jul	Disposals	2,000

Dr		**Computer: accumulated depreciation account**			Cr
20-4		£	20-4		£
12 Jul	Disposals	1,500	1 Jan	Balance b/d	1,500

Dr		**Value Added Tax account**			Cr
20-4		£	20-4		£
			12 Jul	Bank	80

Cash book (receipts)

		Cash	Bank	VAT	Trade receivables	Other income
20-4		£	£	£	£	£
12 Jul	Computer disposal		480	80		400

Statement of profit or loss for the year ended 31 December 20-4		
	Dr **Expense** £	Cr **Income** £
Loss on disposal of computer	100	–

The loss on disposal here is because of under-depreciation; if over-depreciation had occurred, a gain on disposal would be shown as income.

Note that, if Eveshore Growers Limited had not been registered for VAT, it would not charge VAT on disposal of the non-current asset. The loss on disposal would be £200, ie cost £2,400 – (£600 depreciation x 3 years) = carrying amount* £600 – sale proceeds £400 = £200 loss.

*cost less accumulated depreciation

CAPITAL EXPENDITURE AND REVENUE EXPENDITURE

The importance of distinguishing between capital expenditure and revenue expenditure has been highlighted in Chapter 8 (page 143). For example, the purchase of the computer seen in the Case Study is capital expenditure, which is recorded as a non-current asset of the business. Certain costs associated with the delivery and installation of the non-current asset can be capitalised (ie included in the cost of the asset) – for guidance, see the diagram on page 144.

Most non-current assets are depreciated, which means that the costs of the assets are spread over the period during which they are used by the business and charged as an expense to the statement of profit or loss – an application of the **accruals principle**.

ACQUISITION AND CONTROL OF NON-CURRENT ASSETS

Because of the often large amounts of money involved, and the non-routine nature of their purchase, the acquisition of non-current assets is monitored and controlled by the business. In particular, their purchase will have to be approved by the business's managers or owners, or by a committee which appraises capital expenditure projects and decides which will be approved. The stages in the acquisition and control of non-current assets are as follows:

application and authorisation

The section of the business that wishes to purchase the non-current asset must submit an application for capital expenditure to the appropriate level of management:

- the **manager** responsible for a section of the business will be able to approve relatively low-cost items, eg the purchase of a filing cabinet

- the **capital expenditure committee** of a large business will approve significant cost items, eg the proposed installation of a new computer system

- the **owners/directors** will approve the largest applications

Much will depend on the size of the business as to who makes the decisions and how – a small business will do things very differently from a large limited company. Nevertheless, there does need to be an approval process in place for all sizes of business.

The form of the application will vary from a single sheet capital expenditure authorisation form, through to a fully documented proposal which includes an assessment of the likely costs and resources to be used over the life of the asset. Many businesses require two or three prices or quotations to be obtained, so that they can see that they are getting the best value for money.

Before giving their approval to capital projects, particularly those involving large sums of money, the managers responsible for authorising the expenditure will consider a number of wider issues:

- the expenditure must fit in with the business's plans and budgets
- the method of funding (see pages 165-166); the expenditure must be considered
  - is there sufficient money in the bank account?
  - can old assets be sold or part-exchanged to provide some of the money?
  - will a bank or finance company loan need to be arranged?
  - is hire purchase or a finance lease to be used?

■ staffing and training implications
  – will there be redundancies?
  – can staff be retrained? at what cost?
  – will new staff need to be employed? at what pay rates?
■ productivity of the business
  – will the capital expenditure increase the output of the business?
  – will the quality of output be improved?
■ profitability of the business
  – is there a market for the increased output? what will be the sales revenue?
  – by how much will our costs increase?
  – will the business be more profitable?

monitoring and control

Once authorisation has been granted for a particular project, it is important that the actual costs are monitored and controlled against the costs in the original application. For relatively small projects, it is easy to compare the original quotation against the actual price charged. For major projects, where a number of contractors are involved, it will be necessary for the buyer to monitor costs carefully – staff might be appointed specifically for this role. Cost overruns and cost savings need to be investigated to see why they have occurred, and what lessons can be learned for the future.

the use of a non-current asset register

In order to keep a record of non-current assets, many businesses make use of a **non-current asset register** – shown on the next page. This separates out each class of non-current asset – eg premises, vehicles, machinery, computers, office equipment – and records details of each asset owned, in the appropriate class, such as:

■ asset description and/or serial number (a number often marked on the asset in order to give it a positive identification)
■ date of acquisition
■ original cost
■ the method and rate of depreciation
■ depreciation charges for each year of ownership
■ carrying amount, ie cost price less accumulated depreciation
■ funding method, such as cash (which includes payment against an invoice, eg 30 days), part-exchange, part-exchange and cash, or borrowing (loans, hire purchase and finance leases)
■ disposal date
■ disposal proceeds

Details not included in the register would be:

■ revenue expenditure (eg road fund licence on a vehicle not to be included in the asset cost) – see page 144
■ low value assets which are not considered to be material – see page 134

NON-CURRENT ASSET REGISTER

Description/serial no	Acquisition date	Cost £	Depreciation charges £	Carrying amount* £	Funding method	Disposal proceeds £	Disposal date
Office equipment							
Computer, Supra XL	4/1/-1	2,000.00			Cash		
Year ended 31/12/-1			500.00	1,500.00			
Year ended 31/12/-2			500.00	1,000.00			
Year ended 31/12/-3			500.00	500.00			
Year ended 31/12/-4			0.00	0.00		400.00	12/7/-4

* carrying amount, ie cost price less accumulated depreciation

The details of the computer from the Case Study are shown in the non-current asset register. Note that there is no set layout for the register – a business will use whatever method suits it best: some will show each asset over its entire life on a separate page (as shown in the example); others will list several assets on the same page for one year only, carrying forward assets owned at the end of each year to a new page.

The non-current asset register enables a business to keep control of such assets; from time-to-time the accounting staff will ensure that the capital records are being kept up-to-date – in accordance with the organisation's policies and procedures – and will check the physical items of non-current assets listed in the register. Discrepancies may occur because:

- the non-current asset register has not been kept up-to-date
    - new assets have not been recorded
    - sold or scrapped assets have not been written out of the register
    - assets which have become obsolete or inadequate for the job have not been written down in value
- assets have been stolen and their theft has not been reported or recorded
- there are errors in recording details in the register

Accounts assistants are often required to check the non-current asset register against the physical items. Any discrepancies that are identified, if they cannot be resolved, should be referred to the appropriate person – usually the accounts supervisor. It is for the management of a business, or the owners, to decide what action to take over discrepancies. If discrepancies prove to be occurring more frequently than is considered acceptable, it may be appropriate to review the way in which the capital records are maintained and to seek suggestions for improvements from the staff involved.

disposal of non-current assets

An important aspect of the control of non-current assets includes dealing with their disposal in an orderly way. In most cases old assets are replaced at the end of their useful lives with new assets, eg an old computer system is replaced with a new one. Sometimes, however, assets may become surplus to requirements part-way through their lives, eg a section of the business is closed. Whatever the circumstances, it is essential that disposal of assets is handled in such a way that the business receives the maximum amount of cash.

Old and surplus assets may be:

- sold for their scrap value
- used as a part-exchange value to help fund the acquisition of new assets
- sold on the secondhand market
- sold to employees

Before assets are disposed of, the approval of the appropriate person or department must be received. For example, the office manager in a small company may have authority to deal with disposals. In larger companies, a separate department may handle disposals and, for the closure of a section of the business, specialist staff may be brought in to ensure an orderly disposal.

The disposal proceeds, or part-exchange value, must be accounted for correctly through asset disposals account (see pages 97-100). At the same time, the non-current asset register must be updated to:

- identify the correct asset being disposed
- remove it from the register
- record the disposal proceeds and the date of disposal

Note: assets disposed will have a carrying amount of zero at the end of the financial period.

FUNDING NON-CURRENT ASSETS

Funding methods for non-current assets include cash purchase, part-exchange, loans, hire purchase and finance leases. Accounts involved are:

- non-current asset at cost account (eg machinery, vehicles)
- bank/cash account
- loan account

Note: in AAT Assessments you could be asked to identify the most suitable funding method in the context of a business situation.

cash purchase

This is where the business has sufficient cash in its bank account – or in an interest-bearing deposit account – to pay in full for the new asset. Alternatively, a business might buy an asset on standard commercial credit terms, eg 30 days, and then make payment for the asset from the bank account before the end of the term – legal title to the asset is usually acquired at the date of purchase, ie before the date of payment.

part exchange

This is where an old asset is 'traded in' as part of the purchase price of the new asset, the balance remaining due being paid either in cash or by borrowing (the bookkeeping entries for a part-exchange have been seen in Chapter 6); part-exchange is especially common when a new vehicle – car or van – is being purchased.

loans

A loan agreement with a bank or a finance company is a method of funding the purchase of non-current assets, such as vehicles, machinery, computers and office equipment. The bank or finance company lends an agreed sum of money to the business, which uses the funds to purchase the asset.

Ownership of the asset belongs to the business from the start – unlike hire purchase and finance leases – although the bank or finance company will often require security to back their loan. The borrower makes agreed repayments which cover the cost and the interest (which may be fixed for the term of the loan). Loans are available for periods of up to seven years (sometimes longer).

The bookkeeping entries for loans and their repayment are shown on page 23.

Note that a bank overdraft is not the same as a loan – instead it is a short-term facility which allows a business to overdraw its bank account and, usually, is reviewed each year. A bank overdraft is not a suitable funding method for non-current assets.

hire purchase

A hire purchase agreement from a finance company enables a business (the hirer) to have the use of a non-current asset on payment of a deposit. The finance company owns the asset and the hirer makes regular instalment payments – monthly, quarterly or half-yearly – which pay back the cost plus interest over a set period. At the end of the hire purchase period, ownership of the asset usually passes from the finance company to the business. Hire purchase is often used to finance non-current assets such as vehicles, machinery, computers and office equipment.

finance leases

Finance leases are medium term (up to seven years) arrangements used to fund non-current assets such as vehicles, machinery, computers and office equipment. With a leasing agreement, a business (the lessee) has the use of an asset owned by a finance company (the lessor). The lessee makes regular rental payments to the lessor over the period of the lease, which might be up to seven years. There is normally no provision in a finance lease for legal ownership of the leased asset to pass to the lessee at the end of the lease.

Note: in AAT Assessments you will not be required to have detailed knowledge of the accounting treatment for hire purchase and finance leases.

Chapter Summary

- Capital transactions concern all aspects of non-current assets – through purchasing, control and final disposal.

- Tangible non-current assets – such as premises, vehicles, equipment – have a physical existence; intangible non-current assets – such as goodwill – have no physical form.

- A non-current asset register is used to record details of assets.

- Funding methods for non-current assets include cash purchase, part-exchange, loans, hire purchase and finance leases.

Key Terms

non-current assets	non-current assets are usually tangible items that are: – held for use in the production or supply of goods or services – expected to be used during more than one accounting period
non-current asset register	used for control purposes; records details of purchase, depreciation, disposal of all non-current assets owned by a business
hire purchase	agreement between a finance company and a hirer which enables the hirer to have the use of a non-current asset against a deposit and regular instalment payments
finance lease	agreement between a finance company (lessor) and a business (lessee) which enables the lessee to have the use of a non-current asset against regular hire or rental payments

Activities

9.1 Which **one** of the following is a tangible non-current asset?

(a)	Premises	
(b)	Goodwill	
(c)	Trade receivables	
(d)	Bank loan	

9.2 The owner of a taxi company, Mary Sampson, wishes to develop a policy for authorisation of new taxi purchases. Which **one** of the following is most suitable to authorise such purchases?

(a)	The owner of the business, Mary Sampson	
(b)	Her bank manager	
(c)	Her accounts assistant	
(d)	The driver of the vehicle	

9.3 A finance lease is a:

(a) Medium-term agreement where a finance company funds an asset and the business makes instalment payments to buy it	
(b) Medium-term agreement under which the lessee has the use of an asset owned by a finance company	✓
(c) Medium-term agreement under which a bank or finance company lends the funds to a business for it to buy the asset	
(d) Type of hire purchase agreement	

9.4 **(a)** The non-current asset register of Wyvern Building Supplies, a VAT-registered business, is shown below. **You are to** complete the register with depreciation on the non-current asset for the year ended 31 December 20-3.

(b) The asset is sold on 10 February 20-4 for £500 (net of VAT); it is company policy not to charge depreciation in the year of sale. **You are to** complete the non-current asset register showing the asset's disposal.

NON-CURRENT ASSET REGISTER

Description/serial no	Acquisition date	Cost £	Depreciation charges £	Carrying amount £	Funding method	Disposal proceeds £	Disposal date
Office equipment							
Computer, Supra ML	12/3/-1	3,000.00			Cash		
Year ended 31/12/-1			1,500.00	1,500.00			
Year ended 31/12/-2			750.00	750.00			

9.5 QuickPrint Limited is a photographic processing company with a financial year-end of 31 December. On 10 January 20-1 it buys an automated machine to develop and print (d & p) films; the cost is £32,000 (paid by cheque). Depreciation is charged at 40% each year, using the diminishing balance method. It is company policy to charge a full year's depreciation in the year of purchase, but none in the year of sale.

The printing and developing machine works well but it is decided to replace it in 20-4 by a more up-to-date model. The old machine is sold on 17 August 20-4 for a part-exchange price of £5,000.

(a) **You are to** show the journal and accounting entries (cash book not required) to record the machine's:
- acquisition
- depreciation
- disposal

Note: VAT is to be ignored.

(b) Complete the non-current asset register – below – to show the machine's acquisition, depreciation and disposal.

NON-CURRENT ASSET REGISTER							
Description/serial no	Acquisition date	Cost	Depreciation charges	Carrying amount	Funding method	Disposal proceeds	Disposal date
		£	£	£		£	
Machinery							

9.6 John Aziz runs a taxi company called Silver Link Cabs. He started in business on 24 January 20-1 when he bought two taxis, registration numbers WV60 XNP and WV60 YNP, at a cost of £15,000 each (paid from the bank).

John charges depreciation at the rate of 30 per cent each year, using the straight-line method. He charges a full year's depreciation in the year of purchase, but none in the year of sale.

On 17 March 20-3 he buys another taxi, registration number WV13 ZNP, at a cost of £17,500 (paid from the bank). On 13 October 20-3 he sells WV60 XNP for £6,500 (paid into the bank).

You are to show the accounting entries (journal and cash book not required) to record the acquisition, depreciation and disposal of his taxis for the years ended 31 December 20-1, 20-2 and 20-3.

Notes:
- VAT is to be ignored
- use one non-current asset account for all three taxis, one depreciation charges account, and one accumulated depreciation account

9.7 This Activity is about recording information for non-current assets for a business known as Diamond Trading. Diamond Trading is registered for VAT.

The following is a purchase invoice received by Diamond Trading:

To: Diamond Trading Unit 6, Elmtree Estate Wyvern WV5 2LU	Invoice 517 Norse Supplies plc Belmont Road Mereford ME5 4XS		**Date:** 28 March 20-7
Executive desk	Reference 45129X	1	635.00
Delivery		1	25.00
Desk protector mats @ £25.00 each		2	50.00
VAT @ 20%			142.00
Total			852.00
Settlement terms: strictly 30 days net			

The following information relates to the sale of a car:

Registration number	WV14 JEC
Date of sale	10 March 20-7
Selling price	£8,500.00

- Diamond Trading has a policy of capitalising expenditure over £500.
- Vehicles are depreciated at 25% on a diminishing balance basis.
- Office equipment is depreciated at 30% on a straight-line basis assuming no residual value.
- Non-current assets are depreciated in the year of acquisition but not in the year of disposal.

Record the following information in the non-current asset register on the next page.

(a) Any acquisitions of non-current assets during the year ended 31 March 20-7

(b) Any disposals of non-current assets during the year ended 31 March 20-7

(c) Depreciation for the year ended 31 March 20-7

NON-CURRENT ASSET REGISTER							
Description/serial no	Acquisition date	Cost £	Depreciation charges £	Carrying amount £	Funding method	Disposal proceeds £	Disposal date
Office equipment							
Telephone system	30/09/-4	1,500.00			Cash		
Year end 31/03/-5			450.00	1,050.00			
Year end 31/03/-6			450.00	600.00			
Year end 31/03/-7							
Year end 31/03/-7							
Vehicles							
WV14 JEC	15/04/-4	18,000.00			Cash		
Year end 31/03/-5			4,500.00	13,500.00			
Year end 31/03/-6			3,375.00	10,125.00			
Year end 31/03/-7							
WV65 DBC	30/10/-5	12,000.00			Part-exchange		
Year end 31/03/-6			3,000.00	9,000.00			
Year end 31/03/-7							

9.8 A-Z Taxis needs a new taxi to meet an increase in business. The business is profitable but the owner, Ken Molina, doesn't want to use current monies to fund the purchase. Which **one** of the following funding methods would you suggest he considers?

(a)	Cash purchase	
(b)	Purchase on 30 days' credit terms	
(c)	Bank overdraft	
(d)	Hire purchase	

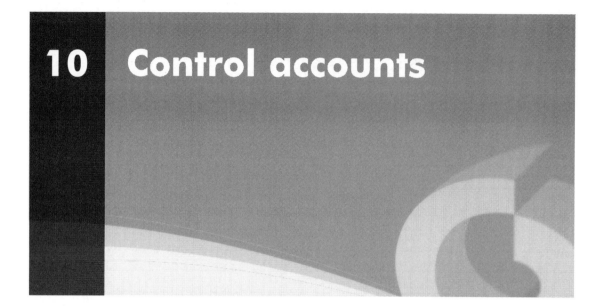

10 Control accounts

this chapter covers...

Control accounts are 'master' accounts which record by means of totals the transactions passing through the accounts that they control.

In this chapter we will look at:

- *the double-entry system and division of the ledger*

- *the concept of control accounts*

- *the layout of sales ledger and purchases ledger control accounts*

- *the use of control accounts as an aid to the management of a business*

- *control accounts and bookkeeping*

- *making reconciliations with*
    - *sales ledger control account to sales ledger*
    - *purchases ledger control account to purchases ledger*
    - *bank account to bank statement*

DIVISION OF THE LEDGER

The double-entry system of bookkeeping involves making two entries in the ledger accounts for each business transaction. The traditional meaning of a ledger is a weighty leather-bound volume into which each account was entered on a separate page. With such a hand-written bookkeeping system, as more and more accounts were opened, the point was reached where another ledger book was needed. Finally, in order to sort the accounts into a logical order, the accounting system was divided into four main sections, and this practice continues today:

- **sales ledger**, containing the accounts of trade receivables

- **purchases ledger**, containing the accounts of trade payables

- **cash book**, containing bank and cash records of the receipts and payments of the business

- **general ledger**, containing all the other accounts

These four divisions comprise 'the ledger', and are illustrated on the next page. Note that sales and purchases ledgers are subsidiary (or memorandum) ledgers, with control accounts (explained in this chapter) held in the general ledger.

THE CONCEPT OF CONTROL ACCOUNTS

Control accounts are 'master' accounts which control a number of subsidiary (or memorandum) ledger accounts.

Control accounts work in the following way:

The control account (also known as a **totals account**) is used to record the totals of transactions passing through the subsidiary accounts. In this way, the balance of the control account will always be equal to the total balances of the subsidiary accounts, unless an error has occurred. Two commonly-used control accounts are:

- **sales ledger control account**, which controls the sales ledger

- **purchases ledger control account**, which controls the purchases ledger

(Later in the chapter we see how VAT control account and payroll control account bring together totals from books of prime entry and accounts.)

DIVISION OF THE LEDGER

sales ledger

Sales ledger contains the accounts of trade receivables, and records:
- sales made on credit to customers of the business
- sales returns by customers
- payments received from customers
- discounts allowed for prompt settlement

Cash sales are not recorded in this ledger.

Sales ledger contains an account for each trade receivable and records the transactions with that customer. The total of the sales ledger account balances should agree with the balance of sales ledger control account in the general ledger.

purchases ledger

Purchases ledger contains the accounts of trade payables, and records:
- purchases made on credit from suppliers of the business
- purchases returns made by the business
- payments made to suppliers
- discounts received for prompt settlement

Cash purchases are not recorded in this ledger.

Purchases ledger contains an account for each trade payable and records the transactions with that supplier. The total of the purchases ledger account balances should agree with the balance of purchases ledger control account in the general ledger.

cash books

Cash Book:

- records all transactions for bank account and cash account

- is also often used for listing the amounts of settlement (cash) discount received and allowed, and for recording amounts of Value Added Tax on cash sales and cash purchases

Note that cash book is included amongst the general ledger accounts for the purposes of a trial balance.

general ledger

The general ledger contains the other accounts of the business:
- sales account (cash and credit sales)
- purchases account (cash and credit purchases)
- sales returns, purchases returns
- expenses and income
- loan
- capital or equity, drawings or dividends (limited companies)
- Value Added Tax or sales tax (where the business is registered for VAT or sales tax)
- non-current assets, eg premises, computers, motor vehicles
- other assets, eg cash, bank balance, inventory
- control accounts, eg sales ledger, purchases ledger

In the illustration on page 173 we have seen how a control account acts as a master account for a number of subsidiary (or memorandum) accounts. The principle is that, if the total of the opening balances for subsidiary accounts is known, together with the total of amounts increasing these balances, and the total of amounts decreasing these balances, then the total of the closing balances for the subsidiary accounts can be calculated.

For example:

		£
Total of opening balances		50,000
Add increases		10,000
		60,000
Less decreases		12,000
Total of closing balances		48,000

The total of the closing balances can now be checked against a separate listing of the balances of the subsidiary accounts to ensure that the two figures agree. If so, it proves that the ledgers within the section are correct, subject to any errors. Let us now apply this concept to one of the divisions of the ledger – sales ledger.

The diagram on the next page shows the personal accounts which form the entire sales ledger of a particular business – in practice there would, of course, be more than four accounts involved. The sales ledger control account acts as a totals account, which records totals of the transactions passing through the subsidiary accounts that it controls. Notice how transactions appear in the control account *on the same side* as they appear in the subsidiary accounts. The sales ledger control account can be reconciled with the balances of the subsidiary accounts which it controls (see below). Thus, control accounts act as an aid to locating errors: if the control account and subsidiary accounts agree, then the error is likely to lie elsewhere. In this way the control account acts as a checking and control device – proving the arithmetical accuracy of the ledger section.

Normally the whole of a ledger section is controlled by one control account, eg sales ledger control account or purchases ledger control account. However, it is also possible to have a number of separate control accounts for sections of the subsidiary ledgers, eg sales ledger control account A-K, purchases ledger control account S-Z, etc. It is for a business – the user of the accounting system – to decide what is most suitable, taking into account the number of accounts in the subsidiary ledgers, together with the type of accounting system – manual or computerised.

From the diagram on the next page the sales ledger control account and sales ledger accounts are agreed at the beginning and end of the month, as follows:

Dr			Sales Ledger Control Account			Cr
20-6		£	20-6			£
1 Jan	Balance b/d	500	31 Jan	Bank		443
31 Jan	Sales	700	31 Jan	Discounts allowed		7
			31 Jan	Sales returns		70
			31 Jan	Balance c/d		680
		1,200				1,200
1 Feb	Balance b/d	680				

Dr			A Ackroyd		Cr
20-6		£	20-6		£
1 Jan	Balance b/d	100	10 Jan	Bank	98
6 Jan	Sales	150	10 Jan	Discounts allowed	2
			31 Jan	Balance c/d	150
		250			250
1 Feb	Balance b/d	150			

Dr			B Barnes		Cr
20-6		£	20-6		£
1 Jan	Balance b/d	200	13 Jan	Bank	195
6 Jan	Sales	250	13 Jan	Discounts allowed	5
			27 Jan	Sales returns	50
			31 Jan	Balance c/d	200
		450			450
1 Feb	Balance b/d	200			

Dr			C Cox		Cr
20-6		£	20-6		£
1 Jan	Balance b/d	50	20 Jan	Bank	50
15 Jan	Sales	200	29 Jan	Sales returns	20
			31 Jan	Balance c/d	180
		250			250
1 Feb	Balance b/d	180			

Dr			D Douglas		Cr
20-6		£	20-6		£
1 Jan	Balance b/d	150	30 Jan	Bank	100
20 Jan	Sales	100	31 Jan	Balance c/d	150
		250			250
1 Feb	Balance b/d	150			

Reconciliation of sales ledger control account		
	1 January 20-6	31 January 20-6
	£	£
A Ackroyd	100	150
B Barnes	200	200
C Cox	50	180
D Douglas	150	150
Sales ledger control account	500	680

The business will decide how often to reconcile (agree) the control account with the subsidiary accounts – weekly, monthly, quarterly or annually. Any discrepancy should be investigated immediately and the error(s) or omission(s) traced.

SALES LEDGER CONTROL ACCOUNT

The layout of sales ledger control account (also known as trade receivables control account) is shown below, with sample figures. Study the layout carefully and then read the text which explains the additional items.

Dr		Sales Ledger Control Account	Cr
	£		£
Balance b/d	2,900	Cash/bank receipts from customers	12,100
Credit sales	14,000	Discounts allowed	290
Returned cheques	930	Sales returns	870
		Irrecoverable debts	1,590
		Set-off entries	250
		Balance c/d	2,730
	17,830		17,830
Balance b/d	2,730		

balance b/d

The figure for balance b/d on the debit side of the control account represents the total of the balances of the individual trade receivables' accounts in the sales ledger. This principle is illustrated in the diagram on the previous page. Remember that, at the end of the month (or other period covered by the control account), the account must be balanced and carried down (on the credit side) on the last day of the month, and then brought down (on the debit side) on the first day of the next month.

Note that it is possible for a trade receivable's account to have a credit balance, instead of the usual debit balance. This may come about, for example, because the customer has paid for goods and then returned them, or has overpaid in error: the business owes the amount due, ie the trade receivable has a credit balance for the time being. Most accounting systems 'net off' any such credit balances against the debit balances to give an overall figure for receivables.

credit sales

Only credit sales – and not cash sales – are entered in the control account because only credit sales are recorded in the sales ledger accounts. The total sales of the business will comprise both credit and cash sales.

returned cheques

If a customer's cheque is returned unpaid by the bank, ie the cheque has 'bounced', then authorisation for the entries to be made in the double-entry system must be given by the accounts supervisor. These entries are:

– **debit** trade receivable's account

– **credit** cash book (bank columns)

As a transaction has been made in a trade receivable's account, then the amount must also be recorded in the sales ledger control account – on the debit side.

irrecoverable debts

The bookkeeping entries for writing off an irrecoverable debt (see Chapter 7) are:

– **debit** irrecoverable debts account

– **credit** trade receivable's account

A credit transaction is entered in a trade receivable's account. This is because the control account 'masters' the sales ledger and so the transaction must also be recorded as a credit transaction in the control account.

> **Tutorial note:** The allowance for doubtful debts – and any changes to the allowance – are never entered in sales ledger control account. This is because the double-entry transactions do not affect the accounts of individual trade receivables – see pages 118-122.

set-off entries

See page 181.

PURCHASES LEDGER CONTROL ACCOUNT

The layout of purchases ledger control account (also known as trade payables control account) is shown below, with sample figures.

Dr		Purchases Ledger Control Account		Cr
	£		£
Cash/bank payments to suppliers	8,200	Balance b/d	5,000
Discounts received	260	Credit purchases	8,500
Purchases returns	1,070		
Set-off entries	250		
Balance c/d	3,720		
	13,500		13,500
		Balance b/d	3,720

balance b/d

The figure for balance b/d on the credit side of the control account represents the total of the balances of the individual trade payables' accounts in the purchases ledger. This principle is illustrated in the diagram on the next page.

Note that it is possible for a trade payable's account to have a debit balance, instead of the usual credit balance – for example, if the supplier has been overpaid. Most accounting systems 'net off' any such debit balances against the credit balances to give an overall figure for payables.

credit purchases

Only credit purchases – and not cash purchases – are entered in the control account. However, the total purchases of the business will comprise both credit and cash purchases.

set-off entries

See page 181.

reconciliation of purchases ledger control account

The diagram on the next page shows how a purchases ledger control account acts as a totals account for the purchases ledger of a business. Reconciliation (agreement) of the balances on the purchases ledger control account and subsidiary accounts is shown on page 181.

Dr	Purchases Ledger Control Account		Cr	
20-6		£	20-6	£
31 Jan	Purchases returns	150	1 Jan Balance b/d	1,000
31 Jan	Bank	594	31 Jan Purchases	1,700
31 Jan	Discounts received	6		
31 Jan	Balance c/d	1,950		
		2,700		2,700
			1 Feb Balance b/d	1,950

Dr	F Francis		Cr	
20-6		£	20-6	£
17 Jan	Bank	98	1 Jan Balance b/d	100
17 Jan	Discounts received	2	3 Jan Purchases	200
31 Jan	Balance c/d	200		
		300		300
			1 Feb Balance b/d	200

Dr	G Gold		Cr	
20-6		£	20-6	£
15 Jan	Purchases returns	50	1 Jan Balance b/d	200
28 Jan	Bank	100	9 Jan Purchases	300
31 Jan	Balance c/d	350		
		500		500
			1 Feb Balance b/d	350

Dr	H Harris		Cr	
20-6		£	20-6	£
28 Jan	Purchases returns	100	1 Jan Balance b/d	300
30 Jan	Bank	200	17 Jan Purchases	500
31 Jan	Balance c/d	500		
		800		800
			1 Feb Balance b/d	500

Dr	I Ingram		Cr	
20-6		£	20-6	£
22 Jan	Bank	196	1 Jan Balance b/d	400
22 Jan	Discounts received	4	27 Jan Purchases	700
31 Jan	Balance c/d	900		
		1,100		1,100
			1 Feb Balance b/d	900

Reconciliation of purchases ledger control account		
	1 January 20-6	**31 January 20-6**
	£	£
F Francis	100	200
G Gold	200	350
H Harris	300	500
I Ingram	400	900
Purchases ledger control account	1,000	1,950

Any discrepancy should be investigated immediately and the error(s) or omission(s) traced.

SET-OFF ENTRIES

Set-off (or contra) entries occur when the same person or business has an account in both subsidiary ledgers – sales ledger and purchases ledger – ie they are both buying from, and selling to, the business whose accounts we are preparing. For example, M Patel Limited has the following accounts in the subsidiary sales and purchases ledgers:

SALES LEDGER

Dr		A Smith		Cr
	£			£
Balance b/d	200			

PURCHASES LEDGER

Dr		A Smith		Cr
	£			£
		Balance b/d		300

From these accounts we can see that:

■ A Smith owes M Patel Limited £200 (sales ledger)

■ M Patel Limited owes A Smith £300 (purchases ledger)

To save each having to send a payment to the other, it is possible (with A Smith's agreement) to set-off one account against the other, so that they can settle their net indebtedness with one payment. The bookkeeping entries in M Patel's books will be:

– **debit** A Smith (purchases ledger) £200

– **credit** A Smith (sales ledger) £200

Note that it is always the smaller of the two amounts owing – here £200 – that is the set-off amount.

The accounts will now appear as:

SALES LEDGER

Dr		A Smith		Cr
		£		£
Balance b/d		200	Set-off: purchases ledger	200

PURCHASES LEDGER

Dr		A Smith		Cr
		£		£
Set-off: sales ledger		200	Balance b/d	300

The net result is that M Patel Limited owes A Smith £100. The important point to note is that, because transactions have been recorded in the subsidiary accounts, an entry needs to be made in the two control accounts:

– **debit** purchases ledger control account

– **credit** sales ledger control account

Set-off transactions should be appropriately documented with a journal entry (see Chapter 11) authorised by the accounts supervisor. The journal entry records the transactions in a book of prime entry and gives the authority to record the transactions in the double-entry accounts.

SOURCES OF INFORMATION FOR CONTROL ACCOUNTS

Control accounts use totals (remember that their other name is 'totals accounts') for the week, month, quarter or year – depending on what time period is decided upon by the business. The totals come from a number of sources in the accounting system:

sales ledger control account

▓ total credit sales (including VAT) – from the 'total' column of the sales day book

▓ total sales returns (including VAT) – from the 'total' column of the sales returns day book

▓ total cash/bank receipts from trade receivables – from the cash book

▓ returned cheques – from the cash book

▓ total prompt payment discount allowed – from the discount allowed column of the cash book, or from discount allowed account

▓ irrecoverable debts – from the journal, or irrecoverable debts account

▓ set-off entries – from the journal

purchases ledger control account

▓ total credit purchases (including VAT) – from the 'total' column of the purchases day book

▓ total purchases returns (including VAT) – from the 'total' column of the purchases returns day book

▓ total cash/bank payments to trade payables – from the cash book

▓ total prompt payment discount received – from the discount received column of the cash book, or from discount received account

▓ set-off entries – from the journal

CONTROL ACCOUNTS AS AN AID TO MANAGEMENT

When the manager of a business needs to know the figure for trade receivables or trade payables the balance of the appropriate control account will give the information immediately: there is no need to add up the balances of all the individual accounts. With a computer accounting system, control accounts can be printed at any time.

The use of control accounts makes fraud more difficult – particularly in a manual accounting system. If a fraudulent transaction is to be recorded on a subsidiary account, the transaction must also be entered in the control account. As the control account will be either maintained by a supervisor, or checked regularly by the manager, the control accounts add another level of security within the accounting system.

We have already seen in this chapter how control accounts can help in locating errors. Remember, though, that a control account only proves the arithmetical accuracy of the accounts which it controls – there could still be errors or omissions (see Chapter 11) within the ledger section.

A further use of control accounts is to help with the preparation of financial statements when a business has not kept double-entry accounts and a trial balance cannot be extracted.

CONTROL ACCOUNTS AND BOOKKEEPING

A business must decide how to use control accounts in its bookkeeping system. The usual way of doing this is to incorporate the control accounts into double-entry bookkeeping.

The control accounts form part of the double-entry system in general ledger. The balances of the sales ledger control account and the purchases ledger control account are recorded in the trial balance or extended trial balance as the figures for trade receivables and trade payables respectively. This means that the individual accounts are not part of double-entry, but are **subsidiary accounts** (also known as memorandum accounts) which record how much each trade receivable owes, and how much is owed to each trade payable. From time-to-time, the balances of the subsidiary accounts are reconciled (agreed) with the balance of the appropriate control account.

The diagrams on the next two pages show how the sales ledger control account and the purchases ledger control account are incorporated into general ledger, with the individual trade receivables' and trade payables' accounts kept in the form of subsidiary accounts.

VALUE ADDED TAX (VAT) CONTROL ACCOUNT

VAT control account (also known as sales tax control account) brings together amounts of VAT (sales tax) from books of prime entry – the day books, the journal and cash book.

It is from VAT control account that the VAT Return is prepared, checked and then sent to HM Revenue & Customs – often quarterly, ie every three months. VAT Return shows:

- either, the money amount due to be paid by the business when VAT collected from sales is greater than the VAT paid on purchases
- or, the money amount due as a refund from HM Revenue & Customs to the business when VAT collected from sales is less than the VAT paid on purchases

The balance of VAT control account must reconcile with the amount shown on the business's VAT Return – any discrepancy should be investigated immediately and the error(s) traced.

- Sales ledger control account incorporated into the double-entry bookkeeping system
- Trade receivables' accounts in the sales ledger

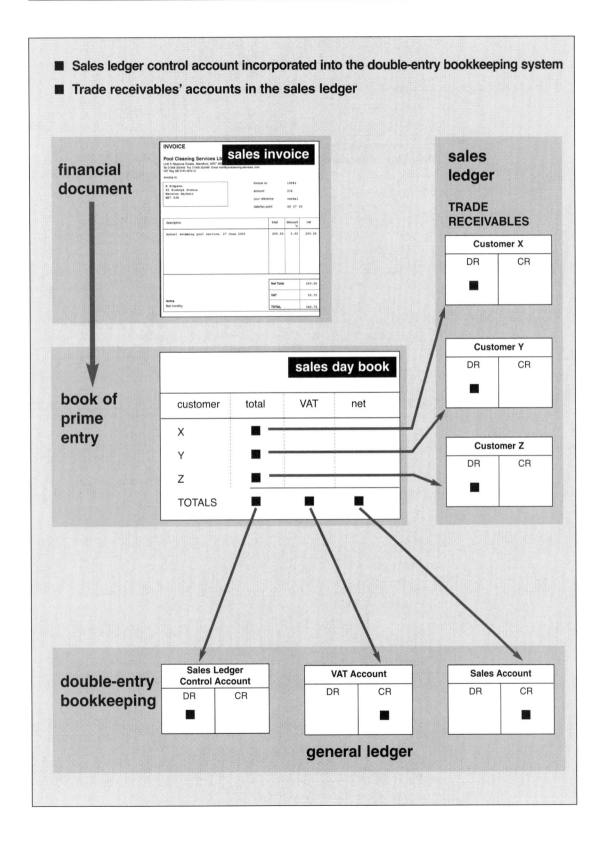

- Purchases ledger control account incorporated into the double-entry bookkeeping system
- Trade payables' accounts in the purchases ledger

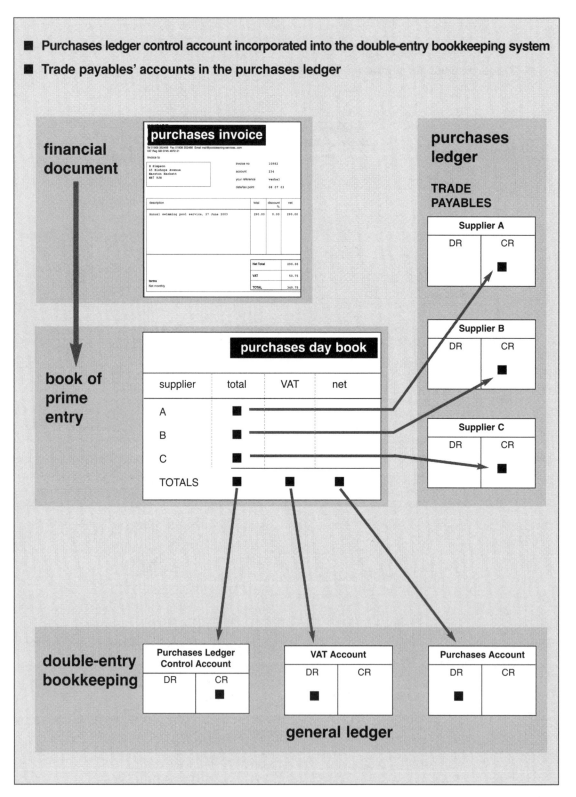

The layout of a VAT control account, with sample figures, is shown below. Study the set-out carefully and then read the text which follows.

Dr		VAT Control Account		Cr
	£			£
Purchases	30,000	Sales		40,000
Sales returns	1,500	Purchases returns		1,000
Cash purchases	4,000	Cash sales		5,000
Other cash expenses	700	Other cash income		300
Balance c/d	10,100			
	46,300			46,300
		Balance b/d		10,100

purchases

This is the VAT paid by the business on its credit purchases.

sales returns

This is the VAT allowed back to customers of the business on the sales returns they make.

cash purchases and other cash expenses

This is the VAT paid on the cash purchases of the business, including other expenses – both capital and revenue – paid for as cash/bank transactions.

sales

This is the VAT charged by the business on its credit sales.

purchases returns

This is the VAT allowed back to the business by its suppliers on purchases returns.

cash sales and other cash income

This is the VAT charged on the cash/bank sales of the business, including other income – both capital and revenue – received as cash transactions.

balance

The balance on VAT control account can be either debit or credit:

- a debit balance brought down indicates that the amount is due as a refund to the business from HM Revenue & Customs
- a credit balance brought down indicates that the amount is due to be paid by the business to HM Revenue & Customs (which is the situation for the majority of businesses)

The balance of the account will be settled with a bank payment either from or to HM Revenue & Customs.

VAT control account in the accounting system

VAT control account is a general ledger account which uses amounts from the books of prime entry – day books, the journal and cash book. The account is the source information for preparation of the VAT Return of the business, which is sent to HM Revenue & Customs. The balance of VAT control account must reconcile with the VAT Return.

PAYROLL (WAGES) CONTROL ACCOUNT

Payroll control account (also known as wages control account) brings together transactions from payroll accounts. The diagram below shows the relationship between the payroll control account and the other payroll accounts. Note that bank account is not shown here, although it is involved in making payroll payment.

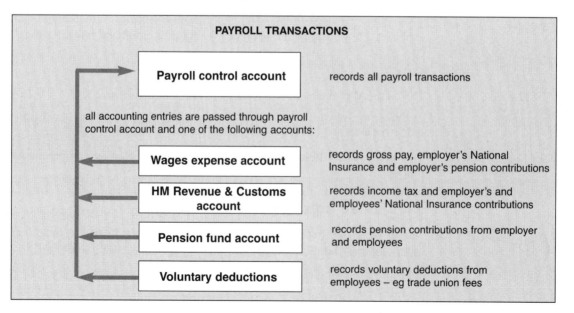

PAYROLL TRANSACTIONS

Payroll control account — records all payroll transactions

all accounting entries are passed through payroll control account and one of the following accounts:

Wages expense account — records gross pay, employer's National Insurance and employer's pension contributions

HM Revenue & Customs account — records income tax and employer's and employees' National Insurance contributions

Pension fund account — records pension contributions from employer and employees

Voluntary deductions — records voluntary deductions from employees – eg trade union fees

An example payroll control account is shown below.

Dr	Payroll Control Account		Cr
20-8		£	
30 Nov	Bank	3,820	
30 Nov	HM Revenue & Customs	1,900	
30 Nov	Pension fund	550	
30 Nov	Trade union fees	55	
		6,325	

			Cr
20-8			£
30 Nov	Wages expense		6,325
			6,325

As you will see from the above, payroll control account records all of the payroll transactions carried out each time the payroll is run. At the end of the process, once all bank payments have been made, the control account balance reverts to zero, ie a nil balance.

PREPARING RECONCILIATIONS

An important part of an accounting system is to carry out checks at regular intervals to ensure that balances are reconciled. If we can show that sections of the accounting system are reconciled we can be reasonably certain that no errors occur within that section – we will be looking in more detail at the correction of errors in the next chapter.

In this section we look at how to make adjustments to reconcile:

- sales ledger control account to sales ledger
- purchases ledger control account to purchases ledger
- cash book bank columns to the bank statement

Whenever a difference is found it needs to be corrected by means of a journal entry – we will look at these in detail in Chapter 11 – or referred to the appropriate person (eg accounts supervisor) for guidance.

sales ledger control account

Discrepancies between sales ledger control account and sales ledger (the accounts of trade receivables) include:

- **credit sales**
  - omitted or understated
  - entered twice or overstated

■ **sales returns**
  - omitted or understated
  - entered twice or overstated

■ **payments received from receivables**
  - omitted or understated
  - entered twice or overstated

■ **discounts allowed to trade receivables**
  - omitted or understated
  - entered twice or overstated

■ **irrecoverable debts**
  - omitted or understated
  - entered twice or overstated

■ **other differences**
  - set-off entries omitted or entered twice, or understated or overstated
  - debit amounts entered on the credit side
  - credit amounts entered on the debit side

The following shows examples of the adjustments that will be necessary to reconcile sales ledger control account to sales ledger.

Examples

The sales ledger has been compared with sales ledger control account and the following differences identified:

1. The total column of sales day book has been undercast (underadded) by £100.

2. £320 of discounts allowed to trade receivables and entered in their sales ledger accounts has not been entered in sales ledger control account.

3. A credit sale of £250 to J Williams has been debited to the account of J Wilson – both are sales ledger accounts.

4. The account of T Basili, £150, has been written off as irrecoverable in sales ledger, but has not been recorded in sales ledger control account.

The total of the account balances in sales ledger is £28,340 debit and the balance of sales ledger control account is £28,710 debit.

The following table shows the three adjustments that need to be made to sales ledger control account.

Adjustment number	Amount £	Debit	Credit
1.	100	✓	
2.	320		✓
4.	150		✓

Tutorial notes:

1. As the total column of sales day book has been undercast (underadded), this error will be carried through into sales ledger control account. It is necessary to increase the amount for sales by debiting sales ledger control account with £100.

2. Discounts allowed is credited to sales ledger control account – here it has been omitted, so the adjustment is a credit of £320.

3. Although there is an error – which needs to be corrected – it is an error within sales ledger, so there is no adjustment to make to sales ledger control account.

4. The irrecoverable debt of £150 must be recorded in sales ledger control account as a credit entry.

All of these adjustments will need to be corrected by means of a journal entry (see Chapter 11) which gives the bookkeeper the authority to record the transactions in the double-entry accounts.

Note that some errors may not be revealed by the reconciliation – adjustment 3 is an example of when sales ledger control account and sales ledger are agreed, but there is an error **within the sales ledger**, which needs to be corrected.

purchases ledger control account

Discrepancies between purchases ledger control account and purchases ledger (the accounts of trade payables) include:

- **credit purchases**
  - omitted or understated
  - entered twice or overstated
- **purchases returns**
  - omitted or understated
  - entered twice or overstated
- **payments made to payables**
  - omitted or understated
  - entered twice or overstated

■ **discounts received from trade payables**

 – omitted or understated

 – entered twice or overstated

■ **other differences**

 – set-off entries omitted or entered twice, or understated or overstated

 – debit amounts entered on the credit side

 – credit amounts entered on the debit side

The following shows examples of the adjustments that will be necessary to reconcile purchases ledger control account to purchases ledger.

Examples

The purchases ledger has been compared with purchases ledger control account and the following differences identified:

1. The total column of purchases day book has been overcast (overadded) by £100.

2. A payment of £200 made to J Smithson has been debited to the account of T Simpson – both are purchases ledger subsidiary accounts.

3. £450 of discounts received from trade payables has been entered on the wrong side of purchases ledger control account.

4. A set-off entry for £450 has been entered as £540 in purchases ledger control account.

The total of the account balances in purchases ledger is £44,235 credit and the balance of purchases ledger control account is £45,145 credit.

The table below shows the three adjustments that need to be made to purchases ledger control account.

Adjustment number	Amount £	Debit	Credit
1.	100	✓	
3.	900	✓	
4.	90		✓

Tutorial notes:

1. As the total column of purchases day book has been overcast (overadded) this error will be carried through into purchases ledger control account. It is necessary to decrease the amount for purchases by debiting purchases ledger control account with £100.

2. Although there is an error – which needs to be corrected – it is an error within purchases ledger, so there is no adjustment to make to purchases ledger control account.

3.   The amount of discounts received should be debited to purchases ledger control account –
     here it has been credited. To correct this error we need to double the amount of £450 to £900
     (if we correct only £450 all that we do is cancel out the error). £900 is debited to purchases
     ledger control account. In practice, rather than showing the difference, it is better to correct
     this error by taking out the wrong amount and recording the correct amount.

4.   Set-off entries are debited to purchases ledger control account. Here the amount recorded
     has been overstated, so we must credit purchases ledger control account with the difference
     being £540 – £450 = £90. Again, it would be better to correct by taking out the wrong amount
     and recording the correct amount.

All of these adjustments will need to be corrected by means of a journal entry (see Chapter 11)
which gives the bookkeeper the authority to record the transactions in the double-entry accounts.

Note that some errors may not be revealed by the reconciliation –
adjustment 2 is an example of where purchases ledger control account and
purchases ledger are agreed, but there is an error **within the purchases
ledger**, which needs to be corrected. Statements received from suppliers are
a further source of information which, when checked against purchases
ledger accounts, will help to reduce errors in the purchases ledger.

cash book bank columns

In a similar way to reconciling control accounts for sales and purchases
ledgers, the bank columns of the cash book can be checked against the bank
statement. Such a reconciliation demonstrates that we can be reasonably
certain that no errors occur within the bank columns of the cash book.
Indeed you may already be familiar, from your previous studies, with the
preparation of a bank reconciliation statement.

A bank statement – which is either posted to customers at regular intervals
or is available online – is the record of customer transactions from the
bank's viewpoint. As such we must remember that a debit balance or entry
in cash book (eg money paid into the bank) will be a credit entry on the bank
statement (from the bank's view it owes the money to the customer); in the
same way a credit balance or entry in cash book (eg a direct debit payment
made) will be a debit entry on the bank statement (the bank has paid money
out of the account on behalf of the customer).

Items appearing on bank statements include a number of different forms of
receipt or payment. These include:

- **cheque** – a written instruction to a bank by a customer to pay a specified
  amount of money to a payee
- **bank transfers, including BACS and Faster Payments** – Bankers
  Automated Clearing Services and Faster Payments are the banks'
  computer payment transfer systems

- **standing order** – regular BACS payments, set up by the customer for the bank to make, usually for fixed amounts
- **direct debit** – regular BACS payments, set up by the organisation receiving the payments and agreed by the customer, for amounts which can be fixed or variable to be paid from the bank account

Discrepancies between the bank columns of the cash book and the bank statement include:

- **unpresented cheques** – cheques issued, not yet recorded on the bank statement
- **outstanding lodgements** – amounts paid into the bank, not yet recorded on the bank statement

These two are called timing differences – because they will correct themselves over time – as they have been recorded in the cash book but are not yet on the bank statement.

Other discrepancies which will need adjustment in the cash book include:

- **bank transfers, including BACS and Faster Payment credits**, such as payments from trade receivables
- **standing order payments**, if not already written up in the cash book
- **direct debit payments**, if not already written up in the cash book
- **unpaid cheques**, that is cheques received by the business and paid in to the bank which have 'bounced'
- **bank charges and interest**, that is service charges to operate the bank account and interest charged on borrowings

If an error is discovered that has been made by the bank, it should be queried immediately and the item and amount should not be entered into the cash book until it has been resolved.

The following shows examples of the adjustments that will be necessary to reconcile the bank columns of the cash book to the bank statement.

Examples

The bank statement has been compared with the bank columns of the cash book and the following differences identified:

1. Bank charges and interest paid of £170 have not been entered in the cash book.

2. A bank lodgement for £1,200 made yesterday is not showing on the bank statement.

3. A payment from a customer by BACS for £450 has not been entered in the cash book.

4. A standing order payment made by the bank for £280 has been incorrectly entered in the cash book as £820.

The balance showing on the bank statement is a credit of £1,900 and the balance in the cash book is a debit of £2,280.

The following table shows the three adjustments that need to be made to the cash book.

Adjustment number	Amount £	Debit	Credit
1.	170		✓
3.	450	✓	
4.	540	✓	

Tutorial notes:

1. As this transaction has not yet been recorded in the business's double-entry accounts, it needs to be shown on the credit side of cash book, and debited to bank charges and interest account in general ledger.

2. This is a timing difference – the cash book is correct and the bank statement will record the lodgement in the next day or so.

3. This transaction needs to be recorded in the business's double-entry accounts as follows:
   - debit cash book
   - credit sales ledger control account

   The amount will also be recorded in the customer's account in sales ledger.

4. Cash book is showing a payment for £540 (£820 – £280) too much. Therefore to correct this a debit is shown in cash book – the other double-entry account needs to be checked to see what amount has been recorded. In practice, rather than showing the difference, it is better to correct this error by taking out the wrong amount and recording the correct amount.

   Adjustment 4 will need to be corrected by means of a journal entry. Adjustments 1 and 3 need to be recorded in the double-entry accounts – many businesses use a bank statement as a 'reminder' about standing orders, direct debits and BACS/Faster Payments receipts that need to be entered into the accounts. No action is needed for adjustment 2, which is a timing difference.

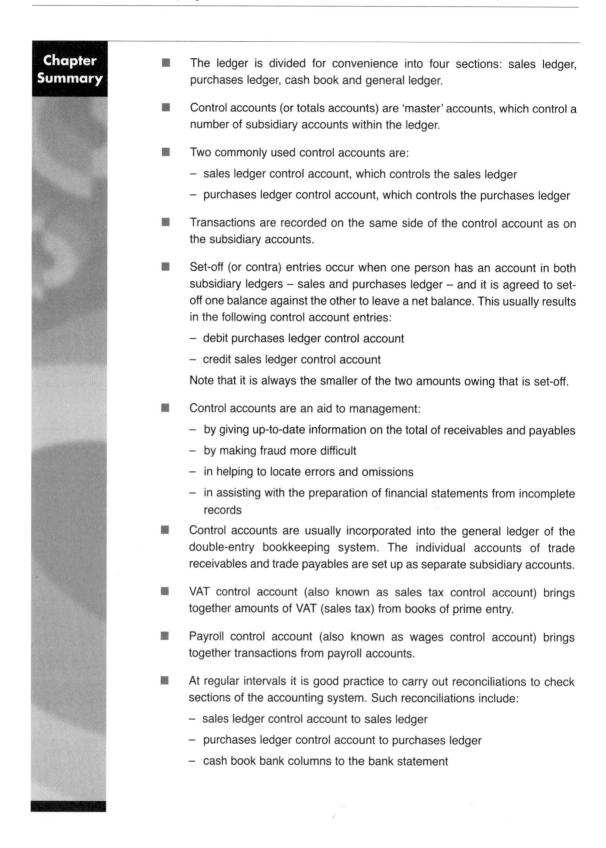

Chapter Summary

■ The ledger is divided for convenience into four sections: sales ledger, purchases ledger, cash book and general ledger.

■ Control accounts (or totals accounts) are 'master' accounts, which control a number of subsidiary accounts within the ledger.

■ Two commonly used control accounts are:

– sales ledger control account, which controls the sales ledger

– purchases ledger control account, which controls the purchases ledger

■ Transactions are recorded on the same side of the control account as on the subsidiary accounts.

■ Set-off (or contra) entries occur when one person has an account in both subsidiary ledgers – sales and purchases ledger – and it is agreed to set-off one balance against the other to leave a net balance. This usually results in the following control account entries:

– debit purchases ledger control account

– credit sales ledger control account

Note that it is always the smaller of the two amounts owing that is set-off.

■ Control accounts are an aid to management:

– by giving up-to-date information on the total of receivables and payables

– by making fraud more difficult

– in helping to locate errors and omissions

– in assisting with the preparation of financial statements from incomplete records

■ Control accounts are usually incorporated into the general ledger of the double-entry bookkeeping system. The individual accounts of trade receivables and trade payables are set up as separate subsidiary accounts.

■ VAT control account (also known as sales tax control account) brings together amounts of VAT (sales tax) from books of prime entry.

■ Payroll control account (also known as wages control account) brings together transactions from payroll accounts.

■ At regular intervals it is good practice to carry out reconciliations to check sections of the accounting system. Such reconciliations include:

– sales ledger control account to sales ledger

– purchases ledger control account to purchases ledger

– cash book bank columns to the bank statement

Key Terms

control account	a 'master' account which controls a number of subsidiary accounts
sales ledger control account	a 'master' account which controls the sales ledger
purchases ledger control account	a 'master' account which controls the purchases ledger
set-off entries	where balances in sales ledger and purchases ledger are to be set-off against one another
subsidiary account	an account which is not part of the double-entry system
VAT control account/ sales tax control account	account which brings together amounts of VAT (sales tax) from books of prime entry
payroll control account/ wages control account	account which brings together transactions from payroll accounts

Activities

10.1 Which **one** of the following is the reason why a sales ledger control account is used?

(a)	To show how much each individual customer owes	
(b)	To show the total sales of the business	
(c)	To enable the manager to know the total of trade receivables	
(d)	To enable the production of individual customer statements	

10.2 Which **one** of the following is the reason why subsidiary purchases ledgers are used?

(a)	To enable the manager to know the total of trade payables	
(b)	To show how much each individual supplier is owed	
(c)	To show potential irrecoverable debts	
(d)	To show the total purchases of the business	

10.3 You have the following information:

• opening payables balances at start of month	£18,600
• cash/cheques paid to trade payables during month	£9,400
• credit purchases for month	£9,100
• purchases returns for month	£800

What is the figure for closing payables balances at the end of the month?

(a)	£18,100	
(b)	£19,100	
(c)	£36,300	
(d)	£17,500	

10.4 Which **one** of the following does not appear in sales ledger control account?

(a)	Irrecoverable debts	
(b)	Discounts received	
(c)	Sales returns	
(d)	Cash/cheques received from trade receivables	

10.5 Prepare a sales ledger control account for the month of June 20-8 from the following information:

20-8		£
1 Jun	Sales ledger balances	17,491
30 Jun	Credit sales for month	42,591
	Sales returns	1,045
	Payments received from trade receivables	39,024
	Discounts allowed	593
	Irrecoverable debts	296

The trade receivables figure at 30 June is to be entered as the balancing figure.

10.6 Prepare a purchases ledger control account for the month of April 20-9 from the following information:

20-9		£
1 Apr	Purchases ledger balances	14,275
30 Apr	Credit purchases for month	36,592
	Purchases returns	653
	Payments made to trade payables	31,074
	Discounts received	1,048
	Set-off of credit balances to sales ledger	597

The trade payables figure at 30 April is to be entered as the balancing figure.

10.7 The sales ledger of Rowcester Traders contains the following accounts on 1 February 20-4:

> Arrow Valley Retailers, balance £826.40 debit
>
> B Brick (Builders) Limited, balance £59.28 debit
>
> Mereford Manufacturing Company, balance £293.49 debit
>
> Redgrove Restorations, balance £724.86 debit
>
> Wyvern Warehouse Limited, balance £108.40 debit

The following transactions took place during February:

3 Feb	Sold goods on credit to Arrow Valley Retailers £338.59, and to Mereford Manufacturing Company £127.48
7 Feb	Redgrove Restorations returned goods £165.38
15 Feb	Received a bank payment from Wyvern Warehouse Limited for the balance of the account after deduction of 2.5% prompt payment discount
17 Feb	Sold goods on credit to Redgrove Restorations £394.78, and to Wyvern Warehouse Limited £427.91
20 Feb	Arrow Valley Retailers settled an invoice for £826.40 by bank payment after deducting 2.5% prompt payment discount
24 Feb	Mereford Manufacturing Company returned goods £56.29
29 Feb	Set-off the balance of Mereford Manufacturing Company's account to the company's account in the purchases ledger
29 Feb	Wrote off the account of B Brick (Builders) Limited as an irrecoverable debt

You are to:

(a) Write up the accounts in the sales ledger of Rowcester Traders for February 20-4, balancing them at the end of the month

(b) Prepare a sales ledger control account for February 20-4, balancing it at the end of the month

(c) Reconcile the control account balance with the subsidiary accounts at 1 February and 29 February 20-4.

Note: VAT is to be ignored on all transactions and day books are not required.

10.8 Which **one** of the following is the reason why a VAT control account is used?

(a)	To bring together amounts of VAT from books of prime entry	
(b)	To calculate the amount of VAT on sales invoices	
(c)	To remind the business when it is time to submit VAT Returns	
(d)	To ensure that the VAT calculated on purchases invoices allows for prompt payment discount	

10.9 This Activity is about preparing reconciliations.

The sales ledger has been compared with sales ledger control account and the following differences identified:

1. The total column of sales returns day book has been undercast (underadded) by £200.

2. A set-off entry for £150 has been omitted from sales ledger control account.

3. The account of D Clarke, £125, has been written off as irrecoverable in sales ledger, but has not been recorded in sales ledger control account.

4. £20 of discounts allowed has been credited to the sales ledger account of K Fairbank instead of the sales ledger account of S Fairweather.

The total of the account balances in sales ledger is £32,705 debit and the balance of sales ledger control account is £33,180 debit.

Use the following table to show the three adjustments you need to make to sales ledger control account.

Adjustment number	Amount £	Debit	Credit

10.10 This Activity is about preparing reconciliations.

The purchases ledger has been compared with purchases ledger control account and the following differences identified:

1. The total of discounts received from trade payables of £240 has been recorded in purchases ledger control account as £420.

2. A payment of £195 has been debited to the purchases ledger account of M Touoson instead of the purchases ledger account of B Toulson.

3. The total column of purchases returns day book has been undercast (underadded) by £400.

4. A set-off entry for £220 has been entered on the wrong side of purchases ledger control account.

The total of the account balances in purchases ledger is £29,640 credit and the balance of purchases ledger control account is £30,300 credit.

Use the table on the next page to show the three adjustments you need to make to purchases ledger control account.

Adjustment number	Amount £	Debit	Credit

10.11 This Activity is about preparing reconciliations.

The bank statement has been compared with the bank columns of the cash book and the following differences identified:

1.   Cheques totalling £2,540 paid into the bank yesterday are not showing on the bank statement.

2.   A direct debit payment made by the bank for £550 has not been entered in the cash book.

3.   A payment cheque to a supplier for £680 has been incorrectly entered in the cash book as £860.

4.   Bank charges and interest of £210 have not been entered in the cash book.

The balance showing on the bank statement is a credit of £1,090 and the balance in the cash book is a debit of £4,210.

Use the following table to show the three adjustments you need to make to the cash book.

Adjustment number	Amount £	Debit	Credit

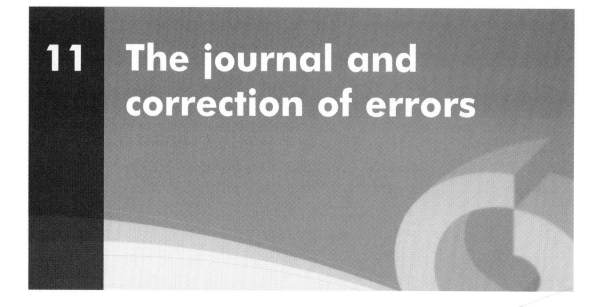

11 The journal and correction of errors

this chapter covers...

The journal is the book of prime entry for non-regular transactions, eg purchase and disposal of non-current assets, correction of errors, end-of-year transfers (such as depreciation and allowance for doubtful debts), and other adjustments.

As a book of prime entry, the journal is not part of double-entry bookkeeping; instead the journal is used to list transactions before they are entered into the accounts. In this way, journal entries record amounts in a book of prime entry and give the bookkeeper the authority to record the transactions in the double-entry accounts.

USES OF THE JOURNAL

The journal provides the book of prime entry for non-regular transactions, which are not recorded in any other book of prime entry. Such non-regular transactions include:

- year-end transfers and adjustments, including accruals and prepayments, depreciation, irrecoverable debts, allowance for doubtful debts, closing inventory

- purchase and sale of non-current assets on credit, and gain/loss on disposal

- correction of errors found in the double-entry system

The reasons for using a journal are:

- to provide a book of prime entry for non-regular transactions

- to eliminate the need for remembering why non-regular transactions were put through the accounts – the journal acts as a notebook

- to give the bookkeeper the authority to record transactions in the double-entry accounts

- to reduce the risk of fraud, by making it difficult for unauthorised transactions to be entered in the double-entry system

- to reduce the risk of errors, by listing the transactions that are to be put into the double-entry accounts

- to ensure that entries can be traced back to an authorised financial document (note that documentation is stored securely for possible future reference)

It should be noted that journal entries – especially those for year-end transfers and adjustments – can have a significant effect on the profits of a business. This aspect, together with pressures put on the accounting staff, are discussed further on pages 226-228.

THE JOURNAL – A BOOK OF PRIME ENTRY

The journal is a book of prime (or original) entry; it is not, therefore, part of the double-entry bookkeeping system. The journal is used to list the transactions that are then to be put through the accounts. The accounting system for non-regular transactions is as follows:

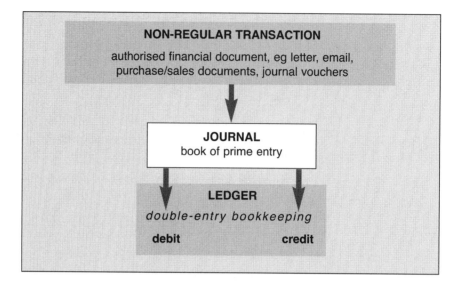

The journal is set out in the following way, with a sample transaction.

Date	Details	Reference	Dr	Cr
20-4			£	£
1 Jul	Vehicle at cost	GL	5,000	
	Bank	CB		5,000

Notes:

- journal entries are prepared from authorised financial documents (which are stored securely for possible future reference)

- the names of the accounts to be debited and credited in the double-entry system are written in the details column; it is customary to show the debit transaction first

- the money amount of each debit and credit is stated in the appropriate columns

- the reference column shows where each account is found, eg GL = general ledger, CB = cash book, SL = sales ledger, PL = purchases ledger; the reference may include an account number

- a journal entry always balances, ie debit and credit entries are for the same amount or total

- it is usual to include a brief narrative (ie a few words) explaining why the transaction is being carried out, and making reference to the financial document whenever possible (you should always include a narrative unless told otherwise)

- each journal entry is complete in itself and is ruled off to separate it from the next entry

Note that any journal entries involving sales ledger control account and purchases ledger control account must also be recorded in the subsidiary accounts in sales ledger and purchases ledger.

YEAR-END TRANSFERS

Many non-regular transactions take place at the end of a business's financial year and need to be recorded in the journal. In this section, we will look at journal entries to account for:

- transfers to the statement of profit or loss
- closing inventory
- accruals and prepayments of expenses and income
- depreciation charges on non-current assets
- irrecoverable debts
- allowance for doubtful debts

As we have seen earlier (Chapter 4), the statement of profit or loss forms part of the double-entry system. Therefore, each amount recorded in the statement of profit or loss must have an opposite entry in another account: such transfers are recorded in the journal as the book of prime entry, as shown by the entries which follow.

transfers to the statement of profit or loss

The three journal entries which follow are examples of year-end transfers which close off income and expense accounts by transfer to the statement of profit or loss. With these examples, the full balance of the account is transferred – we will see how to deal with accruals and prepayments on page 209.

31 Dec 20-4   *Balance of sales account at the year-end, £155,000, transferred to the statement of profit or loss (debit sales account; credit statement of profit or loss)*

Date	Details	Reference	Dr	Cr
20-4			£	£
31 Dec	Sales	GL	155,000	
	*Statement of profit or loss	GL		155,000
	Transfer to the statement of profit or loss of sales for the year			

*Note that, alternatively, this detail may be written as 'Profit or loss account'.

31 Dec 20-4   *The balance of the purchases account at the year-end, £105,000, is transferred to the statement of profit or loss (debit statement of profit or loss; credit purchases account)*

Date	Details	Reference	Dr	Cr
20-4			£	£
31 Dec	Statement of profit or loss	GL	105,000	
	Purchases	GL		105,000
	Transfer to the statement of profit or loss of purchases for the year			

31 Dec 20-4   *Balance of the wages account, £23,500, is transferred to the statement of profit or loss (debit statement of profit or loss; credit wages account)*

Date	Details	Reference	Dr	Cr
20-4			£	£
31 Dec	Statement of profit or loss	GL	23,500	
	Wages	GL		23,500
	Transfer to the statement of profit or loss of expenditure for the year			

closing inventory

31 Dec 20-4   *Closing inventory has been valued at £10,500 and is to be recorded on the statement of profit or loss (debit closing inventory – statement of financial position; credit closing inventory – statement of profit or loss)*

Date	Details	Reference	Dr	Cr
20-4			£	£
31 Dec	Closing inventory – statement of financial position	GL	10,500	
	Closing inventory – statement of profit or loss	GL		10,500
	Closing inventory valuation at 31 December 20-4 recorded on the statement of profit or loss			

The closing inventory is recorded on the statement of financial position as an asset, and will be the opening inventory for next year's statement of profit or loss.

accruals and prepayments

The amounts of accruals and prepayments of expenses and income (see Chapter 5) are recorded in the accounts: such transfers are recorded in the journal as the book of prime entry.

accrual of expense

31 Dec 20-4   *The balance of the telephone account at the year-end is £500 debit. A telephone bill for £100 is received on 4 January 20-5 and relates to costs incurred in 20-4.*

Date	Details	Reference	Dr	Cr
20-4			£	£
31 Dec	Statement of profit or loss	GL	600	
	Telephone	GL		600
	Telephone	GL	100	
	Accrued expenses	GL		100
	Transfer to the statement of profit or loss of expenditure for the year and transfer of accrual to accrued expenses account			

After the journal entry, the telephone account is balanced at the year-end as follows:

Dr			**Telephone account**		Cr
20-4		£	20-4		£
31 Dec	Balance b/d	500	31 Dec	Statement of profit or loss	600
31 Dec	Accrued expenses	100			
		600			600

The journal entry and account:

- ▓ show the transfer to the statement of profit or loss of expenditure for the year
- ▓ show the transfer of £100 to accrued expenses account (shown as a liability on the statement of financial position)

Note that, at the beginning of the new financial year, the accrual is reversed (debit accrued expenses, credit telephone). Then, when the bill is paid (debit telephone, credit bank), the balance of telephone account will fall to zero (see page 68).

prepayment of expense

31 Dec 20-4   The balance of the rent paid account at the year-end is £750 debit. Of this, £675 relates to 20-4, while £75 is a prepayment for 20-5.

Date	Details	Reference	Dr	Cr
20-4			£	£
31 Dec	Statement of profit or loss	GL	675	
	Rent paid	GL		675
	Prepaid expenses	GL	75	
	Rent paid	GL		75
	Transfer to the statement of profit or loss of expenditure for the year and transfer of prepayment to prepaid expenses account			

After the journal entry, the rent paid account is balanced at the year-end as follows:

Dr			Rent paid account		Cr
20-4		£	20-4		£
31 Dec	Balance b/d	750	31 Dec	Statement of profit or loss	675
			31 Dec	Prepaid expenses	75
		750			750

The journal entry and account:

- show the transfer to the statement of profit or loss of expenditure for the year

- show the transfer of £75 to prepaid expenses account (shown as an asset on the statement of financial position)

Note that, at the beginning of the new financial year, the prepayment is reversed (debit rent paid, credit prepaid expenses). Then the amount of rent prepaid will form part of total rent for 20-5 and will be included in that year's transfer to the statement of profit or loss (see page 70).

accrual of income

31 Dec 20-4   *The balance of the commission received account at the year-end is £1,250 credit. A further £250 was received on 10 January 20-5 and relates to work done in 20-4.*

Date	Details	Reference	Dr	Cr
20-4			£	£
31 Dec	Commission received	GL	1,500	
	Statement of profit or loss	GL		1,500
	Accrued income	GL	250	
	Commission received	GL		250
	Transfer to the statement of profit or loss of income for the year, and transfer of accrual to accrued income account			

After the journal entry, the commission received account is balanced at the year-end as follows:

Dr			Commission received account			Cr
20-4		£	20-4			£
31 Dec	Statement of profit or loss	1,500	31 Dec	Balance b/d		1,250
			31 Dec	Accrued income		250
		1,500				1,500

The journal entry and account:

- show the transfer to the statement of profit or loss of income for the year

- show the transfer of £250 to accrued income account (shown as an asset on the statement of financial position)

Note that, at the beginning of the new financial year, the accrual is reversed (debit commission received, credit accrued income). Then, after the entry to record the commission received on 10 January 20-5 is made (debit bank; credit commission received), the balance of commission received account falls to zero.

prepayment of income

31 Dec 20-4   The balance of the rent received account at the year-end is £2,850 credit. Of this, £2,450 relates to 20-4, while £400 is a prepayment of income for 20-5.

Date	Details	Reference	Dr	Cr
20-4			£	£
31 Dec	Rent received	GL	2,450	
	Statement of profit or loss	GL		2,450
	Rent received	GL	400	
	Prepaid income	GL		400
	Transfer to the statement of profit or loss of income for the year, and transfer of prepayment to prepaid income account			

After the journal entry, the rent received account is balanced at the year-end as follows:

Dr			Rent received account		Cr
20-4		£	20-4		£
31 Dec	Statement of profit or loss	2,450	31 Dec	Balance b/d	2,850
31 Dec	Prepaid income	400			
		2,850			2,850

The journal entry and account:

■ show the transfer to the statement of profit or loss of income for the year

■ show the transfer of £400 to prepaid income account (shown as a liability on the statement of financial position, ie at that date the business owes the use of the property to the tenant in the sum of £400)

Note that, at the beginning of the new financial year, the prepayment is reversed (debit prepaid income, credit rent received). Then the prepayment of rent will form part of total rent received for 20-5 and will be included in that year's transfer to the statement of profit or loss.

depreciation charges on non-current assets

As already seen in Chapter 6, the amount of depreciation on non-current assets is debited to depreciation charges account (the annual charge for depreciation) and is then credited to the accumulated depreciation account (which records the total of depreciation for each class of asset):

– **debit** depreciation charges account

– **credit** accumulated depreciation account

31 Dec 20-4   The depreciation charge on machinery is calculated at £400 for the year.

The journal entry for the depreciation is:

Date	Details	Reference	Dr	Cr
20-4			£	£
31 Dec	Depreciation charges	GL	400	
	Machinery: accumulated depreciation	GL		400
	Depreciation charges			
	for year on machinery			

As we have seen in Chapter 6, the amount of depreciation charges is recorded in the statement of profit or loss:

– **debit** statement of profit or loss

– **credit** depreciation charges account

The journal entry for the transfer to the statement of profit or loss is:

Date	Details	Reference	Dr	Cr
20-4			£	£
31 Dec	Statement of profit or loss	GL	400	
	Depreciation charges	GL		400
	Transfer to the statement of profit			
	or loss of depreciation charges for			
	year on machinery			

irrecoverable debts

We have already seen, in Chapter 7, the double-entry transaction to write off a trade receivable's account as irrecoverable:

– **debit** irrecoverable debts account

– **credit** sales ledger control account

15 Dec 20-4 *Write off the sales ledger account of T Hughes, which has a balance of £25, as irrecoverable (ignore VAT).*

The journal entry is:

Date	Details	Reference	Dr	Cr
20-4			£	£
15 Dec	Irrecoverable debts	GL	25	
	Sales ledger control	GL		25
	Account of T Hughes written off			
	as irrecoverable:			
	in the sales ledger			
	– credit T Hughes £25			

At the end of the financial year, the balance of irrecoverable debts account is transferred to the statement of profit or loss as follows:

– **debit** statement of profit or loss

– **credit** irrecoverable debts account

The journal entry for the transfer to the statement of profit or loss is:

Date	Details	Reference	Dr	Cr
20-4			£	£
31 Dec	Statement of profit or loss	GL	25	
	Irrecoverable debts	GL		25
	Transfer to the statement of profit			
	or loss of irrecoverable debts for year			

allowance for doubtful debts

As already seen in Chapter 7, the creation of an allowance for doubtful debts is credited to allowance for doubtful debts: adjustment account (the annual change in the allowance) and is then transferred to allowance for doubtful debts account (which records the accumulated allowance):

– **debit** allowance for doubtful debts: adjustment account

– **credit** allowance for doubtful debts account

31 Dec 20-4 *An allowance for doubtful debts of £500 is to be created.*

The journal entry for the transfer to allowance for doubtful debts is:

Date	Details	Reference	Dr	Cr
20-4			£	£
31 Dec	Allowance for doubtful debts:			
	adjustment	GL	500	
	Allowance for doubtful debts	GL		500
	Transfer of amount for year to			
	allowance for doubtful debts account			

The creation of an allowance for doubtful debts is then recorded in the statement of profit or loss:

– **debit** statement of profit or loss

– **credit** allowance for doubtful debts: adjustment account

The journal entry for the transfer to the statement of profit or loss is:

Date	Details	Reference	Dr	Cr
20-4			£	£
31 Dec	Statement of profit or loss	GL	500	
	Allowance for doubtful debts:			
	adjustment	GL		500
	Transfer to the statement of profit			
	or loss of allowance for doubtful			
	debts adjustment			

An existing allowance for doubtful debts will usually be increased or decreased as the level of trade receivables changes. The bookkeeping entries (see Chapter 7) are:

increasing the allowance

– **debit** statement of profit or loss

– **credit** allowance for doubtful debts: adjustment account

decreasing the allowance

– **debit** allowance for doubtful debts: adjustment account

– **credit** statement of profit or loss

31 Dec 20-5   *The existing allowance for doubtful debts is to be increased by £250.*

The journal entry for the transfer to allowance for doubtful debts account is:

Date	Details	Reference	Dr	Cr
20-5			£	£
31 Dec	Allowance for doubtful debts:			
	adjustment	GL	250	
	Allowance for doubtful debts	GL		250
	Increase for year in			
	allowance for doubtful debts account			

The journal entry for the transfer to the statement of profit or loss is:

Date	Details	Reference	Dr	Cr
20-5			£	£
31 Dec	Statement of profit or loss	GL	250	
	Allowance for doubtful debts:			
	adjustment	GL		250
	Transfer to the statement of profit or			
	loss of increase in allowance for			
	doubtful debts adjustment			

Note that a decrease in the allowance will have the opposite journal entries to these.

PURCHASE AND SALE OF NON-CURRENT ASSETS ON CREDIT

The purchase and sale of non-current assets are non-regular business transactions which are recorded in the journal as the book of prime entry. Only *credit* transactions are entered in the journal (because cash/bank transactions are recorded in the cash book as the book of prime entry). However, a business (or an Activity or an Assessment) may choose to journalise cash book entries: strictly, though, this is incorrect as two books of prime entry are being used.

purchase of non-current asset

15 Apr 20-4   Bought a machine for £1,000 plus VAT (at 20%) on credit from Machinery Supplies Limited, purchase order no 2341.

Date	Details	Reference	Dr	Cr
20-4			£	£
15 Apr	Machinery at cost	GL	1,000	
	VAT	GL	200	
	Purchases ledger control*	GL		1,200
			1,200	1,200
	Purchase of machine on credit			
	from Machinery Supplies Limited:			
	purchase order 2341			

*Instead of entering this transaction in the purchases ledger, an alternative treatment would be to open a general ledger account for Machinery Supplies Limited. This would avoid confusion with trade payables – in the purchases ledger.

Note that, if the business had not been registered for VAT, the full cost of the non-current asset, ie, £1,200, would be recorded in the machinery at cost account and in purchases ledger control account.

sale of non-current asset

20 May 20-4   *A car is sold for £2,500 on credit to Wyvern Motors Limited (no VAT chargeable).*

Date	Details	Reference	Dr	Cr
20-4			£	£
20 May	Sales ledger control**	GL	2,500	
	Disposals	GL		2,500
	Sale of car, registration no QV11 HAB			
	to Wyvern Motors Limited			

**As with the purchase transaction, in order to avoid confusion with trade receivables, a general ledger account could be opened for Wyvern Motors Limited for this sale transaction.

disposal of non-current assets

When a non-current asset is sold or disposed, the double-entry transactions (see pages 97-101) bring together:

■ the original cost of the asset

■ accumulated depreciation over the life of the asset

■ disposal proceeds

31 Dec 20-6   *A machine had been bought on 1 January 20-4 (ie three years ago) for £2,000 (net of VAT). Accumulated depreciation (including the current year) totals £1,200. On 31 December 20-6 the machine is sold for £600 (net of VAT) received into the bank.*

The journal entry is:

Date	Details	Reference	Dr	Cr
20-6			£	£
31 Dec	Disposals	GL	2,000	
	Machinery at cost	GL		2,000
	Machinery: accumulated depreciation	GL	1,200	
	Disposals	GL		1,200
	Bank	CB	720	
	Disposals	GL		600
	VAT	GL		120
	Statement of profit or loss	GL	200	
	Disposals	GL		200
			4,120	4,120
	Sale of machine no. xxxx; loss on disposal £200 debited to the statement of profit or loss account			

(If you wish to check the double-entry transactions for this disposal, they are set out in full on pages 98-100.)

As noted earlier, if the business had not been registered for VAT then the original purchase cost of the machinery and the disposal price would include VAT.

CORRECTION OF ERRORS

In any accounting system there is always the possibility of an error. Ways to avoid errors, or ways to reveal them sooner, include:

- division of the accounting function between a number of people, so that no one person is responsible for all aspects of a business transaction
- regular circulation of statements to customers, who will check the transactions on their accounts and advise any discrepancies
- checking of statements received from suppliers
- preparation of a trial balance at regular intervals
- the use of control accounts
- the regular reconciliation of sales ledger, purchases ledger and bank
- checking cash against cash held
- the use of a computer accounting program

Despite all of these, errors will still occur from time-to-time and, in this section, we will look at:

- correction of errors not revealed by a trial balance
- correction of errors revealed by a trial balance, using a suspense account

errors not revealed by a trial balance

In Chapter 3 we have already seen that some types of errors in a bookkeeping system are not revealed by a trial balance. The main errors are:

- error of principle
- error of commission
- error of original entry
- error of omission
- reversal of entries

Although these errors are not revealed by a trial balance, they are likely to come to light if the procedures suggested above are followed. For example, a customer will soon let you know if her account has been debited with goods she did not buy. When an error is found, it needs to be corrected by means of a journal entry which shows the double-entry transactions that have been made.

We will now look at an example of each of the errors not revealed by a trial balance, and will see how it is corrected by means of a journal entry. (A practical hint which may help in correcting errors is to write out the 'T' accounts as they appear with the error. Then write in the correcting entries and see if the result has achieved what was intended.)

ERROR OF PRINCIPLE

The cost of diesel fuel, £50 (excluding VAT) on receipt no 1234, has been debited to vehicles account; the error is corrected on 20 May 20-4.

Date	Details	Reference	Dr	Cr
20-4			£	£
20 May	Vehicle expenses	GL	50	
	Vehicles at cost	GL		50
	Correction of error: receipt 1234			

With this type of error it is the wrong class of account being used. In this example, the vehicle expenses must be kept separate from the cost of the asset (the vehicle), otherwise the expense and asset accounts will be incorrect, leading to profit for the year being overstated and the non-current asset being shown in the statement of financial position at too high a figure.

ERROR OF COMMISSION

Credit sales of £60, including VAT (at 20%), on invoice no 321, have been debited to the account of J Adams, instead of the account of J Adams Limited; the error is corrected on 15 May 20-4.

Date	Details	Reference	Dr	Cr
20-4			£	£
15 May	Sales ledger control	GL	60	
	Sales ledger control	GL		60
	Correction of mispost in the sales ledger:			
	– debit J Adams Limited £60			
	– credit J Adams £60			

This type of error can be avoided, to some extent, by the use of account numbers, and by persuading the customer to quote the account number or reference on each transaction.

An error of commission can also occur between other accounts, such as expenses or non-current assets. For example, if an expense for advertising has been debited in error to administrative expenses account, this will need to be corrected through a journal entry and the two accounts involved.

ERROR OF ORIGINAL ENTRY

Postages of £45 paid from the bank have been entered in the accounts as £54; the error is corrected on 27 May 20-4.

Date	Details	Reference	Dr	Cr
20-4			£	£
27 May	Bank	CB	54	
	Postages	GL		54
	Postages	GL	45	
	Bank	CB		45
			99	99
	Correction of error: postages of £45 entered into the accounts as £54			

This error could have been corrected by debiting bank and crediting postages with £9, being the difference between the two amounts. However, there was no original transaction for this amount, and it is better to reverse the wrong transaction and put through the correct one. Where figures are reversed there is always a difference of nine (as above), or an amount divisible by nine. An error of original entry can also be a 'bad' figure written on a financial document, eg an invoice, which is entered wrongly into both accounts.

ERROR OF OMISSION

A credit sale of goods, £200 plus VAT (at 20%) on invoice 4967 to H Jarvis, has been completely omitted from the accounting system; the error is corrected on 12 May 20-4.

Date	Details	Reference	Dr	Cr
20-4			£	£
12 May	Sales ledger control	GL	240	
	Sales	GL		200
	VAT	GL		40
			240	240
	Invoice 4967 omitted from accounts:			
	in the sales ledger –			
	debit H Jarvis £240			

This type of error can happen in a very small business – often where the double-entry accounts are kept by one person. For example, a completed sales invoice is 'lost' down the back of a filing cabinet. In a large business, particularly one using a computer accounting system, it should be impossible for this error to occur. Also, if documents are numbered serially, then none should be mislaid.

REVERSAL OF ENTRIES

A payment from the bank of £50 to a supplier, S Wright, on 5 May 20-4, has been debited in the cash book and credited to purchases ledger control and Wright's account in purchases ledger; the error is corrected on 14 May 20-4.

Date	Details	Reference	Dr	Cr
20-4			£	£
14 May	Purchases ledger control	GL	50	
	Bank	CB		50
	Purchases ledger control	GL	50	
	Bank	CB		50
			100	100
	Correction of reversal of entries:			
	in the purchases ledger			
	– debit S Wright £50			
	– debit S Wright £50			

To correct this type of error it is best to reverse the entries that have been made incorrectly (the first two journal entries), and then to put through the correct entries. This is preferable to debiting £100 to purchases ledger control account and crediting £100 to bank account: there was never a transaction for this amount – the original transaction was for £50.

As noted earlier, it is often an idea to write out the 'T' accounts, complete with the error, and then to write in the correcting entries. As an example, the two accounts involved in this last error are shown with the error made on 5 May, and the corrections made on 14 May indicated by the shading:

Dr			Purchases Ledger Control Account				Cr
20-4			£	20-4			£
14 May	Bank		50	5 May	Bank		50
14 May	Bank		50				

Dr			Bank Account				Cr
20-4			£	20-4			£
5 May	Purchases ledger control		50	14 May	Purchases ledger control		50
				14 May	Purchases ledger control		50

The accounts now show a net debit transaction of £50 on purchases ledger control account, and a net credit transaction of £50 on bank account.

ERRORS SHOWN BY THE TRIAL BALANCE: JOURNAL ENTRIES

There are several types of errors revealed by a trial balance; these include:

■ one-sided entry (ie only one of the two parts of a double-entry transaction has been recorded)

■ entry duplicated on one side, nothing on the other (ie two debits or two credits have been recorded for a transaction)

■ unequal entries (ie different amounts have been recorded for the debit and credit entries)

■ account balance incorrectly transferred to the trial balance

When errors are shown, the trial balance is 'balanced' by recording the difference in a suspense account, as shown in the following Case Study.

Case Study

TEMESIDE TRADERS: SUSPENSE ACCOUNT

The bookkeeper of Temeside Traders is unable to balance the trial balance on 30 June 20-4. As the error or errors cannot be found quickly the trial balance is balanced by recording the difference in a suspense account, as follows:

	Dr	Cr
	£	£
Trial balance totals	99,950	100,000
Suspense account	50	
	100,000	100,000

A suspense account is opened in the general ledger with, in this case, a debit balance of £50.

Dr	**Suspense account**	Cr
20-4	£	20-4	£
30 Jun Trial balance difference 50		

A detailed examination of the bookkeeping system is now made in order to find the errors. As errors are found, they are corrected by means of a journal entry. The journal entries will balance, with one part of the entry being either a debit or credit to suspense account. In this way, the balance on suspense account is eliminated by double-entry transactions. Using the above suspense account, the following errors are found and corrected on 15 July 20-4:

- telephone expenses of £55 were not recorded in the expenses account

- stationery expenses of £48 have been debited to both stationery account and bank account

- a payment to a supplier, A Wilson, for £65, has been recorded in the bank as £56

- the balance of rent paid account is £3,100 but it has been recorded in the trial balance as £3,000

These errors are corrected by the journal entries shown on the next few pages.

one-sided entry

Telephone expenses of £55 were not recorded in the expenses account.

As only the bank entry has been recorded, the correcting entry must complete double-entry by debiting telephone expenses account with £55. The correcting journal entry is:

Date	Details	Reference	Dr	Cr
20-4			£	£
15 Jul	Telephone expenses	GL	55	
	Suspense	GL		55
	Omission of entry in expenses account.			

entry duplicated on one side, nothing on the other

Stationery expenses of £48 have been debited to both stationery account and bank account.

As bank account has been debited in error with £48, the correcting journal entry must be in two parts to remove the incorrect entry and record the correct entry.

Date	Details	Reference	Dr	Cr
20-4			£	£
15 Jul	Suspense	GL	48	
	Bank	CB		48
	Suspense	GL	48	
	Bank	CB		48
			96	96
	Correction of error: payment from bank debited in error to bank account			

unequal entries

A £65 payment to a supplier, A Wilson, has been recorded in the bank as £56.
As the credit entry in bank account has been entered incorrectly, the
correcting journal entry must be in two parts to remove the incorrect entry
and record the correct entry.

Date	Details	Reference	Dr	Cr
20-4			£	£
15 Jul	Bank	CB	56	
	Suspense	GL		56
	Suspense	GL	65	
	Bank	CB		65
			121	121
	Payment to a supplier entered in			
	bank account as £56 instead of £65			

account balance incorrectly transferred

The balance of rent paid account has been recorded in the trial balance as
£3,000; further checking shows that the correct balance is £3,100.

To correct this type of error a journal entry is needed in order to take the
wrong amount from suspense account and then to record the correct amount,
ie a two-part journal entry. As rent paid account has a debit balance the
journal entry is firstly to take out the wrong balance (debit suspense account
and credit rent paid account in the trial balance) and then to record the correct
balance (debit rent paid account in the trial balance and credit suspense
account).

Date	Details	Reference	Dr	Cr
20-4			£	£
15 Jul	Suspense	GL	3,000	
	Rent paid	GL		3,000
	Rent paid	GL	3,100	
	Suspense	GL		3,100
			6,100	6,100
	Incorrect balance of rent paid			
	account transferred to the trial			
	balance			

The entries in suspense account are shown on the next page.

suspense account

After the journal entries have been recorded in the double-entry accounts, suspense account appears:

Dr		£		Cr	£
20-4			20-4		
30 Jun	Trial balance difference	50	15 Jul	Telephone expenses	55
15 Jul	Bank	48	15 Jul	Bank	56
15 Jul	Bank	48	15 Jul	Rent paid	3,100
15 Jul	Bank	65			
15 Jul	Rent paid	3,000			
		3,211			3,211

Suspense account

Thus all the errors have now been found, and suspense account has a nil balance.

EFFECT ON PROFIT AND STATEMENT OF FINANCIAL POSITION

The correction of errors, whether shown by a trial balance or not, often has an effect on the profit figure calculated before the errors were found. For example, an undercast of sales account, when corrected, will increase profit and, of course, the profit figure taken to the statement of financial position. Some errors, however, only affect the statement of financial position, eg errors involving trade receivables' and trade payables' accounts. The diagram opposite shows the effect of errors, when corrected, on the profit figure and the statement of financial position.

JOURNAL ENTRIES FOR THE YEAR-END

It should be noted that year-end transfers and adjustments can have a significant effect on the profit or loss figure and the statement of financial position of a business, for example:

- not adjusting for a large accrued expense means that the expense is recorded in the statement of profit or loss at too small an amount (because the accrual has not been included), which will increase the profit figure; also the liability for the accrued expense will not be shown on the statement of financial position.

- not adjusting for a large prepaid expense means that the expense is recorded in the statement of profit or loss at too large an amount (because

statement of profit or loss	correction of error	profit	statement of financial position
	sales undercast/understated	increase	profit increase
	sales overcast/overstated	decrease	profit decrease
	purchases undercast/understated	decrease	profit decrease
	purchases overcast/overstated	increase	profit increase
	opening inventory undervalued	decrease	profit decrease
	opening inventory overvalued	increase	profit increase
	closing inventory undervalued	increase	profit increase/inventory increase
	closing inventory overvalued	decrease	profit decrease/inventory decrease
	expense undercast/understated	decrease	decrease in profit
	expense overcast/overstated	increase	increase in profit
	income undercast/understated	increase	increase in profit
	income overcast/overstated	decrease	decrease in profit
statement of financial position	asset undercast/understated	–	increase asset
	asset overcast/overstated	–	decrease asset
	liability undercast/understated	–	increase liability
	liability overcast/overstated	–	decrease liability

the prepayment has been included), which will decrease the profit figure; also the asset for the prepaid expense will not be shown on the statement of financial position.

It must be remembered that others will be relying on the accuracy of the financial statements – eg owners, managers, lenders, HM Revenue & Customs. The effects of including misleading or inaccurate year-end adjustments include:

■ wrong decisions being made by users because of misinformation

■ non-compliance with regulations – eg legislation and accounting standards

Accounting staff need to ensure that year-end transfers and adjustments are made with integrity (in a straightforward and honest manner) and objectivity (not allowing bias, conflict of interest, or undue influence to override their professional judgement).

With journal entries for year-end transfers and adjustments it is essential to ensure that the business's policies, regulations, procedures and timescales are observed in relation to the preparation of financial statements. Thus journal entries are needed for statement of profit or loss transfers, accruals and prepayments, depreciation, irrecoverable debts and allowance for doubtful debts – all of these must be made at the correct time for the business and for the correct amounts. There are also likely to be pressures at the year-end:

- time pressure for the transfers and adjustments to be made within a tight timescale

- pressure from authority – eg the owners or managers of the business – to report favourable financial results

It is always good practice in a business to ensure that journal entries are checked by an appropriate person before they are entered into the double-entry system. It is all too easy to get a journal entry the wrong way round resulting in an error becoming twice as much as it was in the first place!

- The journal is used to list non-regular transactions.

Chapter Summary

■ The journal is a book of prime entry – it is not a double-entry account.

■ The journal is used for:
  - year-end transfers and adjustments
  - purchase and sale of non-current assets on credit
  - correction of errors found in the double-entry system

■ Correction of errors is always a difficult topic to put into practice: it tests knowledge of double-entry procedures and it is all too easy to make the error worse than it was in the first place! The secret of dealing with this topic well is to write down – in account format – what has gone wrong. It should then be relatively easy to see what has to be done to put the error right.

■ Errors not revealed by a trial balance: error of principle, mispost/error of commission, error of original entry, error of omission and reversal of entries.

■ Errors revealed by a trial balance include: one-sided entry, entry duplicated on one side, nothing on the other, unequal entries, account balance incorrectly transferred to the trial balance.

■ All errors are non-regular transactions and need to be corrected by means of a journal entry: the journal entry gives the bookkeeper the authority to record the transactions in the double-entry accounts.

■ When error(s) are shown by a trial balance, the amount of the error is placed in a suspense account. As the errors are found, journal entries are made which 'clear out' the suspense account.

■ Correction of errors may have an effect on profit calculated before the errors were found, and on the statement of financial position.

■ Period end transfers and adjustments can significantly affect the reported results of an organisation.

Key Terms

journal	the book of prime entry for non-regular transactions
suspense account	account in which to place an error in the trial balance, pending further investigation

Activities

11.1   Which **one** of the following will *not* be recorded in the journal?

(a) Credit purchase of a non-current asset	
(b) Cash sale of goods to a customer	✓
(c) Write-off of an irrecoverable debt	
(d) Correction of an error not shown by the trial balance	

11.2   A trial balance fails to agree by £75 and the difference is placed to a suspense account. Later it is found that a credit sale for this amount has not been entered in the sales account. Which **one** of the following journal entries is correct?

(a) Debit suspense account £75; credit sales account £75	✓
(b) Debit suspense account £150; credit sales account £150	
(c) Debit sales account £75; credit suspense account £75	
(d) Credit sales account £75	

11.3   The trial balance of Thomas Wilson balanced. However, a number of errors have been found in the bookkeeping system:

(a)   Credit sale of £150 to J Rigby has not been entered in the accounts.

(b)   The cost of a new delivery van, £10,000, has been entered to vehicle expenses account.

(c)   Postages of £55, paid by cheque, have been entered on the wrong sides of both accounts.

(d)   A bank payment for £89 from L Johnson, a trade receivable, has been entered in the accounts as £98.

(e)   A bank payment for £125 to H Price Ltd, a trade payable, has been recorded in the account of H Prince.

You are to take each error in turn and:
- state the type of error
- show the correcting journal entry

Notes:
- VAT is to be ignored
- a blank journal entry is given in the Appendix

11.4   Jeremy Johnson extracts a trial balance on 30 September 20-7. Unfortunately the trial balance fails to balance and the difference, £19 debit, is placed to a suspense account in the general ledger pending further investigation.

The following errors are later found:

(a)   A bank payment of £85 for office expenses has been entered in the cash book but no entry has been made in the office expenses account.

(b)   A bank payment for printing of £87 by cheque has been correctly entered in the cash book, but is shown as £78 in the printing expenses account.

(c)   The balance of sales returns account has been recorded in the trial balance as £2,500; further checking shows that the current balance is £2,400.

(d)   Commission received of £25 has been entered twice in the account.

You are to:

·   show the correcting journal entries

·   show the suspense account after the errors have been corrected

Note: a blank journal entry is given in the Appendix.

11.5   Show the journal entries for the following transfers which relate to Trish Hall's business for the year ended 31 December 20-8 (ignore VAT):

(a)   Closing inventory is to be recorded in the financial statements at a valuation of £22,600.

(b)   Telephone expenses for the year, amounting to £890, are to be transferred to the statement of profit or loss.

(c)   Salaries account shows a balance of £22,950, but £980 is owing; the expenditure for the year is to be transferred to the statement of profit or loss.

(d)   Printing expenses account shows a balance of £1,240, but this includes printer rental of £80 in respect of January and February 20-9; the expenditure for the year is to be transferred to the statement of profit or loss.

(e)   Rent received account shows a balance of £4,800, but £400 of this relates to a payment for January 20-9; the income for the year is to be transferred to the statement of profit or loss.

(f)   Depreciation charges on fixtures and fittings for the year are calculated at £500, but no entries have been made in the accounts.

(g)   A machine had been bought on 1 January 20-6 for £5,000. Accumulated depreciation (including the current year) totals £3,750. On 31 December 20-8 the machine is sold for £2,400 received into the bank.

(h)   The following accounts in the sales ledger are to be written off as irrecoverable: Nick Marshall, £55; Crabbe & Company, £30; A Hunt, £40.

These are the only irrecoverable debts during the year; the total is to be transferred to the statement of profit or loss.

(i)   The allowance for doubtful debts is £550; the amount is to be reduced to £450.

Note: a blank journal entry is given in the Appendix.

11.6 This Activity is about recording journal entries.

You are working on the financial statements of a business with a year-end of 31 March. A trial balance has been drawn up and a suspense account opened with a debit balance of £9,700. You now need to make some corrections and adjustments for the year ended 31 March 20-1.

Record the journal entries needed in the general ledger to deal with the items below. You should:

• remove any incorrect entries, where appropriate

• post the correct entries

You do not need to give narratives.

Do NOT enter zeros into unused column cells.

Ignore VAT.

(a) Entries need to be made for an irrecoverable debt of £220.

Journal

	Dr £	Cr £

(b) A purchase of a delivery vehicle for £12,500 has been made from the bank. The correct entry was made to the bank account, but no other entries were made.

Journal

	Dr £	Cr £

(c) No entries have been made for closing inventory for the year ended 31 March 20-1. Closing inventory has been valued at cost at £25,400. Included in this figure are some items costing £1,850 that will be sold for £1,200.

Journal

	Dr £	Cr £

(d) The figures from the columns of the sales day book for 31 March have been totalled correctly as follows:

Sales column	£7,000
VAT column	£1,400
Total column	£8,400

The amounts have been posted as follows:

Cr Sales	£7,000
Dr VAT	£1,400
Dr Sales ledger control	£8,400

Journal

	Dr £	Cr £

11.7 This Activity is about recording adjustments in the extended trial balance and closing off accounts.

You are working on the financial statements of a business with a year-end of 31 March. A trial balance has been drawn up and a suspense account opened with a credit balance of £2,100. You now need to make some corrections and adjustments for the year ended 31 March 20-1.

(a) Record the adjustments needed on the extract from the extended trial balance to deal with the items below.

You will not need to enter adjustments on every line. Do NOT enter zeros into unused cells.

1 Entries need to be made for an irrecoverable debt of £78.

2 A payment of £2,500 for rent has been made from the bank account. The correct entry was made in rent paid account, but no other entries were made.

3 No entries have been made for closing inventory for the year-end 31 March 20-1. Closing inventory has been valued at cost at £42,000. Included in this figure are some items costing £2,300 that will be sold for £1,500.

4 The figures from the columns of the sales day book for 31 March have been totalled correctly as follows:

Sales column	£2,000
VAT column	£400
Total column	£2,400

The amounts have been posted as follows:

Cr Sales	£2,000
Cr VAT	£400
Dr Sales ledger control	£2,000

Extract from extended trial balance

	Ledger balances		Adjustments	
	Dr £	Cr £	Dr £	Cr £
Allowance for doubtful debts		720		
Bank	9,500			
Closing inventory – statement of financial position				
Closing inventory – statement of profit or loss				
Depreciation charges	2,000			
Irrecoverable debts				
Office expenses	5,300			
Rent paid	14,200			
Sales		245,000		
Sales ledger control	47,400			
Suspense		2,100		
VAT		7,300		
Vehicles – accumulated depreciation		6,000		

(b)   The ledgers are ready to be closed off for the year ended 31 March 20-1. Fill in the account names and tick to show the entries to close off the office expenses account. Give an appropriate narrative.

Account	Dr	Cr
Narrative:		

11.8 This Activity is about completing an extended trial balance.

You have the following extended trial balance. The adjustments have already been correctly entered.

Extend the figures into the statement of profit or loss and statement of financial position.

Do NOT enter zeros into unused column cells.

Make the columns balance by entering figures in the correct places.

Extended trial balance

Ledger account	Ledger balances		Adjustments		Statement of profit or loss		Statement of financial position	
	£ Dr	£ Cr	£ Dr	£ Cr	£ Dr	£ Cr	£ Dr	£ Cr
Allowance for doubtful debts		1,700		200				
Allowance for doubtful debts adjustment			200					
Bank		16,200		300				
Capital		20,500						
Closing inventory			18,500	18,500				
Depreciation charges			3,500					
Office expenses	18,600		400					
Opening inventory	12,500							
Payroll expenses	40,800		200					
Purchases	260,000		1,000					
Purchases ledger control		32,500						
Sales revenue		375,000						
Sales ledger control	60,100							
Selling expenses	21,000							
Suspense	1,300		300	1,600				
VAT		2,900						
Vehicles at cost	45,000							
Vehicles accumulated depreciation		10,500		3,500				
Profit/loss for the year								
	459,300	459,300	24,100	24,100				

Answers to chapter activities

CHAPTER 1: THE ACCOUNTING SYSTEM

1.1 **(a)** ledger   **(b)** trade receivable   **(c)** trade payable
     (d) sales day book   **(e)** cash book   **(f)** general ledger *or* nominal ledger
     (g) assets minus liabilities equals capital, *or* assets equals capital plus liabilities

1.2 **(a)** assets – items owned by a business; liabilities – items owed by a business

     (b) trade receivables – individuals or businesses who owe money in respect of goods or services supplied by the business; trade payables – individuals or businesses to whom money is owed by the business

     (c) purchases – goods bought, either on credit or for cash, which are intended to be resold later; sales – the sale of goods, whether on credit or for cash, in which the business trades

     (d) credit purchases – goods bought, with payment to be made at a later date; cash purchases – goods bought and paid for immediately

1.3 **(a)** asset of bank increases by £8,000
           capital increases by £8,000
           asset £8,000 – liability £0 = capital £8,000

     (b) asset of computer increases by £4,000
           asset of bank decreases by £4,000
           asset £8,000 – liability £0 = capital £8,000

     (c) asset of bank increases by £3,000
           liability of loan increases by £3,000
           asset £11,000 – liability £3,000 = capital £8,000

     (d) asset of van increases by £6,000
           asset of bank decreases by £6,000
           asset £11,000 – liability £3,000 = capital £8,000

1.4

(a)	capital	£20,000
(b)	capital	£10,000
(c)	liabilities	£7,550
(d)	assets	£14,100
(e)	liabilities	£18,430
(f)	assets	£21,160

1.5 **(a)** owner started in business with capital of £10,000 in the bank
     (b) bought office equipment for £2,000, paying by cheque
     (c) received a loan of £6,000 by cheque
     (d) bought a van for £10,000, paying by cheque
     (e) owner introduces £2,000 additional capital by cheque
     (f) loan repayment of £3,000 made by cheque

CHAPTER 2: DOUBLE-ENTRY BOOKKEEPING

2.1 (d)   **2.2** (b)   **2.3** (d)

2.4   **JAMES ANDERSON (summary of transactions)**

			Dr				Cr
Account	**20-4**		£	**20-4**			£
Capital				2 Feb	Bank		7,500
Computer	6 Feb	Bank	2,000				
Rent paid	9 Feb	Bank	750				
Wages	12 Feb	Bank	425				
	25 Feb	Bank	380				
Bank loan				13 Feb	Bank		2,500
Commission rec'd				20 Feb	Bank		145
Drawings	23 Feb	Bank	200				
Van	27 Feb	Bank	6,000				

CHAPTER 3: BALANCING ACCOUNTS AND THE TRIAL BALANCE

3.1   (c) Debit £325   **3.2**   (b) Purchases account   **3.3**   (c) Capital account

3.4   **(a)** and **(c)**   **ANDREW JOHNSTONE**

Dr		**Bank account**				Cr
20-4		£	20-4			£
1 Jan	Capital	10,000	4 Jan	Rent paid		500
11 Jan	Sales	1,000	5 Jan	Shop fittings		1,500
12 Jan	Sales	1,250	20 Jan	Comp Supplies Ltd		5,000
22 Jan	Sales	1,450	31 Jan	Balance c/d		6,700
		13,700				13,700
1 Feb	Balance b/d	6,700	2 Feb	Rent paid		500
4 Feb	Sales	1,550	15 Feb	Shop fittings		850
10 Feb	Sales	1,300	27 Feb	Comp Supplies Ltd		6,350
12 Feb	Rowcester College	750	28 Feb	Balance c/d		5,300
19 Feb	Sales	1,600				
25 Feb	Sales	1,100				
		13,000				13,000
1 Mar	Balance b/d	5,300				

Dr		**Capital account**		Cr
20-4		£	20-4	£
			1 Jan Bank	10,000

Dr		**Rent paid account**			Cr
20-4		£	20-4		£
4 Jan	Bank	500	28 Feb	Balance c/d	1,000
2 Feb	Bank	500			
		1,000			1,000
1 Mar	Balance b/d	1,000			

Dr				**Shop fittings account**			Cr
20-4			£	20-4			£
5 Jan	Bank		1,500	28 Feb	Balance c/d		2,350
15 Feb	Bank		850				
			2,350				2,350
1 Mar	Balance b/d		2,350				

Dr				**Purchases account**			Cr
20-4			£	20-4			£
7 Jan	Comp Supplies Ltd		5,000	31 Jan	Balance c/d		11,500
25 Jan	Comp Supplies Ltd		6,500				
			11,500				11,500
1 Feb	Balance b/d		11,500	28 Feb	Balance c/d		17,000
24 Feb	Comp Supplies Ltd		5,500				
			17,000				17,000
1 Mar	Balance b/d		17,000				

Dr				**Comp Supplies Limited**			Cr
20-4			£	20-4			£
20 Jan	Bank		5,000	7 Jan	Purchases		5,000
31 Jan	Balance c/d		6,500	25 Jan	Purchases		6,500
			11,500				11,500
5 Feb	Purchases returns		150	1 Feb	Balance b/d		6,500
27 Feb	Bank		6,350	24 Feb	Purchases		5,500
28 Feb	Balance c/d		5,500				
			12,000				12,000
				1 Mar	Balance b/d		5,500

Dr				**Sales account**			Cr
20-4			£	20-4			£
31 Jan	Balance c/d		4,550	11 Jan	Bank		1,000
				12 Jan	Bank		1,250
				16 Jan	Rowcester College		850
				22 Jan	Bank		1,450
			4,550				4,550
28 Feb	Balance c/d		11,150	1 Feb	Balance b/d		4,550
				4 Feb	Bank		1,550
				10 Feb	Bank		1,300
				19 Feb	Bank		1,600
				25 Feb	Bank		1,100
				26 Feb	Rowcester College		1,050
			11,150				11,150
				1 Mar	Balance b/d		11,150

Dr			Rowcester College			Cr
20-4			£	20-4		£
16 Jan	Sales		850	27 Jan	Sales returns	100
				31 Jan	Balance c/d	750
			850			850
1 Feb	Balance b/d		750	12 Feb	Bank	750
26 Feb	Sales		1,050	28 Feb	Balance c/d	1,050
			1,800			1,800
1 Mar	Balance b/d		1,050			

Dr		Sales returns account		Cr
20-4		£	20-4	£
27 Jan	Rowcester College	100		

Dr		Purchases returns account		Cr
20-4		£	20-4	£
			5 Feb Comp Supplies Ltd	150

(b)

Trial balance as at 31 January 20-4

	Dr	Cr
	£	£
Bank	6,700	
Capital		10,000
Rent paid	500	
Shop fittings	1,500	
Purchases	11,500	
Comp Supplies Limited		6,500
Sales		4,550
Rowcester College	750	
Sales returns	100	
	21,050	21,050

(d)

Trial balance as at 28 February 20-4

	Dr	Cr
	£	£
Bank	5,300	
Capital		10,000
Rent paid	1,000	
Shop fittings	2,350	
Purchases	17,000	
Comp Supplies Limited		5,500
Sales		11,150
Rowcester College	1,050	
Sales returns	100	
Purchases returns		150
	26,800	26,800

3.5

SAMANTHA WILKES
Trial balance as at 31 March 20-4

	Dr £	Cr £
Bank overdraft		2,750
Purchases	14,890	
Sales revenue		35,680
Purchases returns		440
Purchases ledger control		2,360
Office equipment	8,000	
Vehicle	14,000	
Opening inventory	2,810	
Sales returns	550	
Sales ledger control	3,840	
Administration expenses	12,060	
Value Added Tax owing		1,420
Carriage out	740	
Discount received		210
Capital *(missing figure)*		14,030
	56,890	56,890

CHAPTER 4: FINANCIAL STATEMENTS – THE EXTENDED TRIAL BALANCE

4.1 (b) Vehicles   **4.2** (d) Income minus expenses

4.3 Business A: profit £40,000; capital £100,000
Business B: expenses £70,000; liabilities £100,000
Business C: income £70,000; assets £90,000
Business D: expenses £75,000; liabilities £60,000
Business E: loss £10,000; assets £100,000

4.4

			FINANCIAL STATEMENTS			
	Trial balance		Statement of profit or loss		Statement of financial position	
	Debit	Credit	Debit	Credit	Debit	Credit
(a) Salaries	✓		✓			
(b) Purchases	✓		✓			
(c) Sales ledger control	✓				✓	
(d) Sales returns	✓		✓			
(e) Discounts received		✓		✓		
(f) Vehicle	✓				✓	
(g) Capital		✓				✓

4.5 EXTENDED TRIAL BALANCE

NICK JOHNSON

31 DECEMBER 20-3

Account name	Ledger balances		Adjustments		Statement of profit or loss		Statement of financial position	
	Dr £	Cr £	Dr £	Cr £	Dr £	Cr £	Dr £	Cr £
Opening inventory	25,000				25,000			
Purchases	210,000				210,000			
Sales revenue		310,000				310,000		
Administration expenses	12,400				12,400			
Wages	41,000				41,000			
Rent paid	7,500				7,500			
Telephone	1,000				1,000			
Interest paid	9,000				9,000			
Travel expenses	1,100				1,100			
Premises at cost	200,000						200,000	
Machinery at cost	40,000						40,000	
Sales ledger control	31,000						31,000	
Bank	900						900	
Cash	100						100	
Capital		150,000						150,000
Drawings	14,000						14,000	
Loan from bank		100,000						100,000
Purchases ledger control		29,000						29,000
Value Added Tax		4,000						4,000
Closing inventory: statement of profit or loss				21,000		21,000		
Closing inventory: statement of financial position			21,000				21,000	
Profit/loss for the year					24,000			24,000
	593,000	593,000	21,000	21,000	331,000	331,000	307,000	307,000

4.6 EXTENDED TRIAL BALANCE

ALAN HARRIS — 30 JUNE 20-4

Account name	Ledger balances Dr £	Ledger balances Cr £	Adjustments Dr £	Adjustments Cr £	Statement of profit or loss Dr £	Statement of profit or loss Cr £	Statement of financial position Dr £	Statement of financial position Cr £
Opening inventory	13,250				13,250			
Capital		70,000						70,000
Premises at cost	65,000						65,000	
Vehicle at cost	5,250						5,250	
Purchases	55,000				55,000			
Sales revenue		85,500				85,500		
Administration expenses	850				850			
Wages	9,220				9,220			
Rent paid	1,200				1,200			
Telephone	680				680			
Interest paid	120				120			
Travel expenses	330				330			
Sales ledger control	1,350						1,350	
Purchases ledger control		6,400						6,400
Value Added Tax		1,150						1,150
Bank	2,100						2,100	
Cash	600						600	
Drawings	8,100						8,100	
Closing inventory: statement of profit or loss		18,100				18,100		
Closing inventory: statement of financial position	18,100						18,100	
Profit/loss for the year					22,950			22,950
	181,150	181,150			103,600	103,600	100,500	100,500

CHAPTER 5: ACCRUALS AND PREPAYMENTS

5.1 (d) **5.2** (c)

5.3

Dr			Vehicle expenses account		Cr
20-7		£	20-7		£
31 Dec	Balance b/d	1,680	31 Dec	Drawings	420
			31 Dec	Statement of profit or loss	1,260
		1,680			1,680

5.4 **(a)** Expenses in the statement of profit or loss of £56,760; statement of financial position shows accruals of £1,120.

(b) Expenses in the statement of profit or loss of £2,852 (ie £3,565 − £713); statement of financial position shows prepayments of £713.

(c) Expenses in the statement of profit or loss of £1,800; statement of financial position shows prepayments of £150.

5.5 **(a) Rent paid**

	£		£
Bank	11,250	Accrued expenses (reversal)	750
		Statement of profit or loss	9,000
		Prepaid expenses	1,500
	11,250		11,250

(b) Administration expenses

		£			£
20-6 1 Apr	Prepaid expenses (reversal)	250	20-7 31 Mar	Statement of profit or loss	10,825
20-7 31 Mar	Bank	10,400			
20-7 31 Mar	Accrued expenses	175			
		10,825			10,825

(c)

Account	£	Dr £	Cr £
Accrued expenses			175
Capital	75,000		75,000
Discounts received	680		680
Drawings	10,000	10,000	
Interest received	200		200
Machinery at cost	20,000	20,000	
Prepaid expenses		1,500	
Sales revenue	115,000		115,000

5.6 **(a) Rent received**

	£		£
Statement of profit or loss	5,400	Prepaid income (reversal)	450
Prepaid income	900	Bank	5,850
	6,300		6,300

(b) Vehicle expenses

		£			£
20-3 30 Jun	Bank	6,450	20-2 1 Jul	Accrued expenses (reversal)	220
20-3 30 Jun	Accrued expenses	380	20-3 30 Jun	Statement of profit or loss	6,610
		6,830			6,830

(c)

Account	£	Dr £	Cr £
Accrued expenses			380
Capital	30,000		30,000
Cash	250	250	
Discounts allowed	600	600	
Prepaid income			900
Purchases	15,500	15,500	
Sales returns	850	850	
Vehicles at cost	12,000	12,000	

5.7 EXTENDED TRIAL BALANCE

DON SMITH

31 DECEMBER 20-2

Account name	Ledger balances Dr £	Ledger balances Cr £	Adjustments Dr £	Adjustments Cr £	Statement of profit or loss Dr £	Statement of profit or loss Cr £	Statement of financial position Dr £	Statement of financial position Cr £
Sales ledger control	24,325						24,325	
Purchases ledger control		15,408						15,408
Value Added Tax		4,276						4,276
Capital		30,000						30,000
Bank		1,083						1,083
Rent and rates	10,862			250	10,612			
Electricity	2,054		110		2,164			
Telephone	1,695				1,695			
Salaries	55,891		365		56,256			
Vehicles at cost	22,250						22,250	
Office equipment at cost	7,500						7,500	
Vehicle expenses	10,855				10,855			
Drawings	15,275						15,275	
Discounts allowed	478				478			
Discounts received		591				591		
Purchases	138,960				138,960			
Sales revenue		257,258				257,258		
Opening inventory	18,471				18,471			
Closing inventory: statement of profit or loss				14,075		14,075		
Closing inventory: statement of financial position			14,075				14,075	
Accruals				475				475
Prepayments			250				250	
Profit/loss for the year					32,433			32,433
	308,616	308,616	14,800	14,800	271,924	271,924	83,675	83,675

5.8 EXTENDED TRIAL BALANCE

JOHN BARCLAY

30 JUNE 20-3

Account name	Ledger balances Dr £	Ledger balances Cr £	Adjustments Dr £	Adjustments Cr £	Statement of profit or loss Dr £	Statement of profit or loss Cr £	Statement of financial position Dr £	Statement of financial position Cr £
Sales revenue		864,321				864,321		
Purchases	600,128			250	599,878			
Sales returns	2,746				2,746			
Purchases returns		3,894				3,894		
Office expenses	33,947			346	33,601			
Salaries	122,611				122,611			
Vehicle expenses	36,894		1,250		38,144			
Discounts allowed	3,187				3,187			
Discounts received		4,951				4,951		
Sales and purchases ledger control	74,328	52,919					74,328	52,919
Value Added Tax		10,497						10,497
Opening inventory	63,084				63,084			
Vehicles at cost	83,500						83,500	
Office equipment at cost	23,250						23,250	
Land and buildings at cost	100,000						100,000	
Bank loan		75,000						75,000
Bank	1,197						1,197	
Capital		155,000						155,000
Drawings	21,710		250				21,960	
Closing inventory: statement of profit or loss				66,941		66,941		
Closing inventory: statement of financial position			66,941				66,941	
Accruals				1,250				1,250
Prepayments			346				346	
Profit/loss for the year					76,856			76,856
	1,166,582	1,166,582	68,787	68,787	940,107	940,107	371,522	371,522

CHAPTER 6: DEPRECIATION OF NON-CURRENT ASSETS

6.1   (a) £900

6.2   • With diminishing balance depreciation a fixed percentage is written off the diminished balance (carrying amount) of the asset each year.
   • When compared with straight-line depreciation, diminishing balance needs a much higher percentage to be written off each year to achieve the same residual value.
   • Thus the money amounts for diminishing balance are greater in the early years and smaller in the later years when compared with straight-line depreciation.
   • As delivery vans depreciate more in the early years and are unlikely to be kept for the whole of their expected lives, diminishing balance depreciation is a more accurate reflection of their worth than is straight-line depreciation.
   • The depreciation charges will be high in the early years but smaller in the later years; by contrast repair costs are likely to be low early on but will increase in later years. By using diminishing balance depreciation, the total charges to the statement of profit or loss for both depreciation and repair costs is likely to be similar throughout the assets' lives.

6.3   Year 1 £7,000; Year 2 £6,000; Year 3 £5,000.

6.4   **(a)**

Dr			Car accumulated depreciation account			Cr
20-2			£	20-2		£
31 Dec	Balance c/d		3,000	31 Dec	Depreciation charges	3,000
20-3				20-3		
31 Dec	Balance c/d		5,250	1 Jan	Balance b/d	3,000
				31 Dec	Depreciation charges	2,250
			5,250			5,250
20-4				20-4		
31 Dec	Disposals		6,937	1 Jan	Balance b/d	5,250
				31 Dec	Depreciation charges	1,687
			6,937			6,937

(b)

Year	Statement of financial position	
	Dr **Cost**	Cr **Accumulated depreciation**
	£	£
31 Dec 20-2	12,000	3,000
31 Dec 20-3	12,000	5,250

(c)

Dr		Disposals account			Cr

20-4		£	20-4		£
31 Dec	Car at cost	12,000	31 Dec	Accumulated depreciation	6,937
31 Dec	Statement of profit or loss		31 Dec	Bank	5,500
	(gain on disposal)	437			
		12,437			12,437

6.5   **Machinery at cost**

Balance b/d	£20,000		
Bank	£8,000	Balance c/d	£28,000
	£28,000		£28,000

Machinery: accumulated depreciation

		Balance b/d	£6,000
Balance c/d	£7,250	Depreciation charges	£1,250
	£7,250		£7,250

Machinery: depreciation charges

Balance b/d	£2,000	Statement of profit or loss	£3,250
Machinery: accumulated depreciation	£1,250		
	£3,250		£3,250

6.6   **(a)**

Year 1	£3,000
Year 2	£2,250
Total	£5,250

(b) **Vehicle at cost**

Balance b/d	£12,000	Disposals	£12,000
	£12,000		£12,000

Vehicle: disposals

Vehicle at cost	£12,000	Vehicle: accumulated depreciation	£5,250
Statement of profit or loss	£250	Bank/cash	£7,000
	£12,250		£12,250

Bank/cash

Vehicle disposals	£7,000	Balance c/d	£8,400
Value Added Tax	£1,400		
	£8,400		£8,400

(c)

Gain	✓
Loss	

6.7 **Machinery at cost**

Balance b/d	£4,200	Disposals	£4,200
Disposals	£1,200	Balance c/d	£6,000
Bank	£4,800		
	£10,200		£10,200

Machinery: accumulated depreciation

Disposals	£3,150	Balance b/d	£3,150
Balance c/d	£1,500	Depreciation charges	£1,500
	£4,650		£4,650

Machinery: depreciation charges

Machinery: accumulated depreciation	£1,500	Statement of profit or loss	£1,500
	£1,500		£1,500

Machinery: disposals

Machinery at cost	£4,200	Machinery: accumulated depreciation	£3,150
Statement of profit or loss	£150	Machinery at cost	£1,200
	£4,350		£4,350

6.8

Account	£	Dr £	Cr £
Accrued expenses	680		680
Capital	25,000		25,000
Depreciation charges	1,200	1,200	
Drawings	8,000	8,000	
Interest received	200		200
Machinery at cost	6,500	6,500	
Machinery: accumulated depreciation	2,400		2,400
Prepaid expenses	210	210	

6.9   Extended trial balance – see next page

6.10   A letter incorporating the following points:
- Straight-line method at 20% per year = depreciation charge of £200 per year
- Diminishing balance method at 50% per year = depreciation charge of £500 for year 1, £250 for year 2, £125 for year 3, £62 for year 4, and £31 for year 5, leaving a small residual value of £32
- Either method acceptable
- The straight-line method will give larger profits for the first two years
- The cash position is not affected, as depreciation is a non-cash expense (this point should be stressed)

6.9 EXTENDED TRIAL BALANCE

JOHN HENSON

31 DECEMBER 20-1

Account name	Ledger balances Dr £	Cr £	Adjustments Dr £	Cr £	Statement of profit or loss Dr £	Cr £	Statement of financial position Dr £	Cr £
Purchases	71,600				71,600			
Sales revenue		121,750				121,750		
Opening inventory	6,250				6,250			
Vehicle running expenses	1,480				1,480			
Rent and rates	5,650				5,650			
Office expenses	2,220				2,220			
Discounts received		285				285		
Wages and salaries	18,950				18,950			
Office equipment at cost	10,000						10,000	
Office equipment: accumulated depreciation				1,000				1,000
Vehicle at cost	12,000						12,000	
Vehicle: accumulated depreciation				3,000				3,000
Sales ledger control	5,225						5,225	
Purchases ledger control		3,190						3,190
Value Added Tax		1,720						1,720
Capital		20,000						20,000
Drawings	13,095						13,095	
Bank	725						725	
Disposal of non-current asset		250				250		
Closing inventory: statement of profit or loss				8,500		8,500		
Closing inventory: statement of financial position			8,500				8,500	
Depreciation charges			4,000		4,000			
Profit/loss for the year					20,635			20,635
	147,195	147,195	12,500	12,500	130,785	130,785	49,545	49,545

6.11 EXTENDED TRIAL BALANCE

HAZEL HARRIS

31 DECEMBER 20-8

Account name	Ledger balances Dr £	Ledger balances Cr £	Adjustments Dr £	Adjustments Cr £	Statement of profit or loss Dr £	Statement of profit or loss Cr £	Statement of financial position Dr £	Statement of financial position Cr £
Bank loan		75,000						75,000
Capital		125,000						125,000
Purchases and sales revenue	465,000	614,000			465,000	614,000		
Building repairs	8,480				8,480			
Vehicle at cost	12,000						12,000	
Vehicle: accumulated depreciation		2,400		1,920				4,320
Vehicle expenses	2,680				2,680			
Premises at cost	100,000						100,000	
Premises: accumulated depreciation		4,000		2,000				6,000
Bank		2,000						2,000
Furniture at cost	25,000						25,000	
Furniture: accumulated depreciation		2,500		2,500				5,000
Wages and salaries	86,060		3,180		89,240			
Discounts	10,610	8,140			10,610	8,140		
Drawings	24,000						24,000	
Rates and insurance	6,070			450	5,620			
Sales and purchases ledger control	52,130	32,600					52,130	32,600
Value Added Tax		5,250						5,250
Administration expenses	15,460				15,460			
Opening inventory	63,000				63,000			
Disposal of non-current asset	400				400			
Closing inventory: statement of profit or loss				88,000		88,000		
Closing inventory: statement of financial position			88,000				88,000	
Accruals				3,180				3,180
Prepayments			450				450	
Depreciation charges			6,420		6,420			
Profit/loss for the year					43,230			43,230
	870,890	870,890	98,050	98,050	710,140	710,140	301,580	301,580

CHAPTER 7: IRRECOVERABLE DEBTS AND ALLOWANCE FOR DOUBTFUL DEBTS

7.1   (a) Irrecoverable debts – K Shah's account
Tutorial note: where control accounts – see Chapter 10 – are in use, the credit entry will be to sales ledger control account.

7.2   (c) Credit £200

7.3 (a) and **(b)**

- **Statement of profit or loss**
  debit irrecoverable debts, £210
  debit allowance for doubtful debts: adjustment, £500

- **Statement of financial position**
  debit sales ledger control £20,000, credit allowance for doubtful debts £500

7.4

Dr			Allowance for doubtful debts account			Cr
20-5		£	**20-5**			£
31 Dec	Balance c/d	400	1 Jan	Balance b/d		300
			31 Dec	Allowance for doubtful debts: adjustment *(increase in allowance)*		100
		400				400
20-6			**20-6**			
31 Dec	Allowance for doubtful debts: adjustment *(decrease in allowance)*	50	1 Jan	Balance b/d		400
31 Dec	Balance c/d	350				
		400				400
20-7			**20-7**			
			1 Jan	Balance b/d		350

20-5   **Extracts from financial statements produced for year ended 31 December:**
Statement of profit or loss:
   – debit allowance for doubtful debts: adjustment £100
Statement of financial position:
   – debit sales ledger control £8,000
   – credit allowance for doubtful debts £400

20-6   **Extracts from financial statements produced for year ended 31 December:**
Statement of profit or loss:
   – credit allowance for doubtful debts: adjustment £50
Statement of financial position:
   – debit sales ledger control £7,000
   – credit allowance for doubtful debts £350

7.5 **(a)** **Irrecoverable debts**

	£		£
Sales ledger control (Thompson & Co)	110	Statement of profit or loss	255
Sales ledger control (T Aziz)	65		
Sales ledger control (Wyvern Traders)	80		
	255		255

(b) **Allowance for doubtful debts**

		£			£
20-8 31 Dec	Balance c/d	700	20-8 1 Jan	Balance b/d	600
			20-8 31 Dec	Allowance for doubtful debts: adjustment	100
		700			700

(c)

Account	Ledger balances		Adjustments	
	Dr £	Cr £	Dr £	Cr £
Allowance for doubtful debts		600		100
Allowance for doubtful debts: adjustment			100	
Irrecoverable debts			255	
Loan interest	790			
Sales ledger control	28,255			255
Vehicles at cost	12,000			
Vehicles: accumulated depreciation		6,400		
Wages	35,470			

7.6   EXTENDED TRIAL BALANCE

PAUL SANDERS
31 DECEMBER 20-4

Account name	Ledger balances Dr £	Ledger balances Cr £	Adjustments Dr £	Adjustments Cr £	Statement of profit or loss Dr £	Statement of profit or loss Cr £	Statement of financial position Dr £	Statement of financial position Cr £
Purchases and sales revenue	51,225	81,762			51,225	81,762		
Sales and purchases returns	186	254			186	254		
Opening inventory	6,031				6,031			
Discounts allowed and received	324	238			324	238		
Vehicle expenses	1,086				1,086			
Wages and salaries	20,379				20,379			
Electricity	876		102		978			
Telephone	1,241				1,241			
Rent and rates	4,565			251	4,314			
Sundry expenses	732				732			
Irrecoverable debts	219				219			
Sales and purchases ledger control	1,040	7,671					1,040	7,671
Value Added Tax		1,301						1,301
Bank	3,501						3,501	
Cash	21						21	
Vehicles at cost	15,000						15,000	
Vehicles: accumulated depreciation		3,000		3,000				6,000
Office equipment at cost	10,000						10,000	
Office equipment: accumulated depreciation		5,000		1,000				6,000
Capital		25,000						25,000
Drawings	8,000						8,000	
Disposal of non-current asset		200				200		
Closing inventory: statement of profit or loss				8,210		8,210		
Closing inventory: statement of financial position			8,210				8,210	
Accruals				102				102
Prepayments			251				251	
Depreciation charges			4,000		4,000			
Allowance for doubtful debts				52				52
Allowance for doubtful debts: adjustment			52		52			
Profit/loss for the year						103	103	
	124,426	124,426	12,615	12,615	90,767	90,767	46,126	46,126

7.7 EXTENDED TRIAL BALANCE

JAMES JENKINS

30 JUNE 20-5

Account name	Ledger balances Dr £	Ledger balances Cr £	Adjustments Dr £	Adjustments Cr £	Statement of profit or loss Dr £	Statement of profit or loss Cr £	Statement of financial position Dr £	Statement of financial position Cr £
Capital		36,175						36,175
Drawings	19,050						19,050	
Purchases and sales revenue	105,240	168,432			105,240	168,432		
Opening inventory	9,427				9,427			
Sales and purchases ledger control	3,840	5,294					3,840	5,294
Value Added Tax		1,492						1,492
Sales and purchases returns	975	1,237			975	1,237		
Discounts allowed and received	127	643			127	643		
Wages and salaries	30,841				30,841			
Vehicle expenses	1,021		55		1,076			
Rent and rates	8,796			275	8,521			
Heating and lighting	1,840				1,840			
Telephone	355				355			
General expenses	1,752				1,752			
Irrecoverable debts	85				85			
Vehicle at cost	8,000						8,000	
Vehicle: accumulated depreciation		3,500		1,125				4,625
Shop fittings at cost	6,000						6,000	
Shop fittings: accumulated depreciation		2,000		600				2,600
Cash	155						155	
Bank	21,419						21,419	
Closing inventory: statement of profit or loss				11,517		11,517		
Closing inventory: statement of financial position			11,517				11,517	
Accruals				55				55
Prepayments			275				275	
Depreciation charges			1,725		1,725			
Allowance for doubtful debts		150	54					96
Allowance for doubtful debts: adjustment				54		54		
Profit/loss for the year					19,919			19,919
	218,923	218,923	13,626	13,626	181,883	181,883	70,256	70,256

CHAPTER 8: THE RULES OF ACCOUNTING

8.1 (d) Accruals

8.2 **(a)** Materiality: the new machine is a material asset and so should be classed as capital expenditure and depreciated each year over its useful life.

(b) Business entity: car is an asset of John's business, not a personal asset (in any case personal assets, for sole traders and partnerships, might well be used to repay debts of business).

(c) Accruals: expenses and revenues must be matched, therefore it must go through the old year's financial statements.

(d) Going concern: presumes that the business will continue to trade in the foreseeable future: alternative is to use liquidation amounts where the assets may have very different values.

8.3

Statement	Accounting principle
Some items are of such low value that it is not worthwhile recording them separately.	Materiality
The financial statements record and report on the activities of one particular business.	Business entity
Income and expenses are matched so that they relate to the same goods or services and the same accounting period.	Accruals
The presumption is that the business to which the financial statements relate will continue to trade in the foreseeable future.	Going concern

8.4 **(a)** Integrity and **(e)** professional behaviour

8.5

(a)	No compromise of professional judgement	Objectivity
(b)	Transactions are genuine and valid for inclusion in the records of the business	Integrity
(c)	Compliance with relevant laws and regulations	Professional behaviour
(d)	Non-disclosure of information to third parties	Confidentiality
(e)	Knowledge and skill is maintained at the level required to provide a competent professional service	Professional competence and due care

8.6   **(a)**   The purpose of depreciation is to spread the cost of a non-current asset over its useful life.

  (b)   (d) 25% straight-line method

8.7   (c)   Lower of cost and net realisable value

8.8

	£	
• Seeds	1,450	(selling price)
• Fertilisers and insecticides	2,270	(cost price)
• Tools	4,390	(cost price)
	8,110	

8.9 **(a)** this year's profit is overstated by £1,000

(b) next year's profit will be understated by £1,000

8.10 **(a)** Inventory is to be valued at the lower of cost and net realisable value.

(b) (b) £1,260

(c) (d) £40 decrease

(d) decrease

8.11 Cost of computer accounting software

As the cost of the software is relatively low, I recommend that it is treated as revenue expenditure and shown amongst the expenses in the statement of profit or loss. This is in line with the accounting principle of materiality: at a cost of £99 it is not worth recording it separately. Had the cost been much higher, the software would have been treated as a non-current asset and depreciated over its useful life.

8.12 · The first part of the statement is true – capital expenditure is money spent on non-current assets

· Whilst non-current assets are recorded in the statement of financial position, there is a link with the statement of profit or loss in that the depreciation charge will be recorded as an expense

· As all non-current assets having a known useful life must be depreciated (IAS 16), there is a clear link between such non-current assets shown in the statement of financial position and the depreciation charge recorded in the statement of profit or loss

· On disposal of non-current assets the amount of any over or under depreciation is taken to the statement of profit or loss

8.13

		Capital expenditure	Revenue expenditure
(a)	Purchase of machinery	✓	
(b)	Installation of machinery	✓	
(c)	Depreciation of machinery		✓
(d)	Purchase of property	✓	
(e)	Legal fees relating to the purchase of property	✓	
(f)	Repairs to property		✓
(g)	Insurance of property		✓
(h)	Labour costs of own employees used to build extension to property	✓	
(i)	Repainting and redecoration of property		✓

8.14 **(a)** £ 144,000

£240,000 x (100-40)/100

(b) £ 87,500

£105,000 x 100/(100 + 20)

CHAPTER 9: ACCOUNTING FOR CAPITAL TRANSACTIONS

9.1 (a) Premises

9.2 (a) The owner of the business, Mary Sampson

9.3 (b) Medium-term agreement under which the lessee has the use of an asset owned by a finance company

9.4

(a) and (b)

NON-CURRENT ASSET REGISTER							
Description/serial no	**Acquisition date**	**Cost** £	**Depreciation charges** £	**Carrying amount** £	**Funding method**	**Disposal proceeds** £	**Disposal date**
Office equipment							
Computer, Supra ML	12/3/-1	3,000.00			Cash		
Year ended 31/12/-1			1,500.00	1,500.00			
Year ended 31/12/-2			750.00	750.00			
Year ended 31/12/-3			375.00	375.00			
Year ended 31/12/-4			0.00	0.00		500.00	10/2/-4

9.5 (a)

Date	Details	Reference	Dr	Cr
20-1			£	£
10 Jan	Machine	GL	32,000	
	Bank	CB		32,000
	Purchase of machine to develop and print films; capital expenditure authorisation number			

Dr			Machine at cost account			Cr
20-1		£	20-4			£
10 Jan	Bank	32,000	17 Aug	Disposals		32,000
20-4						
17 Aug	Disposals (part-exchange allowance)	5,000				

Depreciation charge calculations

Depreciation at 40 per cent diminishing balance per year is as follows:

  year ended 31 December 20-1 £12,800

  year ended 31 December 20-2 £7,680

  year ended 31 December 20-3 £4,608

Note: the journal entry for the first year only is shown.

Date	Details	Reference	Dr	Cr
20-1			£	£
31 Dec	Depreciation charges	GL	12,800	
	Machine: accumulated depreciation	GL		12,800
	Depreciation charges for *year on machine*			
31 Dec	Statement of profit or loss	GL	12,800	
	Depreciation charges	GL		12,800
	Transfer to the statement of profit or *loss of depreciation charges for year* *on machine*			

Dr	Depreciation charges account				Cr
20-1		£	20-1		£
31 Dec	Machine: accumulated depreciation	12,800	31 Dec	Statement of profit or loss	12,800
20-2			20-2		
31 Dec	Machine: accumulated depreciation	7,680	31 Dec	Statement of profit or loss	7,680
20-3			20-3		
31 Dec	Machine: accumulated depreciation	4,608	31 Dec	Statement of profit or loss	4,608

Dr	Machine: accumulated depreciation account				Cr
20-1		£	20-1		£
31 Dec	Balance c/d	12,800	31 Dec	Depreciation charges	12,800
20-2			20-2		
31 Dec	Balance c/d	20,480	1 Jan	Balance b/d	12,800
			31 Dec	Depreciation charges	7,680
		20,480			20,480
20-3			20-3		
31 Dec	Balance c/d	25,088	1 Jan	Balance b/d	20,480
			31 Dec	Depreciation charges	4,608
		25,088			25,088
20-4			20-4		
17 Aug	Disposals	25,088	1 Jan	Balance b/d	25,088

Date	Details	Reference	Dr	Cr
20-4			£	£
17 Aug	Disposals	GL	32,000	
	Machine at cost	GL		32,000
	Machine: accumulated depreciation	GL	25,088	
	Disposals	GL		25,088
	Machine at cost	GL	5,000	
	Disposals	GL		5,000
	Statement of profit or loss	GL	1,912	
	Disposals	GL		1,912
			64,000	64,000
	Part-exchange of machine to develop and print films; loss on disposal of £1,912 transferred to statement of profit or loss			

Dr		**Machine disposals account**			Cr
20-4	£	20-4			£
17 Aug Machine at cost	32,000	17 Aug	Machine: accumulated depreciation		25,088
		17 Aug	Machine at cost (part-exchange)		5,000
		17 Aug	Statement of profit or loss (loss on disposal)		1,912
	32,000				32,000

(b)

NON-CURRENT ASSET REGISTER							
Description/serial no	**Acquisition date**	**Cost**	**Depreciation charges**	**Carrying amount**	**Funding method**	**Disposal proceeds**	**Disposal date**
		£	£	£		£	
Machinery							
Automated d&p machine	10/1/-1	32,000.00			Cash		
Year ended 31/12/-1			12,800.00	19,200.00			
Year ended 31/12/-2			7,680.00	11,520.00			
Year ended 31/12/-3			4,608.00	6,912.00			
Year ended 31/12/-4			0.00	0.00		5,000.00	17/8/-4

9.6   Depreciation calculations:

	20-1	20-2	20-3	TOTAL
Registration number	£	£	£	£
WV60 XNP	4,500	4,500	–	9,000
WV60 YNP	4,500	4,500	4,500	13,500
WV13 ZNP	–	–	5,250	5,250
TOTAL	9,000	9,000	9,750	27,750

Dr		Vehicles at cost account			Cr
20-1		£	20-1		£
24 Jan	Bank	15,000	31 Dec	Balance c/d	30,000
24 Jan	Bank	15,000			
		30,000			30,000
20-2			20-2		
1 Jan	Balance b/d	30,000	31 Dec	Balance c/d	30,000
20-3			20-3		
1 Jan	Balance b/d	30,000	13 Oct	Disposals	15,000
17 Mar	Bank	17,500	31 Dec	Balance c/d	32,500
		47,500			47,500
20-4			20-4		
1 Jan	Balance b/d	32,500			

Dr	Depreciation charges account			Cr
20-1		£	20-1	£
31 Dec Vehicles: accumulated depreciation		9,000	31 Dec Statement of profit or loss	9,000
20-2			20-2	
31 Dec Vehicles: accumulated depreciation		9,000	31 Dec Statement of profit or loss	9,000
20-3			20-3	
31 Dec Vehicles: accumulated depreciation		9,750	31 Dec Statement of profit or loss	9,750

Dr		Vehicles: accumulated depreciation account			Cr
20-1		£	20-1		£
31 Dec	Balance c/d	9,000	31 Dec	Depreciation charges	9,000
20-2			20-2		
31 Dec	Balance c/d	18,000	1 Jan	Balance b/d	9,000
			31 Dec	Depreciation charges	9,000
		18,000			18,000
20-3			20-3		
13 Oct	Disposals	9,000	1 Jan	Balance b/d	18,000
31 Dec	Balance c/d	18,750	31 Dec	Depreciation charges	9,750
		27,750			27,750
20-4			20-4		
			1 Jan	Balance b/d	18,750

Dr		Vehicle disposals account				Cr

20-3		£	20-3			£
13 Oct	Vehicles at cost	15,000	13 Oct	Vehicles: accumulated depreciation		9,000
13 Oct	Statement of profit or loss (gain on disposal)	500	13 Oct	Bank		6,500
		15,500				15,500

9.7 (a) to **(c)**

NON-CURRENT ASSET REGISTER							
Description/serial no	Acquisition date	Cost £	Depreciation charges £	Carrying amount £	Funding method	Disposal proceeds £	Disposal date
Office equipment							
Telephone system	30/09/-4	1,500.00			Cash		
Year end 31/03/-5			450.00	1,050.00			
Year end 31/03/-6			450.00	600.00			
Year end 31/03/-7			450.00	150.00			
Executive desk	28/03/-7	660.00			Cash		
Year end 31/03/-7			198.00	462.00			
Vehicles							
WV14 JEC	15/04/-4	18,000.00			Cash		
Year end 31/03/-5			4,500.00	13,500.00			
Year end 31/03/-6			3,375.00	10,125.00			
Year end 31/03/-7			0.00	0.00		8,500.00	10/03/-7
WV65 DBC	30/10/-5	12,000.00			Part-exchange		
Year end 31/03/-6			3,000.00	9,000.00			
Year end 31/03/-7			2,250.00	6,750.00			

Tutorial note: the delivery cost of the executive desk is capitalised.

9.8   (d) Hire purchase

CHAPTER 10: CONTROL ACCOUNTS

10.1 (c)   **10.2** (b)

10.3 (d)   **10.4** (b)

10.5

Dr			Sales ledger control account			Cr
20-8		£	20-8			£
1 Jun	Balance b/d	17,491	30 Jun	Sales returns		1,045
30 Jun	Credit sales	42,591	30 Jun	Payments from trade		
				receivables		39,024
			30 Jun	Discounts allowed		593
			30 Jun	Irrecoverable debts		296
			30 Jun	Balance c/d		19,124
		60,082				60,082
1 Jul	Balance b/d	19,124				

10.6

Dr			Purchases ledger control account			Cr
20-9		£	20-9			£
30 Apr	Purchases returns	653	1 Apr	Balance b/d		14,275
30 Apr	Payments to		30 Apr	Credit purchases		36,592
	trade payables	31,074				
30 Apr	Discounts received	1,048				
30 Apr	Set-off: sales ledger	597				
30 Apr	Balance c/d	17,495				
		50,867				50,867
			1 May	Balance b/d		17,495

10.7 (a)   **SALES LEDGER**

Dr			Arrow Valley Retailers			Cr
20-4		£	20-4			£
1 Feb	Balance b/d	826.40	20 Feb	Bank		805.74
3 Feb	Sales	338.59	20 Feb	Discounts allowed		20.66
			29 Feb	Balance c/d		338.59
		1,164.99				1,164.99
1 Mar	Balance b/d	338.59				

Dr			**B Brick (Builders) Limited**		Cr
20-4		£	20-4		£
1 Feb	Balance b/d	59.28	29 Feb	Irrecoverable debts	59.28

Dr			**Mereford Manufacturing Company**		Cr
20-4		£	20-4		£
1 Feb	Balance b/d	293.49	24 Feb	Sales returns	56.29
3 Feb	Sales	127.48	29 Feb	Set-off: purchases ledger	364.68
		420.97			420.97

Dr			**Redgrove Restorations**		Cr
20-4		£	20-4		£
1 Feb	Balance b/d	724.86	7 Feb	Sales returns	165.38
17 Feb	Sales	394.78	29 Feb	Balance c/d	954.26
		1,119.64			1,119.64
1 Mar	Balance b/d	954.26			

Dr			**Wyvern Warehouse Limited**		Cr
20-4		£	20-4		£
1 Feb	Balance b/d	108.40	15 Feb	Bank	105.69
17 Feb	Sales	427.91	15 Feb	Discounts allowed	2.71
			29 Feb	Balance c/d	427.91
		536.31			536.31
1 Mar	Balance b/d	427.91			

(b)

Dr			**Sales ledger control account**		Cr
20-4		£	20-4		£
1 Feb	Balance b/d	2,012.43	29 Feb	Sales returns	221.67
29 Feb	Credit sales	1,288.76	29 Feb	Payments received	911.43
			29 Feb	Discounts allowed	23.37
			29 Feb	Set-off: purchases ledger	364.68
			29 Feb	Irrecoverable debts	59.28
			29 Feb	Balance c/d	1,720.76
		3,301.19			3,301.19
1 Mar	Balance b/d	1,720.76			

(c)

Reconciliation of sales ledger control account		
	1 February 20-4	**29 February 20-4**
	£	£
Arrow Valley Retailers	826.40	338.59
B Brick (Builders) Limited	59.28	–
Mereford Manufacturing Company	293.49	nil
Redgrove Restorations	724.86	954.26
Wyvern Warehouse Limited	108.40	427.91
Sales ledger control account	2,012.43	1,720.76

10.8 (a) To bring together amounts of VAT from books of prime entry

10.9

Adjustment number	Amount £	Debit	Credit
1	200		✓
2	150		✓
3	125		✓

10.10

Adjustment number	Amount £	Debit	Credit
1	180		✓
3	400	✓	
4	440	✓	

10.11

Adjustment number	Amount £	Debit	Credit
2	550		✓
3	180	✓	
4	210		✓

CHAPTER 11: THE JOURNAL AND CORRECTION OF ERRORS

11.1 (b)   **11.2** (a)

11.3 **(a)** *error of omission*

Date	Details	Reference	Dr	Cr
			£	£
	Sales ledger control	GL	150	
	Sales	GL		150
	Sales invoice no .... omitted from the accounts: in the sales ledger – debit J Rigby £150			

(b) *error of principle*

Date	Details	Reference	Dr	Cr
			£	£
	Vehicles at cost	GL	10,000	
	Vehicle expenses	GL		10,000
	Correction of error – vehicle no .... invoice no			

(c) *reversal of entries*

Date	Details	Reference	Dr	Cr
			£	£
	Postages	GL	55	
	Bank	CB		55
	Postages	GL	55	
	Bank	CB		55
			110	110
	Correction of reversal of entries on			

(d) *error of original entry*

Date	Details	Reference	Dr	Cr
			£	£
	Sales ledger control	GL	98	
	Bank	CB		98
	Bank	CB	89	
	Sales ledger control	GL		89
			187	187
	Correction of error – bank payment for £89 received on ......(date)......: in the sales ledger – debit L Johnson £98 – credit L Johnson £89			

(e) *mispost/error of commission*

Date	Details	Reference	Dr	Cr
			£	£
	Purchases ledger control	GL	125	
	Purchases ledger control	GL		125
	Correction of mispost – bank payment			
	for £125 on ..... in the purchases ledger			
	– debit H Price Limited			
	– credit H Prince			

11.4

	Date	Details	Reference	Dr	Cr
				£	£
(a)		Office expenses	GL	85	
		Suspense	GL		85
		Omission of entry in office expenses			
		account			
(b)		Suspense	GL	78	
		Printing expenses	GL		78
		Printing expenses	GL	87	
		Suspense	GL		87
				165	165
		Payment for printing £87			
		entered in printing expenses account			
		as £78			
(c)		Suspense	GL	2,500	
		Sales returns	GL		2,500
		Sales returns	GL	2,400	
		Suspense	GL		2,400
				4,900	4,900
		Incorrect balance of sales returns			
		account transferred to the trial balance			
(d)		Commission received	GL	25	
		Suspense	GL		25
		Commission received entered twice			

Dr	Suspense account			Cr
20-7		£	**20-7**	£
30 Sep	Trial balance difference	19	(a) Office expenses	85
(b)	Photocopying	78	(b) Photocopying	87
(c)	Sales returns	2,500	(c) Sales returns	2,400
			(d) Commission received	25
		2,597		2,597

11.5 (a)

Date	Details	Reference	Dr	Cr
20-8			£	£
31 Dec	Closing inventory – statement of financial position	GL	22,600	
	Closing inventory – statement of profit or loss	GL		22,600
	Inventory valuation at 31 December 20-8 transferred to the financial statements			

(b)

Date	Details	Reference	Dr	Cr
20-8			£	£
31 Dec	Statement of profit or loss	GL	890	
	Telephone expenses	GL		890
	Transfer to the statement of profit or loss of expenditure for the year			

(c)

Date	Details	Reference	Dr	Cr
20-8			£	£
31 Dec	Statement of profit or loss	GL	23,930	
	Salaries	GL		23,930
	Salaries	GL	980	
	Accrued expenses	GL		980
			24,910	24,910
	Transfer to the statement of profit or loss of expenditure for the year, and transfer of accrual to accrued expenses account			

(d)

Date	Details	Reference	Dr	Cr
20-8			£	£
31 Dec	Statement of profit or loss	GL	1,160	
	Printing expenses	GL		1,160
	Prepaid expenses	GL	160	
	Printing expenses	GL		160
			1,320	1,320
	Transfer to the statement of profit or loss of expenditure for the year and transfer of prepayment to prepaid expenses account			

(e)

Date	Details	Reference	Dr	Cr
20-8			£	£
31 Dec	Rent received	GL	4,400	
	Statement of profit or loss	GL		4,400
	Rent received	GL	400	
	Prepaid income	GL		400
			4,800	4,800
	Transfer to the statement of profit or loss of income for year and transfer of prepayment to prepaid income account			

(f)

Date	Details	Reference	Dr	Cr
20-8			£	£
31 Dec	Depreciation charges	GL	500	
	Fixtures and fittings: accumulated depreciation	GL		500
	Depreciation charges for year on fixtures and fittings			
31 Dec	Statement of profit or loss	GL	500	
	Depreciation charges	GL		500
	Transfer to the statement of profit or loss of depreciation charges for year on fixtures and fittings			

(g)

Date	Details	Reference	Dr £	Cr £
20-8				
31 Dec	Disposals	GL	5,000	
	Machinery at cost	GL		5,000
	Machinery: accumulated depreciation	GL	3,750	
	Disposals	GL		3,750
	Bank	CB	2,400	
	Disposals	GL		2,400
	Statement of profit or loss	GL		1,150
	Disposals	GL	1,150	
			12,300	12,300
	Sale of machine no ....; gain on sale £750 credited to the statement of profit or loss			

(h)

Date	Details	Reference	Dr £	Cr £
20-8				
31 Dec	Irrecoverable debts	GL	125	
	Sales ledger control	GL		125
	Accounts written off as irrecoverable: in the sales ledger			
	– credit Nick Marshall *£55*			
	– credit Crabbe & Company *£30*			
	– credit A Hunt *£40*			
	Total *£125*			
31 Dec	Statement of profit or loss	GL	125	
	Irrecoverable debts	GL		125
	Transfer to the statement of profit or loss of irrecoverable debts for year			

(i)

Date	Details	Reference	Dr £	Cr £
20-8				
31 Dec	Allowance for doubtful debts	GL	100	
	Allowance for doubtful debts: adjustment	GL		100
	Decrease for year in allowance for doubtful debts			
31 Dec	Allowance for doubtful debts: adjustment	GL	100	
	Statement of profit or loss	GL		100
	Transfer to the statement of profit or loss of decrease in allowance for doubtful debts			

11.6 (a) Journal

	Dr £	Cr £
Irrecoverable debts	220	
Sales ledger control		220

(b) Journal

	Dr £	Cr £
Vehicles	12,500	
Suspense		12,500

(c) Journal

	Dr £	Cr £
Closing inventory – statement of financial position	*24,750	
Closing inventory – statement of profit or loss		*24,750

*lower of cost and net realisable value: £25,400 – £650

(d) Journal

	Dr £	Cr £
Suspense	1,400	
VAT		1,400
Suspense	1,400	
VAT		1,400

11.7   (a)   Extract from extended trial balance

	Ledger balances		Adjustments	
	Dr £	Cr £	Dr £	Cr £
Allowance for doubtful debts		720		
Bank	9,500			2,500
Closing inventory – statement of financial position			*41,200	
Closing inventory – statement of profit or loss				*41,200
Depreciation charges	2,000			
Irrecoverable debts			78	
Office expenses	5,300			
Rent paid	14,200			
Sales		245,000		
Sales ledger control	47,400		400	78
Suspense		2,100	2,500	400
VAT		7,300		
Vehicles – accumulated depreciation		6,000		

*lower of cost and net realisable value: £42,000 – £800

(b)

Account	Dr	Cr
Statement of profit or loss	✓	
Office expenses		✓
Narrative: Transfer to the statement of profit or loss of expenditure for the year		

11.8 Extended trial balance

Ledger account	Ledger balances		Adjustments		Statement of profit or loss		Statement of financial position	
	£ Dr	£ Cr	£ Dr	£ Cr	£ Dr	£ Cr	£ Dr	£ Cr
Allowance for doubtful debts		1,700		200				1,900
Allowance for doubtful debts adjustment			200		200			
Bank		16,200		300				16,500
Capital		20,500						20,500
Closing inventory			18,500	18,500		18,500	18,500	
Depreciation charges			3,500		3,500			
Office expenses	18,600		400		19,000			
Opening inventory	12,500				12,500			
Payroll expenses	40,800		200		41,000			
Purchases	260,000		1,000		261,000			
Purchases ledger control		32,500						32,500
Sales revenue		375,000				375,000		
Sales ledger control	60,100						60,100	
Selling expenses	21,000				21,000			
Suspense	1,300		300	1,600				
VAT		2,900						2,900
Vehicles at cost	45,000						45,000	
Vehicles accumulated depreciation		10,500		3,500				14,000
Profit/loss for the year					35,300			35,300
	459,300	459,300	24,100	24,100	393,500	393,500	123,600	123,600

Tutorial notes:

- two amounts are shown on the same line in the adjustments column for closing inventory: the debit entry is shown in the debit column of the statement of financial position; the credit entry is shown in the credit column of the statement of profit or loss (see the journal entries in this Chapter)

- in suspense account the debit balance of £1,300 is cleared by the credit adjustments for £400, £200 and £1,000 (total £1,600), and the debit adjustment of £300

- depreciation charges and allowance for doubtful debts are adjusted in the way that has been shown in Chapters 6 and 7

Appendix:
photocopiable resources

These pages may be photocopied for student use, but remain the copyright of the author. It is recommended that they are enlarged to A4 size.

These pages are also available for download from the Resources Section of www.osbornebooks.co.uk.

The forms and formats include:

Dr ———————————————— account   Cr

Date	Details	Amount	Date	Details	Amount
		£			£

Dr ———————————————— account   Cr

Date	Details	Amount	Date	Details	Amount
		£			£

Dr ———————————————— account   Cr

Date	Details	Amount	Date	Details	Amount
		£			£

Dr ———————————————— account   Cr

Date	Details	Amount	Date	Details	Amount
		£			£

Journal

Date	Details	Reference	Dr	Cr
			£	£

Journal

Date	Details	Reference	Dr	Cr
			£	£

Journal

Date	Details	Reference	Dr	Cr
			£	£

Journal

Date	Details	Reference	Dr	Cr
			£	£

284

EXTENDED TRIAL BALANCE name .... date ....

Account name	Ledger balances		Adjustments		Statement of profit or loss		Statement of financial position	
	Dr £	Cr £	Dr £	Cr £	Dr £	Cr £	Dr £	Cr £
Closing inventory: statement of profit or loss								
Closing inventory: statement of financial position								
Accruals								
Prepayments								
Depreciation charges								
Irrecoverable debts								
Allowance for doubtful debts								
Allowance for doubtful debts: adjustment								
Profit/loss for the year								

NON-CURRENT ASSET REGISTER

Description/serial no	Acquisition date	Cost £	Depreciation charges £	Carrying amount* £	Funding method	Disposal proceeds £	Disposal date

*carrying amount: cost less accumulated depreciation

Index

for your notes

for your notes

for your notes

for your notes

for your notes

for your notes

for your notes

for your notes

for your notes